THE BEST OF 'DEAR BILL'

The Best of
DEAR BILL

Richard Ingrams
and
John Wells

Illustrated by
BRIAN BAGNALL

SPHERE BOOKS LIMITED
PRIVATE EYE

Sphere Books Ltd, 27 Wrights Lane, London W8 5TZ

First published in Great Britain by
André Deutsch Ltd and
Private Eye Productions Ltd 1986
Published by Sphere Books Ltd 1987

TRADE
MARK

Printed and bound in Great Britain by
Richard Clay Ltd, Bungay, Suffolk

CHATEAU
ST. DENIS

1979
BOTTLED

10 Downing Street
S. W. 1.   94 FLOOD STREET
LONDON SW3

Dear Bill,   18 MAY 1979

So sorry I couldn't make it on Tuesday. The Major rang me last night to report, and obviously I missed a jolly good day. I haven't played down at Sandwich since '68, when poor old Archie Bracketts dropped down dead at the fourteenth. I remember we drove over to the Dolphin afterwards and had a slap-up meal, which I am sure is what Archie would have wanted had he been alive.

Anyway, as you may have seen in the *Telegraph*, all hell has broken loose around here since we were last able to have a chat over lunch that day at the Army & Navy. M. has become Prime Minister, and it's caused no end of a flap. Telephone never stops ringing. All my daffs got trampled by a lot of bloody pressmen on election day. I actually spotted some photographer johnny from the *Sun* nipping up the fire-escape trying to catch Carol starkers in the bath, dirty bugger.

To cap it all, we've now had to ship the whole shooting match over to Number Ten, and I don't know yet whether I'm coming or going. The bloody fools from Pickfords seem to have lost that set of Ping Irons Burmah gave me when I handed in my cards. What with decorators, policemen and politicos running about all over the place, Number Ten is the worst shambles I've seen since the Dieppe show in '42. What's more, there doesn't seem to be a decent local, and they've even got some Ministry of Works chappie called Boris to take care of the garden, so any hope I had of taking off a peaceful hour or two in the greenhouse is out of the window.

Anyway, back to Tuesday. Why I couldn't make it was that M. insisted I turn up for some kind of State Opening of Parliament or other. I had assumed now the election was over I would be excused this kind of thing, but oh no. I had just carried my spare clubs out to the jalopy when heigh ho! — up goes a window and M. is giving me my marching orders. It's off to Moss Bros. for the full kit, and at that moment, I don't mind telling you, I couldn't help thinking pretty enviously of you, Monty and the Major enjoying a few pre-match snifters at the 19th without a care in the world.

It took ages to get kitted out. The staff at Moss Bros. all seem to be gyppos these days, and there was a bit of a communications problem. But eventually I managed to get a cab back to the House of Commons, only to find that I'd left my Invite at Downing Street. I told the chap on the door that I was Mr Thatcher, and he said, 'That's what they all say'. After about 20 minutes they

6

agreed to go and get M. out to vouch for my *bona fides* and, as you can imagine, I wasn't top of the popularity stakes at that particular juncture!!

M. then had to go off to do her stuff, so I just mooched around for a while, looking for a watering-hole. What a place, Bill! If you ask me, it's just an antiquated rabbit warren — miles and miles of corridors, with chaps in evening dress wandering about like a lot of super-annuated penguins. Luckily I eventually bumped into a familiar face in the shape of George Brown. He seemed to know his way around, and we ended up in a nice little bar overlooking the river, with an awfully jolly crowd of chaps who were watching the show on the TV.

It all seemed to go quite smoothly, but I was a bit miffed to see M. fussing over that fellow Stevas, and taking the fluff off his collar. To tell you the truth, I don't like the cut of that chap's jib. If you ask me, he's not absolutely 100%, and when I said as much a lot of the fellows at the bar agreed.

On a more serious note, do tell Monty and the Major that I am definitely on for the 24th. I've checked with M's secretary, and there's absolutely nothing in the book. So I'll get the usual 11.08 from Charing Cross, and if Monty could pick me up at Tonbridge, we'll meet you in Ye Olde Shippe In Ye Bottle at 12.00 sharp. (I wonder if they've still got any of that Glen Keswick we had the night poor old Tuppy bought it?) Must close, as M. has got some Hun coming to dinner and I've got to do my stuff again. I sometimes wonder who won the bloody war!

Yours aye!

DENIS

10 Downing Street
Whitehall

1 June 1979

Dear Bill,

What can you think of me? I tried desperately to get through at Ye Olde Shippe but no joy. Some foreign chappie in the kitchen who wasn't making much sense thought you'd all gone off in a charabanc to Deal, and I knew that couldn't be right. Anyway, the Major rang me next morning and I gather I missed another cracking day out at Littlestone.

As I tried to explain to the Major, who sounded rather plastered even at breakfast time (!), I got hauled in to do my stuff at HQ. It really is the most extraordinary building: looks like an ordinary house from outside, give or take a bobby on the front door, but when you get in it's just like a lot of board-rooms, very similar to the set-up at Burmah, and very difficult to find the smallest room. We're really camping on the top floor and there are endless arguments between M. and that Stevas chap about wallpaper.

Anyway, come the twenty-fourth, M. announces at breakfast that I'm on parade that evening for 'bridge building'. Something cold in the dining room with Ted Heath. To be perfectly frank I don't know what it was all about. Ted was supposed to bring some sort of pianist woman, but she cried off at the last minute. To put the tin hat on it, M. got tied up with her hanging bunch at the House, and rang through to me and told me to hold the fort. Ted arrived a quarter of an hour early, so yours truly was well and truly lumbered.

I took him upstairs into what they call the blue room and offered him a drink, but he refused rather huffily, saying, 'Most people know I'm on a diet.' He then gave me a shirty look when I helped myself to a stiff one. Then there was a deathly hush from both ends of the wicket. Finally, to break the ice, I asked him if he ever played golf. He said, 'No'. The hush resumed. Then he looked at his watch and asked rather testily, 'Have you any idea why that woman wants to see me?' I was still trying to haul that one in when he looked at me in an odd sort of way and said, 'Do you work here? In my day I must say we had a rather younger crew.'

A pretty tricky situation, as you can imagine, Bill. Not unlike the time the Vicar mistook your good lady for the barmaid of the Bull. Fortunately young Cosgrove got us off the hook by coming in and saying that Margaret had rung to say that there were more delays and we were to start without her. So there we were. Cosgrove emptied the ashtrays and took himself off, and I suggested we should make a move downstairs to get stuck in to the buffet. As I opened the double door into the dining room, blow me if Boris, the new gardener, didn't pop up from behind some flower arrangement, playing out a length of flex to a wall-socket and explaining to me in that peculiar accent of his: 'Zis dropical daffodil cannot survive wizzout heat.'

When I turned round, would you believe it, there was Heath tucking in his bib in M's chair at the head of the table. Anyway, I rang the bell and Cosgrove came in with the Avocado a la Prawns. Heath took one look at his and waved it away, saying: 'Do you realise that the calorie content of one of those is the equivalent of two double whiskies?' This seemed a useful cue for me to go and refill my glass, and since M. wasn't there I saw no harm in bringing the bottle to the table. I was the recipient of another fishy glare from our sea-faring friend.

'These European Elections are the most crucial historical turning point since I took Britain in,' Heath then announced. Well, Bill, I don't mind confessing I was pretty nonplussed as to what to reply to this. However, inspiration came, and I said I had once played at Le Touquet but couldn't make head or tail of the course being laid out in metres. Heath peered at me for several seconds, then said: 'You really ought to meet Denis Thatcher. I gather he's a golf nut. Can't talk about anything else.' Then, leaning forward confidentially, he added: 'Between ourselves, I gather he likes his drink.'

Before I could put my oar in on that one, in stomped Boris, who fiddled about with the daffodils and said would we mind speaking up. Pretty rum, eh Bill? But I've been told to keep a low profile by the Boss, so low profile it shall be. When Cosgrove brought in the cold pork and Russian Salad Heath took one look at it, gave a snort, and shouted: 'She may not have much of a grasp of common courtesy but I bloody well have. Sod this for a lark, I'm going.' As you can imagine, Bill, I was pretty relieved to see the back of the fellow and what's more when M. showed up two hours or so later she didn't seem too put out. I was very baffled by the piece in the *Telegraph* next morning headed 'Mystery surrounds Heath/Thatcher Summit', but these newspaper johnnies are a closed book to me.

As I told the Major, June the Tenth it is. Stoke Poges come hell or high water. Dinner at the French Horn. My shout.

Yours aye!

DENIS

10 Downing Street
Whitehall

15 June 1979

Dear Bill,
I hope this reaches you, as I gather the postal johnnies are playing silly buggers yet again.

By the way, whatever you do don't ring the home number again, at least for a bit! I gather the Major got an earful when he rang up on Budget Night. According to the Boss, any more calls after two a.m. and I'm for the high jump. From the sound of things the old boys was a bit plastered. (Was that you playing the piano in the background?) I tried to explain you only wanted to convey your congratulations on the Budget, but M. was absolutely livid and came all the way up to the boxroom in her slippers to read the Riot Act. Oh dear.

A propos the Budget, I was in a spot of hot water myself. I happened to be talking to some chaps in the RAC Club a couple of days before the Big Day, and Reggie Stebbings — very intelligent chap in insurance who's got his ear to the ground — said he wouldn't be half surprised if they didn't bump up the price of booze and he was thinking of popping down to Barrett's to lay in a goodly store.

Well, I asked Her Ladyship that evening if she thought there was any truth in it, and did she hit the roof! Official Secrets Act, Queen Juliana, contempt of Court, Muldergate, she threw the lot at me. In the end I wished I hadn't opened my mouth. A few minutes later in comes Howe from next door. I don't know whether you know him — some sort of lawyer by trade, harmless enough but a bit of a worrier, rather under his wife's thumb I always think. 'Well, PM,' he says, bouncing in through the door, 'the boffins have worked it all out and I can't see why we shouldn't get away with it, at least for a few months.' 'Drink?' I suggested, trying to put him at ease and swinging open the cabinet. 'Yes,' says the little chap, 'sixty p. on a bottle of Scotch.'

At this point M. gave him one of her looks and took him off to the Holy of Holies, but I'd already twigged what was in the wind and bustled out to ring you lot and tip you the wink. As bad luck would have it, Boris was in the process of dismantling the telephone, so no joy. He told me it's his hobby, and apparently he's building his own 'ham' transmitter out of old egg-boxes on the roof. Anyhow, down to the Liquormart in a jiffy, three crates in the boot — I reckon it was a saving of about ten quid — not to be sniffed at in these hard times, as the Major would say! Just backing into the only parking space available outside Number Ten when who do I collide with but old Howe standing on the pavement outside Number Eleven waving a tatty briefcase about, grinning like the proverbial Cheshire Cat and having his picture taken by the usual bunch of yobs with flash-bulbs.

Not my day as it turned out. No sooner had I started to unload than they turned round and snapped away at me. Front door opens, out pops the Boss. Lot of poppycock about tradesmen coming to the wrong address, going round the back, told to go to Number Nine, anyway I was to take it all back this minute, me left looking a damn fool. Not easy you know, Bill, all those bloody tourists looking on.

After all this, as you can imagine, I can't wait for Wednesday. Eastbourne it is. Lunch at the Grand and drinks on the way back with the Major's father at the Home.

T. T. F. N.

Yrs aye,

DENIS

13 July 1979

Dear Bill,

Sorry about going AWOL on your Rotary. Usual thing, last-minute *froideur* from M. Of course I could go, but . . . Probably just as well in view of what transpired. I gather from the Major things got a bit out of hand and the bread rolls were flying. If I'd been there no doubt we'd have made the front page of the *Daily* bloody *Mirror*. Ah well, cakes and ale in very limited supply.

The Major told me you'd had a bit of a barney over those Boat People being let in. It must seem very rum from down there, and I don't want you to think I'd let the side down. On the contrary.

When the whole thing blew up in the first place M., as you know, put her foot down. Very right and proper. God knows the place is swarming with darkies of all 57 varieties as it is. I foam at the mouth on that topic as everyone in the Clubhouse will testify, especially when I've had a snort or two, and M. is basically in agreement, whatever she has to say in public. Strong support from K. Joseph.

Basically it was all Cosgrove's fault. Last Wednesday had been absolutely beastly: baking hot and all sorts of Union hobble-dehoys tramping in and out with smelly socks, leaving a ghastly pong about the place. Proprietor displeased as you can well imagine; yours truly upstairs having completed *Telegraph* crossword puzzle except for three clues, tongue hanging out.

The plan was for Cosgrove to leave us a slap-up cold buffet with all the trimmings. M. had asked Stevarse round — not my favourite person in all the world — and I'd intended to take a plate upstairs with a noggin or two out of my cache in the attic and watch the International Golf on the box.

Alas. The moron Cosgrove had gone to a religious poetry reading. Cupboard bare. Stevarse mincing about putting the pictures straight and making damnfool jokes to cover up, but M. white at the gills. I suggested we all amble up to Wilton Street for a snack, but oh no. Stevarse on dangers of conspicuous extravagance. As bachelor he has far better scheme. Magic Number. A1 Chinese Takeaway delivered to Your Door. Orders Grand Feast for Three Persons: Sweet and Sour Lobster Tails, Crispy Balls, Peking Hot Crab — you know the form. In the meantime, Carrington shimmers in in his brothel creepers. Stevarse very miffed as the boss seems to have taken rather a shine to P.C.

(Peter Carrington turns out to be a very nice sort of chap, no side whatsoever, and he was at Eton with Sticky Wilkinson, so Sticky tells me, although Carrington didn't remember the name.)

Come nine-thirty, everyone a bit squiffy. Stevarse's jokes all

falling very flat. Carrington getting no end of giggles from M. with impersonations of Q. Hogg etc. Suddenly serious note struck by Carrington. Boat People drowning like rats. Reminiscences of time Out East. Loyal little Ghurkas, Chindits etc. To tell the truth Bill, I began to feel a bit of a lump in the throat. Took me back, I don't mind telling you. Old days in Burma, etc. Carrington removed spectacles, wiped eyes.

At this juncture, bell rings and enter Chinese nosh-wallah with steaming cartons and obliging manner. Clearly no stranger to Stevarse, who tucks ten pound note in his top pocket and sends him on his way rejoicing. 'There you are, Margaret,' says our Norm. 'Lot more where he came from. Very co-operative little people. Clean as a whistle. No local resentment. Try their hand at anything.' M. seemed hesitant, but it suddenly struck me that it all made sense. Do you remember the last time we played at Deal? Couldn't get a caddy for love or money. Why not let these Boat Johnnies in and hey presto, caddy problem solved. Emboldened by the odd snort of Old Stag's Breath, and possibly just a touch blotto, I embarked on a harangue. Everyone spellbound. Haven't had a better reception since Reggie Stebbings's wife's funeral. Carrington misty-eyed. Stevarse arguing plausibly in favour of servant problem for returning tax-exiles, good gimmick etc. All turn to M. for response.

Chews on lobster leg for a bit, wipes chin, then says: 'All right. How many?'

I must confess I stumped off up to Bedfordshire in something of a glow. Not often one has one's hand on the National Tiller, what? I think I may be cut out for this decision-making lark after all. M. filthy headache next morning, but no reversal of policy.

More soon. '

Yours till Hell freezes over,

DENIS

10 Downing Street
Whitehall

27 July 1979

Dear Bill,

What topping weather we've been having, and golly do I envy you the afternoon at Broadstairs! As you know, I tried to get away, only to be given a very severe wigging from the Boss about fuel conservation and an immediate directive to remove the personalised number plates from the Rolls. (My initials apparently open to misconstruction!!)

All in all, not a good week, Bill. I find a lot of the time hanging rather heavy on my hands. Westminster seems a particularly bad area for greenfly, and the roses in the garden were covered in the little blighters. Anyway, I took it into my head to get the old stirrup pump out of the attic and give them a good drench with the new Fisons CHX03. Blow me, no sooner had I got the bucket out — old Boris happy as a grig other end of the garden reading one of those foreign newspapers — than the window goes up and Her Ladyship is banging on about sodding things up with the Ministry of Environment — who does what — hard enough to get civil servants as it is etc. Ah me.

What I can't understand is that they seem to be massacring the Civil Servants like flies. I don't know whether you've seen that chappie Keith Joseph on the telly at all, but in my book he really is a bit of a four-letter fellow, and what's more, for our own private consumption, I'd be very surprised if they'd let him in at Hampstead Golf Club. Carrington, who I really have got to like awfully, calls him the Mad Monk, after that Svengali chap who put the kibosh on the Tsar. He's been in and out of the place like the proverbial dose of salts. Cut this, cut that, sell off the Post Office, railways back to Private Enterprise, North Sea Oil back to the Americans. Where will it all end, I ask you, Bill?

Mind you, they've obviously got to do something, the way things are going.

Emboldened by my intervention on behalf of the little yellow-skinned folk in the boats, I told them all as much the other night. M. had asked HQ staff back to the house for a bacon sandwich and a glass of port after the day's work — to celebrate old Thorneycroft's seventieth birthday — no sign of him packing it in, I regret to say — and the Mad Monk dropped by with a list of new cuts, including the Lifeboat Service, the Fire Brigade, and Museums. Stevarse and Carrington got very shirty about this, the former banging on in his usual arty-crafty mimsy manner about our bloody heritage. I ask you, Bill, who really gives a hoot about a lot of old Greek Jars and bits of bric-a-brac? I didn't say anything at this stage, but I could see Humpty Dumpty, i.e. Thorneycroft, getting a bit hot under the collar, and the situation began to look a bit ugly.

However. Somebody, it may have been Carrington, started in about all the dire consequences that would inevitably ensue from the Monk's cuts. Higher school meals, higher council house rents. 'Look here,' I said. Sudden hush. 'I was talking to my friend the Major last night on the phone.' They all looked a bit blank at this, so I seized the moment for another quick snort to oil the wheels. 'Very nice chap,' I explained. 'Used to be in the RASC and then went into biscuits. Now he's flogging greenhouses in Tunbridge Wells.' More blank looks. 'He lives in a little village just outside Hastings. Do you know, there's a chap living in a council house in the Major's village — can't remember the name off-hand' — which I couldn't: Wittering? Twittering? Remind me. No matter. 'Anyway, there's a chap living in a council house in this place who earns £400,000 a year, moon-lighting with one thing and another, Daimler outside the door, kids at public school, obviously goes all over the world: now, I think this is the point, these council house buggers have obviously got jam on it. Motor-driven shower goes wrong in his bloody solarium — there's some wretched man from the council round in five minutes to fix it. If you seriously think a few quid on the rent is going to hurt these spongeing sods you must all be mad.'

Harsh words, you may think, Bill, but honestly, the trouble with Carrington, charming drinking companion though he may be, is that his experience of the ordinary man in the street is precisely nil. To be fair to him, I think he took the point. Stevarse made funny faces and looked at the ceiling, but otherwise there was a feeling my words had gone home. I tottered off to bed then, but there was a good deal of laughter and merriment below for some time, and I got the impression that things are going our way.

By the by, I was talking to one of those Press johnnies who ring up from time to time trying to trip me up, and he told me that there's a marvellous clover-leaf course outside Barflor, or somewhere like that, in Normandy. You can get over quite easily on the Hovercraft — licensed all the way across — and it sounds just the thing for a thirsty lot like us: he said a double gin is fifteen pee and over on the other side it's all in francs. Bit of a change from the Old Mermaid. Would you have a word with the Major and see whether it might be feasible?

Yours in the pink,

DENIS

10 Downing Street
Whitehall

10 August 1979

Dear Bill,

Sorry I haven't been in touch before but I've been laid up with Lusaka Tummy ever since our return from the Dark Continent. God, what a trip! I must say I was jolly glad to set foot on British soil once more.

You know me, Bill, I've never had much time for our Dusky Cousins and this latest outing only went to confirm what everyone else calls my prejudice, but what you and I and the Major know full well is just plain common sense. To begin with

14

it's bloody hot, Bill. 150°in the shade and there's precious little of that. After ten minutes in the hotel I was completely dehydrated and gasping for a long cool lotion, not to say two or even three. I rang for room service and this waiter Johnny staggered in dressed up as a rear admiral, took a quid off me and I never saw the blighter again.

That's the sort of thing that happens in these parts.

Peter Carrington was the only one who had the right approach, I thought. You probably saw that the Nigerians had the bright idea of grabbing all of BP's assets. Can you imagine that, Bill? We go out there with all the kit, teach them how to burrow down and suck it up, and then the shifty little buggers turn round and seize it just as soon as our back's turned. Anyway, Carrington was at this reception along with me and the Boss, and he went up to their Ambassador or whatever and gave the fellow a good dressing-down.

When he'd finished, I came over and gave him a piece of *my* mind. M., however, intervened while I was in mid-stream and afterwards I was given a bit of a wigging and told to keep out of that sort of thing. But I still think I did right, Bill. You treat these buggers firmly and they respect you for it.

I gather a lot of people think the Boss has backed down a bit on this Rhodesia business. Fact of the matter is, Bill — but for Christ's sake keep it under your hat — that she had no choice. I can tell you this because of what happened on Day 2.

After breakfast (half a paw-paw and a pretty odd-looking sausage) I'm given my marching orders by M. Report 09.00 hours to the Royal Victoria Zambian Championship Links 10 miles out of town (get the old boy out of the way, what?). To be candid, Bill, I was glad to escape from the cocktail circuit and get

a breath of fresh air on the golf course — or rather Hot Air, what?

You could have knocked me down with a feather when I discovered who my partner was — none other than HRH the D of E, no less, who as it turned out was in the same boat as yours truly, i.e. Not Wanted On Voyage, putting foot in it all over the shop and generally sticking out like a sore thumb at a wedding party. We got on like a house on fire from the start, Bill. I tell you, he's one of us, and a damn good egg who likes a snort as much as the next man.

You can tell why Zambia has so an Arnold Palmer. The fairways have got about as much grass on them as Margate beach when the tide's out, and the so-called greens are made of lino. You hit a perfect pitch-shot, only to see a herd of wildebeeste or some such charging across in a cloud of dust and gobbling up the balls as if they were mushrooms.

After two holes, having lost all his Maxflies, the Duke turned to me and said: 'Sod this for a lark, Thatcher. Where's the watering-hole?' (That's the way he talks.) He'd taken the words from my mouth, Bill, and in no time at all we were ensconced on the verandah of quite a decent club-house (run by a frightfully nice man from Carshalton who was in the Royal Artillery with Reggie Stebbings. Small world, eh Bill?)

Anyway, the Duke and I got chatting about this and that and the other and he let slip that he doesn't think too much of these Front Line Presidents or whatever they call themselves either. His solution for Rhodesia's the same as mine:

Re-organise the country.

Lift the sanctions.

Sod the lot of them.

The snag is this, Bill. HM, as he calls her, is in fact frightfully keen on all the Commonwealth shindig. Loves the whole palaver. White Goddess drops out of sky in great silver bird, crowds turn out, hordes of little piccaninnies waving Union Jacks, naked women dancing up and down shaking their whatsits — she laps it up, Bill, would you believe it? Kaunda, Nyerere, all of them, the bee's knees in her book. Won't hear a word against them. No choice for me but to tell M. what the form is. No more of this Carrington malarkey, kiss and make up with Kaunda and eat humble pie.

End result — all the nig-nogs beaming and smiling and singing ghastly songs, while M. and I put a brave face on it.

By the way, Bill. When HRH and I were having our chinwag at the nineteenth he passed on to me a little tin of ground rhinoceros horn. 'Very tricky to get,' he says, 'with all these preservation orders about the place.' Damn me if M. doesn't mistake the stuff for Coffee-Mate and puts it in the Gold Blend. Result: four days chained to the Mahogany! Absolute hell, Bill.

Should be back in circulation in a couple of days so I'll see you at Sandwich on the 18th. I've brought you back a little souvenir — a bottle of the local fire-water made out of fermented bamboo shoots — and it packs a powerful punch. Two snorts and you're out like a light.

Yours, aye

DENIS

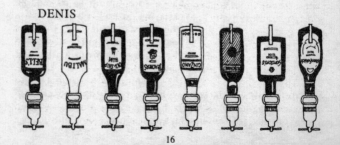

31 August 1979

Dear Bill,

We got back from Scotland on the Flying Fornicator at seven o'clock this morning, and I'm still feeling pretty groggy. However much I hate this place, a week on the Isle of Muck or whatever it's called makes it seem like a positive Shangri-La.

I'm very confused about the whole thing, but it seems to have all been Macmillan's fault. He told the Boss that the done thing was a week in Scotland every August going after the grouse. Damn silly idea if you ask me, especially when all good men and true are out on the links at the Royal and Ancient.

I never caught the name of our host, but he had a handle to his name and used to be something very big in M's lot. He lives in the most ghastly God-forsaken castle on this frightful island covered with boulders and fir trees and not so much as a putting green in sight, somewhere out in the Celtic twilight you get to in a little aeroplane from Glasgow.

You know me, Bill. I can't tell a grouse from a bloody emu and I haven't fired a shot in anger since we went on that TA booze-up with the Major's mob at Deal. However, when I asked to be let off games, M. got unbelievably shirty. Down to the gun-room by the ear, kitted out in His Lordship's spare waterproofs and a damn silly hat with a lot of flies stuck in it, all several sizes too big. I ask you, Bill. Good thing none of the photographer johnnies were about otherwise I should have made the front page of *Gay News*, I can tell you. M's argument that it was no use being in a sulk, gratitude to our host and so forth: all I had to do was stand by the little flag and blast off a couples of times to show willing.

What we had to be grateful for I really don't know. Everything they say about the Scots is absolutely true. Lord Whatsisname's idea of a snort looks as though a gnat's pissed in the bottom of the glass. Luckily, prior to the Shooting Expedition, I struck up a great friendship with the Factotum, who used to work for Royal Dutch, and he loaned me an awfully ingenious flask that fitted down the gumboot, filled with his favourite tipple, made at a secret still up in the hills somewhere. I meant to bring you back some, but unfortunately I got rather depressed on the train. Sorry about that.

Anyway, picture the scene. Rain bucketing down. His Lordship's reachmedowns leaking like the proverbial colander. M. got up in her best tweeds with a macintosh hat, deep in conversation with His Nibs. Yours Truly skulking in the butts under the watchful eye of one Ben Rubinstein, the local ghillie. Not one of the most talkative of souls, Bill: the odd grunt and a yellow-toothed snarl was about the sum of his repertoire.

After an eternity of waiting, barbaric cries from the under-growth, a few bedraggled boiler fowl come winging in, barely visible in the mist. Auld Ben strikes me heavily between the shoulder blades and grunts something in Gaelic which I fail to catch, fowling-piece discharges into the butts, Auld Ben casts eyes heavenwards. Obviously no confidence in Bwana. Thoughts of D.T. at this juncture need not be described.

Scene Two. Another part of the forest. Same set-up: winds up to Force Nine, rain now horizontal, specs entirely steamed up, Wellingtons filling nicely. A few sheep cropping the rocks. Lord Thingummybob plainly in his element, talking to M. about the old days with Winston. At that point, Bill, something snapped. No one watching, so I gave old Snaggleteeth five quid and the gun, and buggered off back to the castle.

Hot bath, dry togs, large noggin of firewater, and settled down in Back Nursery to watch International Golf. Much to my relief my absence did not appear to have registered with the Big White Chief, or indeed Mine Host. Ghastly dinner of boiled birds, all bones and buckshot, no fizz in sight. Sympathetic shrugs from kilted majordomo, but the message is No Can Do. Meanwhile Lord Whatsisname is telling M. how much he approves of axeing the students, far too many long-haired clever dicks about the place as it is. High time student grants were cut out altogether and they were all turned over to potato picking. (Not a bad wheeze when you think of it, Bill. Half the cheek you and I have encountered over the past few years has come from that sort of person.)

Reggie says there's rather a nice little indoor driving range near London Airport. Would that be a possible venue to bob back a few scoops?

Yours, through a glass darkly,

DENIS

10 Downing Street
Whitehall

28 September 1979

Dear Bill,

It seems donkeys' years since we had a proper pow-wow and a few snorts. To be perfectly frank I'm beginning to feel like the Man in the Iron Mask locked up in this confounded talking shop. For your ears only, Eric my bodyguard is the most bloody awful drip I have ever encountered. His latest wheeze is to try and get me onto the water wagon. It's got to the stage where I can't open the drinks cabinet without him giving me a beady look and going 'Tut tut

tut!' Bloody fool. I told him frankly Bill that I wasn't going to stand for it: by the time you get to our age either you can take it or you can't.

Can you imagine it, Bill? Every time I go down to the Club for elevenses this flatfoot comes plodding along behind me with his socks hanging down, looking exactly like that flasher who used to hang about near the fifteenth at the Royal and Ancient and who gave Daphne such a nasty turn that time you and I got unavoidably detained.

I've been trying to keep my head below the parapet this week anyway during the Rhodesian Gathering. But it's been real murder. Every night I've had to get done up in my Mess kit for one or other of the Paramount Chiefs. Needless to say, the festivities have not gone by without the odd clanger being dropped by yours truly. For one thing they all look exactly the same to me except for the fat one, and for the life of me I can't understand a word any of them says.

On Wednesday for example we all had to go to Buck House for a stand-up scoff in one of the larger rooms at the back. As bad luck would have it, I got stuck with a little sky-pilot chap in glasses whose name I didn't catch, and who seemed nice enough in his way. Low Church, and spoke very well of the missionaries. I asked him if he ever played golf and he didn't seem to catch on, so after a while I tried again. 'What do you think of this Prime Minister bloke you've got over there — Ian Smith?' (Bit of an H.M.G. [Home Made Gent] in my opinion but I obviously didn't say as much.) Next thing I know I'm left holding our black friend's plate of chicken curry and he's out the door like a streak of greased lightning. Scene Two, a few moments later — self propping up mantelpiece with D of E discussing life under the iron heel, up pops Peter Carrington, accoutrements askew, exceedingly fussed. Do I realise I have ruined entire conference by insulting the Prime Minister? It turns out, you see Bill, that the chap I was talking to was none other than Bishop Whatsit, who was now very miffed and downstairs in the yard talking about flying the whole delegation back to Nyasaland. I refrained from saying that it might be a jolly good thing if they all buggered off for the duration, and had to go downstairs cap in hand and plead temporary insanity due to war wound playing up. But I said to Peter Carrington afterwards that they really ought to get themselves sorted out. After all, how was I to know it was the PM? Bishops are one thing, and Prime Ministers are another. You and I would have thought it pretty odd in the old days to have a padre on the Burmah Board, let alone running the whole bang-shoot.

(Incidentally, Bill, between ourselves, did you know that one of M's jobs was appointing the Archbishop of Canterbury? I took the liberty of putting forward old Archie Wellbeloved now that he's retired: I know he often gives the impression he's not all there, but he's pretty good through the green and preaches a very

nice little sermon, as you and I discovered at the Wilkinson funeral: all in the Saloon Bar by twelve on the dot, as I recall. However, I was told that I was talking out of turn again, that everything had been fixed and this goof from St Albans with the talkative wife had it in the bag all along.)

Anyway, the whole African Circus has struck camp now and sodded off. The Captains and the Kings depart, eerie silence falls etc. etc. and the Boss seems to have patched up some sort of deal about sanctions. But quite honestly Bill, what difference will it make with a full-scale Zulu war raging to and fro and the British box-wallahs getting the hell out of it as fast as their sun-bronzed knees can carry them? I was saying to Boris only the other day, while I was helping him fix his new television aerial on the roof, it beats me why we have to get mixed up in that sort of caper when we're in it up to here as it is with British Leyland and so on. He made the point I might have a word with M. along those lines, but he's a bachelor of course and doesn't understand the form.

Talking of that, if Daphne's off again on her travels, why don't you and I have a little stag outing on one of those Thomson's Winterbreaks? You have to be at Luton at five o'clock in the morning, but I gather the booze flows as per normal once you're aloft. They tell me they have a very good offer of three days in Corfu all in for £92.50, where, as you know from the Major's reminiscences, they have that extraordinary course with ponds instead of bunkers. According to my informant, a Greek chap I ran into at the Club, the place is swarming with frogs, who set up their caterwauling whenever a ball lands anywhere near.

Yours in high dungeon,

DENIS

10 Downing Street
Whitehall

12 October 1979

Dear Bill,
Do you remember that chap Maurice Picarda who used to run a couple of garages near Sevenoaks? Rough diamond, especially

20

after a tincture or two — you probably recall the embarrassing evening at The Feathers with Polly Mountjoy, and whatever happened to her, by the way? — but he could putt like a demon and I've always had rather a soft spot for the old boy, not to say his missus, who is a sweetie. Anyway, he wrote me a frightfully decent letter the other day. His point was this. Were we Conservatives or weren't we?
If we were, what the hell was Geoffrey Howe doing farting about with Company Perks, i.e. free cars? The tone of the letter, I confess, was very emotional, and he ended up by calling us a bunch of half-crazed sods.

Funnily enough, Howe happened to call by just before lunch and, emboldened by the pre-prandial lotion, I broached the topic, adding a point of my own, to wit who on earth could afford to buy these British Leyland limos at ten grand a time, and if it wasn't for the company perks the whole shooting match would go bust.

Odd chap Howe. Some kind of lawyer. Nothing against lawyers myself. Do you remember that solicitor in Fairlight who got done for fiddling the bar accounts? Awfully amusing chap, used to write to me from prison. Howe, anyway, seemed to take my point, and I was encouraged to go on and outline to him our old strategy at Burmah when every member of the Board automatically got a Rover. In the Major's firm, you remember, wives and children were similarly provided for. I also made him laugh no end with my old story about Sticky's trick with the cheque-stubs.

The long and the short of it is, Bill, that when he finally went off to the trough with M. — she was a bit late — Howe was absolutely roaring to do a U-turn on the whole thing. Sure enough, come closing time, Boss a new woman. No more nonsense of that sort. I rang Picarda to tell him the glad tidings. He sounded absolutely chuffed to naafibreaks, and has promised me a free limo on the strength of it. How about that, eh Bill? Who says Conservative Government isn't working?

Next week I'm afraid is a washout. Bloody bloody Blackpool. On parade every day, I imagine, so you can count me out vis a vis the nine holes you proposed at Wimbledon. Am I dreading it, Bill! Out every night, trailing along in the perfumed wake, pressing the flesh, grin grin, Young Conservative Pressure Group For Change from Penge, Wine and Cheese at the Top Rank Bingo Hall (no wine, precious little cheese), Stevarse traipsing about like a Piccadilly Penguin with an orange up its arse. I'll let you know, Bill, I'll let you know.

Meanwhile, spare a thought for your erstwhile chum in the snug,

DENIS

10 Downing Street
Whitehall

26 October 1979

Dear Bill,

I hope you got the p.c. from Blackpool and Daphne wasn't too shocked — or is she not back yet from Bermuda? I've always liked that joke and I thought the drawing of the surgeon had a look of the Major about it.

The whole shemozzle ran pretty true to form, as you may have appreciated from what they showed on the telly. The tricky part as far as yours truly was concerned was staying awake during the long stretches after lunch. I was under a seven line whip from the Boss on that topic: my orders were to sit up under the lights in full view of the cameras and 'try to look compos mentis', laugh at the right places and so-called 'jokes', and clap at the appropriate moments. No easy brief, Bill, as you will appreciate, especially after taking a few tinctures at lunchtime.

Incidentally, I fell in with a most amusing little fellow called Palmer who claimed to have served under the Major at Caterham, and said he was never a major at all, but actually RSM in charge of stores! What about that, eh Bill? Next time I see the old boy I shall certainly rib him about it. Any rate, Palmer and I got on like a house on fire and found a charming little antiquey sort of snug just off the front where you could get Glen Morangie and not have to rub shoulders with creeps like Stevarse and Heseltine. Honestly, Bill, what a couple of four-letter fellows. I can't think

why the Boss brings in that class of person. By God, have you got to watch them in the rough!

One person I have taken a terrific shine to is old Willie Whitelaw. A real gent of the old school, and what's more with a very decent handicap. Like me, the poor old buffer is much afflicted with the Special Branch. His is called Muffler and is, if anything, more grotesque in appearance than my frightful Eric. He

22

has already spoiled more than one potentially excellent afternoon by lurking about outside the Clubhouse improperly accoutred. We've hatched a plan to give them both the slip one day and pop down to Worplesdon for a few holes (inter nos).

Whitelaw I thought made the only good speech in the whole ballsaching business, saying what he was going to do to the hooligans, i.e. give them a short sharp taste of their own medicine and put a stop to all this namby-pamby do-gooder type of caper recommended by our friends on the *Guardian*. Incidentally, what about Princess Margaret calling the Irish pigs, eh? Glad to see I'm not the only one to put my foot in it over the bog-trotters. Absolutely right, of course: pigs is what they are, and always have been, and if one can't say what one thinks after a cocktail or two what's the point in being alive? As per usual these Press people were lurking behind every bush waiting to pounce. Buggers. I had half a mind to scribble a note to HRH expressing solidarity, but M. squashed it, needless to say.

Did you get a circular from Whiffy about a Burmah Piss-Artists' Reunion at the Savoy? I thought it might be very agreeable if I can get someone to babysit with Eric: still trying to persuade me to sign the pledge, producing awful literature showing the havoc wrought by the demon alcohol. I think one of the snaps is of old Heatherington who used to be a regular at The Feathers.

Yours in spirit,

DENIS

10 Downing Street
Whitehall

9 November 1979

Dear Bill,

I'm beginning to think that Boris is really the only sound man we have in our little Colditz set-up here in Downing Street. He took an extraordinarily dim view of the arrival of the Yellow Peril last week. Boss and Carrington rolling about like puppies waiting to have their tummies tickled by Mr Hu Flung Dung. Yours truly was wheeled out, despite protests, for the Muster Parade. That thing they say about not being able to tell them apart is absolutely true, you know. Hordes of little men poured into the Talking Shop. Fingers crushed to jelly, cramp in jaw muscles from grinning, just about to take refuge in the back pantry with the tincture bottle when Stevarse throws arm round shoulders, cuddles up close and tells me we're off to the Ballet at Covent

Garden. Bang goes my evening with the Celebrity Golf. Boris suggested I should take a portable into the back of the box — he knows all about that sort of thing because they have it in Russia — but I decided reluctantly that M. was in no mood to be trifled with, especially after that speech of Chairman Hu which caused great amusement among those Chinese speakers present and came out in translation as something to do with her wanting to wear Winston's trousers. However, Boris did fit me up with something in a flask to deaden the pain during the long hours of culture that lay ahead.

We got into our box all right, and I managed to bag a seat at the back where it was quite dark, behind a fat chap with bushy eyebrows who seemed to know all about it. After ten minutes of standing up and sitting down, just like that bit in the Marx Brothers film, the orchestra struck up and the curtain rose. Whereupon two dozen or so Bertie Wooftahs came prancing on pretending to be flowers. Bloody fools. I think I must have dozed off at that point. The next thing I knew, the fat man was nudging me and saying my snores were disturbing the dancers. I watched Hu for a bit after that, and I came to the conclusion that these Chinese chaps can sleep with their eyes open. No wonder they did so well against the Chindits. Apropos, frightfully sad about old Templar turning his toes up.

Stevarse, needless to say, flooded out in the interval into the little dining room they have at the back; in raptures about the whole shebang, fluttering around Hu like the proverbial moth. Wasn't he entranced by the Palais Glide and so forth, and throwing in a lot of French expressions that took a bit of fielding by the interpreter. I may say I succeeded in spending Acts II, III and IV in a nice little fizz-shop up in the Gods with a very cheery old body called Mrs Bloomer, who said they might all look very cultivated but you should see the mess after they've gone: cigar butts, rubber johnnies, everything apparently. At the end of it all I squeezed back behind Fatty in time to catch the Finale, which consisted of the same bunch of pansies dressed up as horny-handed sons of toil doing ring a ring o'roses round the village well.

I asked Stevarse afterwards if there was any chance of pulling the whole place down as part of Margaret's cuts, but he got frightfully sniffy and said it would be over his dead body. Which is OK in my book, but I didn't say that.

See you on the 12th at Squiffy's. Promise no shop.

Yours,

DENIS

Dear Bill,
Sorry about M's tetchiness when you phoned on Wednesday night, but things have been somewhat hectic of late and we've been a bit bogged down in the rough. Any little thing sets the old alarm bells going, and your query about why no more tax cuts after the Guildhall shindig on the telly clearly caught M. on the wrong foot. I should have warned you, I suppose, because I got a nasty nip in the seat of the pants only the day before.

As you know, Bill, economics have never exactly been my best shot, but this MLR caper is really too rum for words. I don't know whether I've mentioned it, but I have a very accommodating little bank manager I've discovered at my local NatWest round the corner in Victoria. Name of Furniss and keeps a very decent sherry in the safe. Nor is he averse, I may say, to one or two during working hours, which makes for a most relaxing relationship, I think you'll agree. Anyway, I popped in to pass the time of day on the way to lunch with Sticky at Simpson's, and the conversation eventually came round to my account, which just between the two of us is looking quite healthy at present, thanks to one thing and another.

Why not, says our banking friend, taking a sip of the amber tincture, slosh a bit of the current over into the deposit? 'As from today', he says, pulling out a sheaf of publicity bumf from head office, 'we're giving you a nice fat thirteen and a half per cent before tax, and that can't be bad in anyone's language.' Well, Bill, I thought that sounded a very sensible wheeze. Virtually no expenses nowadays, as many five-course dinners as you can eat, crates of the stuff appearing from well-wishers, not to mention the odd cadeau from tradesmen, and all the rest on HMG. I was always brought up to believe in the piggy bank. 'Put something away for a rainy day,' was what Uncle Jonah used to say: damn shame he never lived to spend it. (Liver, as you may remember, ran up the white flag. But cheerful to the last.) Put the money where it can do something. Very roughly, on the back of an envelope, I reckoned by next year I should be able to bung on a good six noughts, always assuming my mental arithmetic was accurate.

Be that as it may, inflation's no bloody joke — witness poor old Maurice Picarda having the receiver in at Tonbridge and forced to bring forward his holiday plans somewhat sharpish. Now you won't believe this, Bill, but when I got back to the shop I found Howe *a deux* with the Boss, having what I took to be a bit of a barney. When I had helped myself to a generous lotion to keep me going till they opened, I strolled in to see if I could offer any assistance. Although he's very quiet about it, I think Geoffrey Howe values my advice: voice from the grass roots and so forth, car to the shop floor. I make my entrance. Comes a pause. Both looking a bit down in the mouth. 'Well,' says I, 'I think things are going our way at last.' 'Oh,' says M., 'and why do you think that?' So, as you can imagine, Bill, I spooled out the yarn about my little chat with Friend Furniss and the thirteen and a half per cent business, thinking in all innocence that that was the name of the game.

Would you believe it, Bill, the Boss absolutely hit the ceiling. Howe all white and trembly, spectacles steaming on the nose, looking at me as much as to say, 'Why couldn't you keep your bloody trap shut?', and me giving him my 'How was I to know?' look. Turns out the last thing they want to know about is lending rates. M. absolutely Gale Force Eight, next thing we know the mortgages will be going up. Very foolish, looking back, but I put forward the argument that this might be no bad thing, instancing the Major doing so well with his own show, the Tonbridge Reliable. (Weren't you on the Board of that for a while? I think I was.) My God, did the solids hit the fan! I was treated to a sixteen and a half minute lecture on money supply, MLR, some boffin called Friedmann, all of which didn't make any sense to me, and a similar diatribe harping on my various shortcomings, which were all too painfully familiar. Howe didn't exactly come rushing to my support, I must say. But I realised he'd been having his ear pretty effectively chewed off before I blundered in.

Did I tell you I'm beginning to have my doubts about Peter Carrington? I rather think he may have done the dirty on us over the Rhodesia show. I had my suspicions about the Padre chap, Mazaratti or whatever he calls himself, but my hunch is that Carrington has patched up some sort of deal behind our backs with the fat one. I can't see what he hopes to get out of it, that's what puzzles me. But ah me, such is life.

Any chance of Daphne being back at Christmas? I thought we might try and fit in a few rounds at Lamberhurst over the Festive Tide, but the Boss may want to go to Chequers. Not my C of T at all. Full of draughty corridors, portraits of Disraeli, very antique shoppy. Boris I know is dreading it.

My best to Daphne if you're ringing the Bahamas.

TTFN,

DENIS

10 Downing Street
Whitehall

7 December 1979

Dear Bill,

I say, I think the Boss did the right thing vis a vis that swine Blunt, don't you? Did you see him on the TV by any chance? Crikey, what a roarer. I don't know how he ever passed his medical for the Palace. When the whole thing blew up I told the Boss not to go into bat on that one. Exceedingly sticky wicket. Have no qualms, said I, about dropping him right in it. And I've certainly been proved right.

The whole business struck me as very rum. Wilson pops up and says he knew about it all along, shifty little stoat. (I always thought the Sergeants' Mess didn't go along with that sort of thing!) And then it all, comes as a complete surprise to old Home. As you know, Bill, I've always taken the line that Home was a gent, and gents told the truth. And yet, do you know, watching him on the box I could have sworn the old fraud was lying in his teeth. Anyway, it all appears to have been mopped up now, and I wasn't in the mood to raise it with the Proprietor, as her nerves haven't been all they might have been of late and the balloon is likely to go up at the slightest provocation.

The thing is, Bill, I'm not absolutely certain where we are. M. did her table-thumping number at the Common Market get-together in Dublin as you saw, without, it seems, anything very clear emerging, at least not from where I'm sitting. I had been hoping for a bit of a beano beside the Liffey, particularly after that glorious three days — or was it a week? — with you and Daphne the time we ran into the Major's mother in the Shelbourne when she fell over at four o'clock in the afternoon and had to be laid out on the tea-trolley, but anyway, F. O. said no can do, danger to life and limb, too much of a burden on security forces, so I popped down to Lamberhurst in the old Rolls and watched events wrapped around a bottle of Old Grandad. But not

27

before being stuck for the best part of half an hour in one of the downstairs offices with that frightful HMG Roy Jenkins, who apparently runs the whole Common Market racket at their end and had come round to put the Boss in the picture. Talk about dropping names, Bill! We were ankle-deep in them, e.g. did I know any of the French Rothschilds? I said the only Rothschild I ever knew was that awfully decent little pawnbroker in Sandwich where you got that simulated mink for Daphne after the Rotary Dinner went wrong.

As I was saying, I can't help feeling a bit mystified by it all. Howe has a frightful haunted mien, and Joseph looks to me as though he was ripe for the Bin. As Picarda quite rightly complained in a lengthy reverse-charge call from Malta, all this talk about cutting taxes for our people seems to have gone for a burton, and now the teenage boffins in M's think-tank are talking about putting them up again! One hesitates to talk about the old girl being blown off course, but that's the way it's beginning to look. They keep going on about cutting the money supply, but I've never really understood how that was supposed to be achieved, unless of course you go round with collecting bags, as with saucepans during the war, gathering the surplus fivers all together in a heap and setting fire to the lot. I made this point to Howe the other day when he was hanging about in the hall, and he went very quiet. It made me wonder whether he understood it at all.

By the way, Bill, the Festive Tide being almost upon us, could you wangle us a crate or two of the Club port for distribution amongst my intimate circle? Just pop in the usual card and sign them for me if you would be so kind. I simply can't bear the thought of traipsing round Harrods with Eric in tow in his flat hat, not to mention the smell of all those Arabs. Good will to all men, I agree, but there are limits. Quite honestly I am beginning to dread the whole grisly business. Mark is threatening to descend with one of his hideous harem, and him and M. together, as you know, is oil and water. Must go now, Boris is leading me astray with a new consignment of Mother Russia's ruin.

Hope this finds you in the pink,

Your old chum,

DENIS

21 December 1979

Dear Bill,

Oh God! I expect you saw that I made page two of the *Telegraph*. Not exactly calculated to ease my lot with the Boss over Yule. Talk about shits of hell: Fleet Street takes the biscuit. God knows I'm let off the leash seldom enough as it is, sitting in Downing Street all day long being told to lift my feet up every time little Cosgrove comes by with the hoover, and now this comes up.

What happened, Bill, was as follows: as you probably know, I've been toddling along to the Savoy for donkeys' years for some little do that Squiffy gets together in aid of Mentally Handicapped Referees or something of that nature, and I've never thought a thing about it. Quite a decent set of chaps, a few snorts, odd familiar face, all very agreeable. This year, it so happened, thanks to M's elevated status, one of the organisers who I think runs a garden centre just outside Maidstone said would I mind getting up on my hind legs and saying a word or two after the loyal toast. Anything on a sporting theme, absolutely off the record, press wallahs excluded and so on and so forth. I should have seen his form a mile off: a real greaser of the old school and HMG to boot.

Anyway the time trickled by, and come the great day mind still a perfect blank. Boris gave me quite an amusing story about a Chinaman which wasn't really suitable, but as luck would have it I ran into Hector Bellville in the bar as both of us had arrived rather early, and he was frightfully steamed up about the Olympics. Wasn't it a bit rich for the Russians to be practising all their general ghastliness and at the same time telling us that it's verboten for the All Black And Tans or whatever they're called — I can never remember which are ours and which are the Kiwis' — to go out to South Africa and kick the ball about with Brother Boer.

By about seven when the others arrived I felt pretty strongly on this issue and after a dozen or so glasses of plonk accompanying whatever it was we were given to toy with over dinner, I was raring to go. Honestly, Bill, I really believed I was on home ground. And judging by the ovation I got from the comrades and the odd bread roll flying through the air I formed the impression I'd gone down rather well. Some silly bugger wrapped himself up in the tablecloth afterwards, occasioning a certain *froideur* from the Toastmaster, but otherwise the horseplay was very mild and a good time was had by all — or so I thought.

Imagine my feelings when I was having one for the road in a little broom cupboard with Hercot and Co afterwards, when the garden centre fellow came creeping up, laid a hand around my shoulders and said he'd been so bowled over by my harangue that he'd taken the liberty of ringing up a friend of his on *The Times*, and that the chap had been absolutely cock-a-hoop, high time somebody spoke up, my views would reach a wider audience etc.

The memory of breakfast next morning is still too painful to be raked over in full: suffice it to say that the decibel counter shot right off the dial. Did I realise that Africa was an unexploded bomb and that I was jumping up and down on it in hobnailed boots, or words to that effect. I said nothing, and at the first lull in the firing put down smoke and retired upstairs to do my devotions. Eric was very decent. He came up after me looking very shaken and said would I like to spend a few days with him and his mother.

In view of this little misunderstanding, I deemed it prudent not to put my oar in on the Affaire Soames — though, to my mind, Bill, Carrington and the Boss are in the rough without a mashie on this one. Soames is a perfectly nice chap, but as I was saying to Boris, can he stand the excitement of Rhodesia? You'd never guess it from looking at him, but he's already had one very nasty brush with the Reaper, brought on, I surmise, by over-doing it in Brussels on all fronts, not but what he still remains a doughty quaffer of the snorts, presumably on the grounds, though I haven't taxed him on this, that if you've got to go you've got to go. All very well in Sloane Square, Bill, but what happens when a Fuzzy-Wuzzy jumps out from behind a bush, as occurred when I myself was playing golf with the D of E in Lusaka, waving an assegai and shouting 'Whoah ho ho!' or words to that effect?

It's exactly the same as bloody Ulster. Before we know where we are, Bill, we'll be bogged down in Coonsville just like the Frogs at Dien Bien Phu, to general international hilarity on all sides. It just peeves me that thanks to some bloody little garden centre wallah from Maidstone I am going to be held responsible for it.

If I don't see you before, the merriest of Christmasses to you and yours, and don't do anything I wouldn't do.

Yours,

DENIS

CHATEAU
ST. DENIS

1980
BOTTLED

CHEQUERS

4 January 1980

Dear Bill,

You must think I'm an absolute four-letter fellow for letting you and Daphne down over the Boxing Day tinctures. but *force majeure* intervened yet again. I sent you a p.c. to explain the last-minute change of plan but I imagine you won't have got it. In our neck of the woods we haven't had a delivery or collection as far as I can see for the last fortnight apart from the buff envelopes from the GPO threatening one with death by a thousand cuts. If you ask me, the whole so-called workforce have now got it into their Neanderthal skulls that they are entitled to a month's free holiday over Christmas and the New Year. What it means in real terms is that people like you and me, Bill, are forced to sit on our backsides doing absolutely sod-all when we could be usefully employed.

Everything was reasonably under control until Boxing Day morning, when young Mark, the son and heir, who had to my profound relief failed to respond to his mother's unambiguous directives to join us over the festive board, drove in unannounced in one of his souped-up BRMs, knocking over two of the Elizabethan bollards planted outside this monstrosity by one of the former incumbents. At his side, need I say, a very solid looking air-hostess from Air Danske with whom, it seemed, he had struck up an acquaintance on one of their scheduled flights. His mother had been up working for some three or four hours in the Baldwin Room, so I was obliged, if you please, to bustle down and play mine genial host.

God, Bill, what a ballsacher! Great Dane entirely mute, refusing all refreshment, prodigal son full of interminable anecdotes re his latest business venture viz advertising felt-tip pens on his bloody racing car. All the time, I must say, stuffing his face with a massive fry-up very decently conjured into existence out of hours by Mr Wu, the Filipino custodian in the employ of the National Trust, which quite put me off my first snort of the day. I was about to recommend a wash and brush up prior to his being received into the maternal bosom when M. anticipated my thoughts by sweeping in, dressed to the nines and muttering about Afghanistan. I could see at a glance that she was slightly less than delighted by the scene that met her eyes, particularly when Miss Piggy failed to respond in any way, staring sulkily at her shoes and gripping her Air Danske travelling bag. I thought it prudent at this point to toddle off, feeling as I always do rather defenceless in a dressing-gown and slippers.

While slipping into the tweeds, I discovered from Boris — he, lucky man, was able to spend Christmas entirely alone in the attic — that some celebration was afoot, and we were entertaining the Carringtons to lunch. My spirits couldn't have been much lower, but I realised on arriving in what passes for the drawing-room that things were more disastrous than even I had feared. Mr Wu had failed to clear away the little red ropes that normally keep the public off the furniture, and the central heating had packed it in a few hours earlier. It's always pretty chilly in this ghastly mausoleum even when it works, and by now you could see your breath.

The Danish Bacon was still in situ: it seemed that Mark had put in a word on social poise, and the sulky expression had given way to a glassy and immutable smile. All Peter Carrington's very remarkable powers of diplomacy, successful though they may have been with the Coons, seemed to be making little impact on the Anglo-Danish front. Doubles seemed to be in order. Lady Carrington, who is really a very good sport, got down on her hands and knees in the grate and tried to get a fire going out of some old National Trust literature and a model of *Morning Cloud* left behind by Heath. Mark meanwhile had done something to appease the maternal wrath by producing a presentation hamper from Harrods, now enshrined in the place of honour under the Christmas tree.

Lunch, in our overcoats, was not the happiest of occasions, and Mr Wu's curried turkey croquettes were by no means the success they might have been. For long periods there was no sound but the clink of cutlery on plates, and curious looks were exchanged between M. and the Danish Bacon. After Mr Wu, now in a mood of suppressed hysteria, had handed round the cold Christmas pud and we had drained four bottles of very decent Chateau Talbot out of the cellar, Mark volunteered to burrow underneath the tree, and came back with a huge box of Harrods' Al Koran Drambuie-Filled Chocolate Bonbons. 'Here you are, Ma' — pushing them in her face — 'your favourites', at which a carbon-copy invoice fluttered into M's lap, clearly made out to 'Mrs M. Thatcher' of Downing Street for 250 nicker, overprinted with a red rubber stamp expressing hopes of an early settlement of the account.

As you know, Bill, I am always an optimist. I had hoped that M. would restrain her feelings at least until the departure of our guests, but I was wrong and we were instantly bent to ground level in the fury of a real Force-Eighter. Thank God for Boris and the little billiard-room-cum-cocktail-lounge under the roof, installed by the Lady Falkender for her personal researches.

On a warmer note, I've been looking through some of these holiday brochures. If Daphne's wanderlust is still unabated, how about you and me sampling the Off Season Duty-Free on the

Isola d'Elba? A magnificent new 18-holer, all mod cons, six days from £299.73.

Vive le Sport.

Yours till the cows come home,

DENIS

10 Downing Street
Whitehall

18 January 1980

Dear Bill,

I must say the news as the year begins is enough to make one embark on the bare bodkin routine. M. is frightfully steamed up about the Russian Bear. Quite right too in my book. Boris of course is biased on this one, but as one who knows his Burma and has seen Johnny Gurkha on the job, I see the whole thing as crystal-clear. Peter Carrington dropped in the other night with his missus for a bite. A very nice chap, no side at all, told me he *did* remember Sticky at Eton, but more of that anon when we meet. Lady C. is an absolute brick, and while she and M. went off to powder their noses I took the opportunity of putting in my two-pennyworth. As I told him, with the help of the very serviceable *Reader's Digest World Atlas and Restaurant Guide* your Tunbridge Wells friend kindly slipped into my arms after that shindig at the Pantiles, Warm Water Ports is the name of the game. Ever since the days of Ivan the Terrible, I explained over a tincture or twain, what the Russky has always craved is somewhere to keep his fleet where it isn't too cold. Archangel and so forth often frozen up about Christmas time. What more natural then than for the Red Menace to come rolling through the Khyber, next stop Colombo, and there's your W.W.P?

Carrington seemed very receptive to my little geography lesson, which I hope provided a salutary antidote to what he gets fed by the assorted Moles, Pinkoes and Wooftahs at the F.O. As he did not reply in so many words, merely drumming his fingers on the tabletop and looking at the ceiling — always a sign in my experience that the little grey cells are working flat out — I was emboldened to propose something short and sharp. No earthly use, I ventured to suggest, in buggering about banning the export of breakfast cereals, they can always fill up with lentils. Withdrawing our show-jumping team from the Olympic Caper seems equally pointless, pissing in the wind, only leave the way open for the Japs to nab all the silver pots and trophies. Far better a quick blitz with half a dozen ICBMs, only language these chaps understand. Witness A. Hitler, failure to deal with menace of.

I could see Carrington absorbing all this, eyes tightly closed in concentration. However, when we joined the Boss and Lady C. for the After Eights, the conversation turned to the rights and wrongs of index-linked perks for non-residential ex-industrialists. I now learn that as far as the Red Menace is concerned there are plans afoot to cancel the forthcoming visit of the Leningrad Formation Ice-Skating Team. That'll stop the Mongol Hordes in their tracks, eh Bill? Poor old Colombo is all I have to add.

Perhaps you detect a note of cynicism creeping in. I found myself in the lift at Number Ten the other day with old Howe. I don't know if you remember him: glasses, brothel-creepers, quite a decent bird in the main but hardly one for a night of mischief at the Pig & Whistle. He seemed to think, poor jerk, that I had some influence with M., and weighed in on the steel strike. As you know, M's line on this is the Three Wise Monkey Gambit — not the Government's baby, let the  buggers fight it out among themselves and so forth. Howe seemed to have got it into his head that it *was* somehow the Government's responsibility in view of the fact that the Government was actually the employer and would have to foot the bill, whatever they decide. Quite a sound point, Bill, I think you'll agree.

However the Boss is not, as you know, over-open to persuasion. I told Howe that as a married man he ought to know that when dealing with the fair sex the only option open is to sit on arse, keep head down and wait for wind to change: not then to be too surprised, when this happens, if your point of view is claimed to have been hers all along.

So, if you ask me, little Len Murray will be toddling round for a tincture within the very foreseeable future.

The Major has opened a book on the Fatty Soames In Coonsville saga. I've given him evens on our portly friend having to be winched out by helicopter as the blood rises around his knees. However, let's hope for everyone's sake that they can patch up some sort of semblance of a settlement and get the hell out of it before that scenario actually goes into production.

Give my regards to civilisation when you get there, and bring me back a bottle of that 200-proof if you have room in your little zip-bag.

Yours, holding the fort,

DENIS

Dear Bill,

Ta for the p.c., which, alas, was not received at our breakfast table with quite the mirth I'm sure you intended. Boris insisted on showing it to M., hoping to curry favour, and her response was grim in the extreme. Would I kindly see to it in future that if my golfing friends wish to send obscene material through the post they do so in a sealed package. Quite enough trouble as it was without giving the Press another stick to beat us with. Nil desperandum, however. Boris and I found the dusky lady absolutely irresistible, and have got her propped up on the mantelpiece in our little den in the attic.

The Boss is over the moon with the War Fever. I must say I am all in favour of buggering up the Olympics. For a start it always occupies the TV to the exclusion of better things, e.g. Angela Rippon and *Pot Black*, and then again, what's the point of a huge jamboree like that if it excludes the only decent game, and indeed one of the oldest, ever invented? So full marks to the Boss for her firm stand in Round One. I did opine, over a Twiglet, that the idea of putting the whole bang-shoot into Olympia seemed a bit outre. Those sort of places are always booked up months in advance anyway with DIY conventions, Health Food weirdoes and Caravan Shows, as the Major discovered when he and Picarda had that wheeze for flogging the cargo of reject Japanese greenhouses to the unsuspecting populace.

The Boss however would hear none of it, and poor little Cosgrove had to ring round every Bingo Hall and Greyhound Stadium in the country and ask if they had any cancellations. Result: no can do all round. My proposal for International Golfing Tournament sponsored by one of the big snort merchants instantly vetoed.

Ding, Ding, Round Two. Various elderly Senior Citizens summoned round. From their appearance in the hall I took them to be a British Legion delegation whose home had fallen under the axe, come to plead for mercy. Not so. Every one of the old buffers had at some time twinkled round the track bearing the Olympic Torch. Frogmarched en masse into Boss's sanctum, yours truly roped in to pass round warm sherry, M. sweeps in giving her Virgin Queen, reads them all the Riot Act, no truckling to Russian Bear or Government rug pulled from under young Gymnasts in no uncertain manner. At this, one cherry-nosed old party having trouble with his hearing-aid made point that they were all booked into Moscow Hilton, whole caper insured at Lloyds fifty-six million pounds, loss in souvenirs alone would bankrupt country, and anyway Hitler not such a bad fellow, made trains run on time. No wonder the Boss got nowhere. Cherry-nosed party blows noisily through pipe, unaware of Gorgon glance which would have turned anyone more alert to stone. Cosgrove told me old codger won a bronze for hop skip and jump in 1911. Incredible, isn't it?

Only decent chuckle material we've had was provided by M's creepy little chum Stevarse. All of us here, or Boris at least, knew perfectly well the Budget was going to clash with the Enthronement highjinks at Canterbury. Indeed, when the thing originally cropped up, Howe sought me out personally for a gut reaction. What would be drinking man's view? With a flash of insight I suggested double-booking: with two functions on same day any reasonable man can get out of both by saying he's at the other one. Howe agreed, observing that three hours amid the flowered hats in Canterbury Cathedral listening to *Hymns A&M* not his idea of bliss. I omitted to counter that a similar period locked in the Distinguished Strangers' Pen wearing the Moss Bros. bib and tucker listening to him drooling on over the little red box not exactly mine.

All would have been hunky-dory had it not been for our friend Stevarse who came mincing round reeking of garlic after a troughful of Risotto with our iceycreamio chums Saatchi and Saatchi. I spotted he was up to something from the way he was wringing his hands like a sky-pilot on the make. 'What an opportunity', he tells the Boss, all misty-eyed, 'to show that spiritual values not dead, religion meaningful role to play in the Eighties, Ayatollah not entirely barking up wrong tree, materialism on the run etc.' Quite honestly, Bill, it made me feel sick. But as you know, the Boss took a shine to Stevarse from the start — God knows why. Clear as the balls on a dog the man's an A1 bumsucker. So you can cross March 25th and March 26th off the map as far as I'm concerned.

Give my regards to Mrs Nightingale at the Lamb & Flag and ask her if she still remembers the night we played Spudarse along the top of the Saloon Bar after Rollo Wittaker's funeral.

Yours in the Lord,

DENIS

15 February 1980

Dear Bill,

Glad to hear you and Daphne are back on terra firma and, according to the Major, black as a couple of coons. It must be a touch disheartening to find so little changed during your absence, i.e. steelmen's pickets at every corner baying defiance.

Who, you might ask, is behind this ongoing balls-up? None other than our old friend Sir Keith Joseph, Svengali, the Mad Monk, assisted by friend Howe, who, I am beginning to opine, has very little going on between the ears. So, according to the latest bulletin, it's full steam ahead now for New Laws. Pickets illegal, proles absolutely at liberty to strike providing no inconvenience caused.

Last Tuesday evening I happened to stumble on the Monk spelling out this latest lunacy to the Boss over a lotion in her little sitting-room upstairs. You should see him in action, Bill: it's quite a sight. Eyes rolling, fingers scratching at the roots of his curly locks, then leaping up, and pacing about overturning everything that isn't nailed to the floor. Rather like that peculiar brother of Maurice Picarda's who set up as a shrink in Bournemouth. (Wasn't he struck off?)  M. watches, teeth agleam, eyes filled with admiration, rabbit hypnotised by snake syndrome. I was helping myself to a large brownie from the lotion cupboard and doing my best to keep the blood pressure normal. However, when he paused for breath I decided to put my oar in. All very well wheeling out the senile beaks like Gaffer Denning: what if revolutionary mob raises two fingers? My query was obviously seen as only an irritation. The Bold Baronet muttered something about crossing that bridge, fullness of time, majority of unions law-abiding etc. Boss looking firmly at toe-cap, jaw set. Yours truly ploughs on with history lesson. E. Heath, Industrial Relations Court, Pentonville Martyrs. Our Lot made to look bloody idiots.

Silly of me as it turned out. Always unwise to refer to M's sea-faring predecessor. Solids hit airconditioning in no uncertain manner. Anything that went wrong that time all Heath's fault, my views irrelevant and unwished for, yours truly there to be seen but not heard, ideally neither.

I did have a quiet word with Jim Prior however by the back door, and he said he thought the Monk was due for a spell in the funny farm. Apparently, during their meeting, though this is absolutely for your ears only, Prior enquired what happened if there was a General Strike? Cannot arrest whole population. Not enough bobbies to go round. Joseph's solution: recruit more bobbies. I ask you, Bill! Not that the Monk's legislation will ever come to pass in any shape or form, but it does make you yearn for the old days of Peterloo and so forth, when they knew how to do these things.

Oh, by the way, Boris is fairly certain that the Special Branch are listening in on our phone calls. Apparently, thanks to this new micro-chip technology, certain keywords will start the spools going round in their cellar. So don't be too surprised if you find my conversation somewhat guarded. The Major was very mystified, particularly by the noise of Boris clattering about with his de-bugging kit. However, the folowing code will apply in future: The Boss equals 'Ethel'. The Major equals 'our mutual friend'. Golf equals 'Boardroom meeting'. This should do for a start. See you at the Driving Range on Friday and ask Mrs Ferguson to line them up at the bar. It is my intention to get really plastered.

Your old chum,

DENIS

10 Downing Street
Whitehall

29 February 1980

Dear Bill,

Sorry to be a bit short on the phone. I knew perfectly well what you wanted to know, but with the Boss in a dudgeon at my elbow my replies had perforce to be somewhat clipped. All I can say is that it hasn't been entirely disagreeable to see another member of the family, to wit the son and heir, taking it in the neck for a change.

As you know, Bill, Mark and I have never exactly hit it off. I could have overlooked his chucking golf lessons after only two sessions on the links, but when he used the set of half-size clubs from Hamleys I gave him for his seventh birthday to light the bonfire with I realised that we would have to go our separate ways. Nothing he has done since has ever given me cause to revise my opinion. Still, there it is. New wine and old bottles, as somebody said. As for bringing the little bugger to heel, I long since banished that idea from the realm of possibility. Not that his mother's ever had a great deal of time for him either, between ourselves, though she did kick up a bit rough when he started on this Fangio business in the first place. Quite understandable in the circs: animal instinct to preserve our young. Even though the sight of the little swine makes one want to puke, one doesn't like the thought of him going over the hard shoulder and snuffing it in a blaze of publicity.

I remember at the time I was detailed to have a man-to-man chinwag about it all and try to steer his thoughts into dress-designing or accountancy. Needless to say, the whole exercise was a non-event. He just sat there with a sulky sort of look sipping his rum and coca-cola and inferring that I was some sort of alcoholic idiot spending the twilight of my life staggering from green to green with various derelicts and deadbeats. Some truth in it, I suppose, if I am to be perfectly honest, but I was buggered if I was going to take it from a long-haired spotty-faced whipper-snapper like that who doesn't know his arse from his elbow.

Anyway after that I took the view that as far as I was concerned he could go to hell in a handcart. He was fairly hard put to it to do a three-point turn in any case, so no one seemed very anxious to come up with the spondulicks. Even the rubber johnny merchants gave him the thumbs down, and you couldn't go much lower than that, eh? (I must say, even I would have qualms about allowing my first-born to hurtle round Brands Hatch at a hundred mph flogging French letters to the great unwashed.)

I was therefore not displeased when old Eric, my bodyguard, who usually toddles down to the corner to pick up the evening edition, showed me the item about this big Jap conglomerate Phuwhatascorcha Co. offering to put something up front in return for him modelling their electrically-heated rain-hats. I said to Boris, 'He could do a lot worse than that.' Besides which, it did cross my mind that there might be the odd free trip for yours truly to the Land of the Rising Sun where, as you know, if the Major is to be believed, there are many avenues to be explored by the fun-loving golf enthusiast and *bon viveur*. (Not a word to Bessie etc!) M. didn't seem too miffed at the time, it being no great loss, in her view, were young Mark to be permanently exported to Japan and points East.

As usual, all would have been well had it not been for the filthy reptiles of Fleet Street. Before you could say Red Robbo every jumped-up dirty-necked little leader-writer was sniggering away about the Japanese Connection, Pissing on the Flag, what's wrong with British electrically-heated rain-hats and so forth, conveniently forgetting that no self-respecting British company woud touch the little bugger with a bargepole. Labour mob up on their feet like a pack of monkeys at the zoo, pelting the Boss with anything they can lay their hands on. Proprietor inevitably displeased. I am summoned to the Snug, nicely woozy on Boris's vodka, to do my heavy father bit. Helter-skelter to Flood Street, Boris at the wheel, enter over back wall to avoid press, tear new pair of cavalry twill trousers from arsehole to breakfast table, finally track down son and h. slouched in front of TV amid litter of beer cans.

To my amazement, immediate cave-in on all fronts. No question of embracing Nips if M. doesn't like it, has British sponsor up sleeve. It occurred to me on the way back to the Lubjanka there might be a catch in it, and indeed there was. Next thing we know Mark emerging from Massage Parlour to maximum publicity brandishing offers from some seedy Soho tit-and-bum wallah who publishes *Men Only* in his spare time. I don't know if you've seen *Men Only* recently, Bill, but it has rather changed since the days when you and I would peruse a dog-eared black-and-white copy in the Mess over a snort or two. I sent Eric down to W.H. Smith to pick up a sample but what he found within clearly distressed the poor old boy terribly. I'm a broad-minded chap myself, Bill, as you know, but some of the material puts one in mind of old Army days doing a Clap Round on the Reeperbahn. Moments later, Mark on the phone. 'Okay? Hope M. is now satisfied, real bunk-up for British magazine publishing. Soho Johnny nice bloke, anxious to come round for a snifter at Number Ten.'

Result inevitable. No official intervention from M. Mark agrees to sever connections with porn-wallah, future silence assured in exchange re-opening unlimited credit facilities M's account Harrods, Man About Town Tailoring Company, Talbot Winemart etc. Don't say the Young Tories don't know their 'A' level Economics.

Yours very affectionately,

DENIS

10 Downing Street
Whitehall

14 March 1980

Dear Bill,
Hats off to Fatty Soames. I must say he fooled me. There was time, as you know, when Boris and I were absolutely at one in thinking the old boy would be winched out of Rhodesia by a chopper as the blood rose over his knees. As it is, the stage seems well and truly set for our overweight chum to climb into his feathered hat and watch the flag pulled down with a modicum of

41

dignity. The D of E rang to say he was under some pressure from the better half to turn out for the Last Post but that he was, entre nous, resisting it. His plan now is to try and winkle out one of the younger generation to go and stand in on behalf of the Great White Mother Across The Sea.

I find the whole thing extraordinarily puzzling, Bill. After all, we had been led to suppose that this Mugabe character was the devil incarnate, hands steeped in gore, loincloth laden down with Moscow gold etc. etc. so I was a bit nonplussed when little Carrington came bouncing in rubbing his hands and saying everything was tickety-boo. I could see at once that the Boss didn't share his enthusiasm, so I suggested to our noble friend that a lotion might not come amiss. A generous brownie and soda made his eyes gleam somewhat, and he raised the Waterford crystal to remark, 'Well, Prime Minister, here's to the new Democratic People's Republic of Zimbabwe!' He then drained the tumbler, while the Boss continued to give him one of her looks. 'I thought, Peter,' she said, in a frostyish tone, 'our money was on the Bishop.' 'But don't you see?' the modern Metternich exclaimed, extending his glass for a refill, 'that's what it's all about, Baby Doll. Free and Fair Elections! May the best man win!' It crossed my mind at this point that he might have had one or two before he arrived — some kind of FO celebration. M. however remained unmoved. 'I don't like it one little bit,' she said. 'Kindly make it clear to him that one step out of line and he will get it very hard over the knuckles.' Carrington wisely refrained at this juncture from pursuing the point further, and turned the conversation to events nearer home.

I took the liberty of pouring a little cold water over Carrington myself on the way out to the lift. I don't know if you know, but the Major's brother Clem who went off to Rhodesia after the 39–45 show and did very well out of copper sulphate has been making noises for some time about catching the first plane out, and now that Comrade Mugabe has assumed the reins of office I imagine he'll be over any minute. The point I put to Peter Carrington is that they're obviously not going to be able to run the country without the Major's brother and his ilk, so he shouldn't be too cock-a-hoop. I formed the impression, as he got into the lift with some difficulty, that he frankly didn't give a bugger. 'Well,' he shouted, as the doors began to close, 'it's not my responsibility now, chum! Get the British bobbies back, and if all the suburban riff-raff who went out to feather their beastly little nests get chopped up into tiny bits by the natives, I personally shall not lift a finger to prevent it.' With this the doors closed, the lift lurched downwards and he sank, swaying, out of sight.

I must say, Bill, I was a bit shocked by his attitude. I went straight back upstairs, opened another bottle, and wrote a firm note to Carrington suggesting the moment Clem hits Gatwick we should all get together at the Army & Navy and give him the benefit of a view from the grass roots.

Gilmour and Carrington are all very well in their way, but, like Sticky, they tend to take a rather lofty view of things.

Yours pro tem,

DENIS

10 Downing Street
Whitehall

28 March 1980

Dear Bill,

Stroll on, what a week! I don't know whether you've ever been to an Archbishop's Enthronement, but I would strongly advise against it. The charabanc left Downing Street at some Godforsaken hour, very depressing drive through the East End, bloody cold to boot, and M. plainly narked at being called away from affairs of State. Eric insisted on sitting in the front so as to take the first impact of any assassination attempt, and I was stuck in the back between Boris and the Boss. As B. is on the bulky side you can imagine I emerged somewhat crushed outside the Archiepiscopal digs. Needless to say, we were early. The Boss always has to leave two hours in case of punctures, acts of God, earthquakes etc.

You know the form at these sky-pilots' get-togethers — remember the grisly evening we once spent with the Bishop of Deal the time he blessed the Golf Course, silly bugger? (Who's daft idea was that?) I knew perfectly well that all we were going to get while we were kicking our heels was a thick glass of warm cooking sherry and as we went through the oaken door I was feeling pretty depressed, I don't mind admitting. Mrs Runcie, reeking of some tarty scent, was doing the honours in a silly hat with fruit on, and Runcie himself was hovering about in a long purple get-up rubbing his hands and showing his teeth. I took the Boss aside and began to tell her she'd picked a wrong 'un and they should have had old Archie Wellbeloved, senile or not senile, but I was sent away with a flea in my ear as per usual and told not to be preposterous.

At this juncture all eyes turned to the door at the arrival of Royalty and the Number Two Seed tottered in looking very merry in a veil. I was just thinking, Bill, what a relief she hadn't brought that frightful little nancy-boy with her when she made a bee-line for me, ignoring the grinning Bish, and led me discreetly into a corner behind the bust of some bearded buffer from Victorian days. 'You and I are going to go out into the garden and admire the daffodils,' she hissed through clenched teeth, a note of great firmness in her voice, and before I knew it, she had a firm grip on my arm and was steering me through the French windows. Once outside, her manner changed. 'God, what a relief,' she breathed. 'If they think we're going to get through three hours of all that jiggery-pokery without a couple of big ones they must be out of their tiny minds.'

I know a cry for help when I hear one, Bill, and in no time at all we had swung a leg over the garden wall, shot down a little cobbled alleyway, and were lining them up in the firelit snug of the Miller's Arms.

Very approachable lady, Bill. Full of good tales, and as you will have gathered from the above, not averse to the odd snort. We managed to take on board half a dozen large G and Ts before a breathless Eric, his tie and raincoat in disarray, burst through the curtain to announce that Stevarse had observed our departure and ratted on the Boss. Would we kindly take our seats as the balloon was going up? I don't remember a great deal of the ceremony. I must have dropped off I think while a whiskery old Greek was saying a word or two on behalf of our sundered brethren in the East. I found it all very confusing. As I said to Princess Margaret, I thought it was meant to be a CofE beano, and yet the place was swarming with RCs, Methodists and God knows what.

Back at the Barracks I was inevitably called into the study and given a wigging for going AWOL, but fortunately I had the Prerogative to fall back on, Royal Will not to be denied etc. Didn't go down too well, but better than nothing.

A few brief hours of troubled sleep and then back into the bib and tucker for little friend Howe's hour of glory. I have never understood why he can't just get up and say 'A quid on fags, couple of quid on petrol etc.', and then sit down again. Instead of which we are treated to a ballsaching lecture beforehand on the state of the nation with special reference to such fascinating topics as International Monetary Trends, Excess Surpluses and Taking Up The Slack. Thank goodness I am beginning to know the ropes. I always choose a seat at the back of the gallery on the gangway, and after a suitable interval I get a very nasty frog in the throat, of the type that prevents other members of the audience from catching the jewels being scattered below. Stifling the sounds in vain with a hanky, and amid sympathetic murmurs, I then bang out through the swing doors, and away like the clappers to the House of Lords' Lounge, where there is always a very decent crowd watching the Racing, and even a hot line to Joe Coral's.

 Wilson was sitting in a corner looking rather under the weather with a bottle of brandy in one hand and a balloon glass in the other, and I got chatting to him. Quite a decent cove, Bill. Very fond of golf and used an umbrella to show me a wheeze for getting out of a bunker in the rain with a number three lofting iron. At about five o'clock they started serving tea and cakes, and I asked him what had happened in the Budget, but he said he didn't know and didn't give a bugger. I know you'll find it hard to believe, Bill, but I think he's one of us. One of these days I really feel we ought to invite him down to Littlestone. I'd give a great deal to see the Major's face when we stomp in with his arch-enemy in tow.

All best to Daphne. Wrap up well.

Yours,

DENIS

CHEQUERS

11 April 1980

Dear Bill,

I'm sorry Hoddinott was so miffed about the liquor run to Number Ten. Tell him I'll see him right with a couple of blueys next time I'm down at Worplesdon. My fault entirely. I should have explained about bringing it round the back. As it was I gather he started lugging crates out of his hatchback bang outside the front door on Budget Eve and all the tourists began to cheer. Thinking there was some pro-Tory demo organised by Saatchi & Saatchi afoot, M. stuck her head out of the first-floor window to acknowledge the greetings of the Faithful, and there's poor old H. struggling to get his arms round a Europack of litre-size Mother's Ruin. We were definitely not amused.

H. got a flea in his ear before being duffed up by the Special Patrol Unit, always on the lurk with weighted truncheons looking for a spot of fun. I hurried down to try and rescue the booze at least, but every bloody bottle had already been impounded by the Commissioner, and all I got was six of the best from the Boss, and three days in Coventry.

A propos the Budget, the general consensus at the watering holes would appear to be that our lawyer friend Howe could have done a damn sight worse. I had a word with Mine Host at the Waggonload of Monkeys in Great Missenden, and his view was that it was high time somebody got a grip on the strikers and came down on their free hand-outs and that anyone who was prepared to go out and give the so-called workers a good solid boot in the balls had his vote. A bit extreme, you may think, but I find more and more of our sort talking in that vein on my whistle-stop tours of the local hostelries.

By the way, Bill, you might be interested to hear that Howe very sensibly consulted me as part of his grass roots soundings before toddling down Mount Sinai with his battered old bag. We found ourselves sitting next to each other at one of those ghastly receptions for some visiting potentate at the Fishmongers' Hall and he asked me would I go white about the gills if he slammed fifty pee on a bottle of snorts. I spotted his drift at once. Obviously the mandarins had got the wind up at the last minute: drinking man's backlash, heels dug in, consumption peaks off, etc. By way of reply I recalled the case of that old sawbones who was always propping up the bar at Rye. Furnival? Bulstrode? Anyway I think he turned his toes up a few years ago after a prolonged period of St Vitus Dance and DTs. (I always remember M. used to object to the fumes when he was feeling her chest in a professional capacity.)

Anyway, one Budget night I shall never forget, old Venables or whatever his name was banged on the bar with his knobkerry and announced to all and sundry that enough was enough. In protest at yet another imposition by the Chancellor he wanted everyone to witness that he was about to sink his final snort this side of the grave. He then filled a beermug with Stag's Breath, drained the lot, and was duly carried out by some of his medical chums who knew the form. But, as I said to Howe, and this was the point, precisely three nights later there he was back on his stool, looking like death warmed up and paying his surcharge like the rest of us.

Howe obviously got the message. Not that I'm in favour of it, you understand, Bill, but as I said to Boris, what's fifty pee nowadays? Give it to the cloakroom wallah at the Savoy and he'll spit in your eye.

A quiet Easter in the main. Mark, thank the Lord, has gone off to practise his reversing and three-point turns at a disused airport somewhere near Kidderminster. M. had that smarmy bloke from Brussels, Jenkins, down to chew the fat vis a vis our European Contributions, and the only excitement came when Wilson, who has a little hideyhole just up the road from here, rang up during the Boat Race to propose a round of golf with some Lebanese friends of his on Bank Holiday Monday. Needless to say, M. put the kibosh on this 'for security reasons'. What she means is the Press might get hold of it, further ridicule and contempt etc. for fraternising with the other side, even though Wilson himself hates the Unions as much as you or me, and told me in strict confidence that that secretary of his there was all the trouble about actually voted for our side last time round.

Ah well, see you at the Reunion on the 14th.

Yours aye,

DENIS

10 Downing Street
Whitehall

25 April 1980

Dear Bill,

Sorry I couldn't make the Reunion. For once the coast was clear on the Proprietor front, but bloody Boris had been tinkering with the Rolls all weekend and when it came to the count-down she spluttered a bit and then conked out. All done up in my bib and tucker, juices going nicely at the thought of snorts to come, and the old girl dies on me. Boris crawled underneath, followed by yours truly, in a bit of a temper by this time, but no joy. Next train wouldn't have got me down till after midnight, limos all tied up, Mr Patel of the minicabs celebrating Pakistani New Year. I rang through to the Lady Hamilton Suite at the Anchor but as usual only got some Filipino cove with a very limited grasp of the language. In the end Boris and I mooched off in the direction of the bright lights, v. down at heart, and after one or two scrapes ended up in some refurbished Georgian joint in Mayfair with a lot of sweaty Arabs throwing their money away as if there was no tomorrow.

Talking of Arabs, I thought Peter Carrington went a bit far grovelling to the Chief Wog about the Death of a Princess. I told him so myself when he dropped in for a hamburger and a glass of port conjured up by the Boss for the Salisbury briefing. He said he hated doing it, but the Children of Allah v. touchy and there

47

was a lot of money involved. I suppose it makes sense though honestly, when you think of the way we used to handle the buggers in Benghazi it's jolly weird I think you'll agree . . . Do you remember the night the Colonel squirted the fire extinguisher all over the dhobi wallah? Through the window like a dose of salts, as I recall. No apologies on that occasion.

Meanwhile we're all supposed to be getting steamed up about the Hostages. The Boss, as you may have noticed, is v. carried away, everything within our power to support friend Carter in his hour of need etc. Sanctions, naval blockade, threat of nuclear bombardment. Fortunately I managed to get my oar in before everybody went quite over the top. Carrington, as I think I've told you, is a very approachable geezer, and I broached matters with him when we found ourselves shoulder-to-shoulder in the downstairs gents at Number Ten.

My theme, Bill, was this. You and I know brother Wog and what an excitable little chap he is. Threaten him with a big stick and the danger is that before you can say knife you'll have him whirling like a dervish, eyes flashing fire, bonfire of American flags blazing away on every side, situation v. disagreeable. The other point I pressed home on our friend, who very decently agreed to follow me up to the boxroom for a nocturnal lotion, was that trying to impose sanctions was about as much good as flogging rubber johnnies in a monastery. You try and stop the Japs, for instance, piling in, all spectacles and flashing gold teeth, if they sniff a market for their motorbikes and electric xylophones. Ditto the Frog. Ditto practically everyone you can think of, viz BP in Rhodesia.

Replenishing our friend's toothmug with another generous shot of the duty-free, I made my third point — in my view the clincher. All very well for Carter to ask everyone to rally round for his Middle Eastern adventures, but what happened at Suez? In we go, grin grin from Uncle Sam, shit hits fan and you can't see the buggers for dust. In plain man's language, you've got to watch the Yanks in the rough.

Carrington seemed very receptive, I must say, to all of the above. What's more, he agreed with me wholeheartedly as we negotiated our way down the stairs from the attic that there's something bloody rum about a bloke of Carter's age going round holding hands with his wife in public.

Neither of us had any idea it was so late, but when I attempted to unravel the various chains and bolts on the front door, imagine my surprise when the burglar alarm system went off with the noise of fifty fire-engines going flat out. Eric was first down the pole, cloth cap and dressing-gown with Luger at the ready, what a prize ass that man is, closely followed by the Boss, hair in curlers, poker in hand, eyes flashing killer rays. Carrington's powers of diplomacy enabled him to shimmer through the crack unharmed, leaving yours truly to take it in the neck as per usual.

By the bye. Did you see that fellow Mugabe going on about

being in love with Fatty Soames? Is it me, Bill, or is everyone going completely barmy?

Yours to the death,

DENIS

10 Downing Street
Whitehall

9 May 1980

Dear Bill,

Forgive me for not answering all of your telephone calls during the crisis, but M. was hoping Carter would ring any minute on the hot line and things, at this end at least, were a trifle tense. I gather the Major was a bit carried away after the CD practice at Maidstone and was trying to get through for a nuclear sitrep. What the poor old bean doesn't quite grasp is that I'm often just as much in the dark as you lot. As indeed is M. She was absolutely hopping mad hearing about Carter's hostage rescue attempt on the wireless, but I pointed out that even Vance wasn't au fait with events so it was hardly surprising if Carter failed to give the tip-off to his friends and allies around the globe.

I don't know whether I've ever mentioned it before, Bill, but Carter has always struck me as a very rum sort of cove, ever since that time he went around holding hands with his wife. M.

continues to go into bat for him in the H of C, but from where I'm sitting it's pretty clear he's a bit top-heavy on the loony end of things. Carrington admitted as much himself when he called in to collect his shoes which he left behind the week before. But his reading is that if Carter starts feeling unwanted and unloved something might crack and he'd press the red one. Hence the general closing of ranks and rallying round, even by Giscard who hates his guts. I suppose this is a sound approach. Do you remember the time Sticky's brother who was head of that big ball-bearings firm in the Midlands got it into his head that everybody had it in for him? Took all his clothes off and went through the ornamental flowerbeds outside the works with a Rotaator. They had to take him away. (Is he out? No matter.)

Boris is rather coming round to this Ayatollah bloke. As, I may

49

say, am I. If you're going to have a sky-pilot in the driving seat, far better the mad Mullah than some awful wet blanket like that prize ass Runcie. My own view of the Islam problem is that they made a great mistake from the word go by putting a ban on snorts. Four wives quite a sound idea if you've got the constitution that can stand it, but how they manage it without booze, God only knows! I said to Carrington, if only these students and muftis and so forth were allowed the odd snifter, come half-past five the pickets outside the Embassy would melt away leaving the place wide open for taxi-borne rescue missions of a civilised nature. I don't know whether he passed on to Carter my scheme for parachuting in crates of the duty-free, but it seemed a good idea at the time. I mean, even you or I, Bill, would be whirling like bloody dervishes if we couldn't adjourn every so often for a sip of the sparkling sherbet, especially in the sort of weather they have down there.

A propos the Major's birthday celebrations on 14th May. I gather the plan is to RV for pre-lunch lotions at the Cat and Hamster in the Pantiles at 11.30 sharp. Technically speaking I am under house arrest that day, but Eric and Boris between them have devised an ingenious little escape wheeze which involves me donning a false beard and walking confidently out of the front door to be driven off by Boris in Arab gear at the wheel of the Rolls. (Eric meanwhile to create a diversion by sitting in my den hammering at the typewriter.) Boris says that anyone nowadays done up in wog paraphernalia gets automatic VIP treatment, waved through checkpoints without question etc, so the scheme should be foolproof. Fingers crossed nonetheless.

Yours aye,

DENIS

10 Downing Street
Whitehall

23 May 1980

Dear Bill,
I don't want to speak out of turn, but my clear impression is that we've got the buggers on the run at long last. I don't think I've had a chance to put pen to paper since the SAS dust-up at Prince's Gate. Best thing since the Coronation. High time a few wogs bit the dust and thank God there was a British finger on the trigger. I just hope that ass Carter recognises that when it comes to mowing down the Dervish Britain can still teach the rest of the world a lesson or two. By the by, did you feel a mite let down by old Whitelaw after the curtain finally descended? I know he was

being got at by all those sneering little reptiles from Fleet Street but, as I said to M., why couldn't he come straight out with the joyful tidings about the wog cull, i.e. that the little fellows had been lined up in the corner and rat-a-tat-tat, and that the only reason the last one got out in one piece was that they thought he was one of ours? Instead of which, we got the pussy-footing stuff about sub judice and the Ministry of Defence. What's old Oyster Eyes got to be ashamed of? I told Carrington that if I'd had any say in it they'd have lugged them out, all two and a half brace of them, and had our masked friends from the SAS round for a photo-call with their boots planted on the day's bag. What, Bill? I'm beginning to think Whitelaw deep down may be a bit of a wet. A decent enough old stick and a demon with the mashie, no doubt, but inclined to fluff his putts.

If it hadn't been for our little contretemps on the Major's birthday I'd have had a damn good laugh over that other lot of untouchables, the TUC. What about little Murray, then, swanning it in Madeira when the so-called Day of Action is looming up? I don't know whether you recognised it from the photographs, but that was the hotel where Sticky got such a nasty bout of the Pharaoh's Revenge in '69. He said it was the sea-food, but I suspected an overdose of the local hooch as usual. I remember it set him back £40 a night – even in those days, when £40 was a lot of money. A pretty classy sort of joint, and I must say I'd be pretty shirty if I was still on the Burmah Board, getting away from it all for a three-week mid-Spring mini-break, only to find the Cloth Cap Brigade sitting out there as bold as brass puffing a Corona Corona by the pool and snipping their snortoes in the Members' Enclosure. For once the Press johnnies did an absolutely splendid job bearding the little fellow and buggering up his holiday good and proper. I shouldn't think he'll go back to Madeira in a hurry. Next year Southend more likely, I'd have thought, Bill. Bag of whelks and a knotted hankie on the promenade would be more his line of country.

As to the schemozzle on the Major's birthday, the whole thing was a complete balls-up from the word go. What I overlooked was that May 14th happened also to be the TUC's Day For Playing Silly Buggers. I generally see eye to eye with Boris, but when he came in with the early morning snort and a packet of fags on a tray to announce that he was regretfully withdrawing his services in solidarity with the aspirations of something or other, I absolutely blew my top. To no avail, of course. One thing I've learned about the Russians from Peter Carrington is that once they dig their heels in there's no moving them. However, I was determined not to let the Major down and was just donning the Arab kit, prior to shimmering out of the front door as planned, when Eric came in and started kicking up the most godawful fuss about security. In the end he insisted on accompanying me in the passenger seat, wearing the false beard. I got to the garage without too much trouble, but no sooner had I screeched to a halt outside Number

Ten and thrown open the door for Eric to scramble aboard than the Third World War broke out. Violent explosions, smoke, hooded black figures running to and fro, tin-openers applied to the roof, a complete re-run of the Prince's Gate lark, ending with self and Eric face down in the gutter, hands strapped behind our backs, listening to some straight talk from a chap in a balaclava helmet. Boss inevitably shirty about the whole thing, and my Insurance Company proving very tricky about what's left of the Rolls.

After it was all over I must say the Corporal in charge of the Squad was most apologetic, and after a few shots in the pantry we got talking about this that and the other. He said morale was very high in the Unit, and if only the Boss would blow the whistle he reckoned they could give the entire IRA the Prince's Gate treatment over a weekend, and everything would be tickety-boo. I promised to put in a word once things had calmed down a bit upstairs. Alas, M. is still fuming over our little escapade during old Tito's funeral. How was I to know that she'd be coming back on an earlier plane before we had a chance to get Maurice Picarda's musical lady friend out of the Cabinet Room? Ah well, these things are sent to try us, I suppose.

What about Royal St George's for the Open? We could stay in that very decent little pub in the Sandwich kept by the widow Venables.

Yours in the Pink,

DENIS

10 Downing Street
Whitehall

6 June 1980

Dear Bill,

Flaming June, eh? A propos, did you see us on the TV? I don't know whether I've mentioned two little wop fellows who loom fairly large in M's life, but they're called Saatchi and Saatchi – I think one's called Luigi and the other one's called Alberto, but it could be the other way round. Anyway, whenever there's not much going on, they ring up and come oiling in with some new publicity stunt.

I was dosing the greenfly out the back with that frightfully good aerosol defoliant that Picarda got the recipe for from some boffin on the run from Porton Down, and most of the indoor staff being down at the betting shop it fell to my lot to open the front door. Lo and behold the Corsican Brothers. Shiny suits, carnations, rings a-sparkle on every finger, teeth a-gleam. How nice to see me, great pleasure, arm pumped up and down, waft of parma violets. Do you remember that couple of spivs who used to hang about the nineteenth at Huntercombe just after the war flogging nylons? Very much the same style of cove.

The name of the game, it transpires on this occasion, is an outing to Madame Tussaud's in the Marylebone Road to be fitted out for the waxworks show. Pale pink Rolls at our disposal, the Brothers falling over each other among the cushions in the back, opening champagne, demonstrating stereophonic sound system electric windows, just like a couple of monkeys. Eric crammed in a corner of the back seat, looking very disapproving. Rolls purrs to a silent halt, welcoming committee sidle out from the shadows. Lord Someone-or-other presented with great relish by Luigi, or it may have been Alberto, and we are all swept in under the canopy.

I hadn't been since the days when Uncle Jonah used to dump me there while he popped off to his little rendez-vous during the afternoons, but it's a pretty tatty sort of place, Bill. What struck me was that it was impossible to tell who anybody was actually meant to be. I thought I spotted old Wilson, admittedly looking a bit waxen and glassy, but when I read the label underneath it turned out to be Bertrand Russell. Anyway M. seemed pretty taken by the whole set-up, good old laugh at the Royals etc, booze flows very freely, tape measures and calipers out, glass eyeballs produced from tray and held up for matching purposes, small samples of hair, eyebrows etcetera snipped away. In the end I began to quite enjoy it.

By the by, one of the Bertie Wooftahs on duty took me aside and explained how they do it. There being a pretty constant turnover in celebrities, and naturally wishing to save on the spondulicks, apparently, Bill, they recycle the bodies. Just between the two of us, M. was going to be knocked together out of an old Barbara Castle, and they'd got a Jeremy Thorpe that would be 'just the thing' for me. Honestly, Bill, it gave me quite a turn, thinking of changing trousers with that bounder.

Come the great day of the unveiling before the world's press. Usual turnout from the reptile house, all well and truly lubricated by Luigi and Alberto prior to kick-off. I was standing there inspecting the exhibits, thinking that a sharpener wouldn't come amiss and trying to work out who was meant to be who, when I noticed M. whispering in an off-hand manner to Lord Tussaud and waving a hand airily in my direct-

ion. Whereupon, Bill, blow me if two burly little fellows in brown overalls don't move across the stage towards me, lift me sharply off my feet and before I can protest I am upended and bundled off, I presume towards the melting pot. Luckily a few brisk obscenities were enough to convince them of their mistake, and they put me down with no great ceremony, but not before the reptiles had sniggered their fill.

It turned out, Bill, that the Proprietor in her infinite wisdom had given instructions that yours truly was once more Not Wanted On Voyage in a Cabinet situation. However, as the rest of them look like something out of the window of the gents outfitters in Sevenoaks, I can't say I felt unduly miffed at the exclusion.

From your vantage point, Bill, it may look, in a more general context, as if we're on the rocks with this 20% inflation, recession looming, etc. All I can say is that you wouldn't think so if you were here. Optimism is the keyword, and come July the word is that everything is going to look different. The Mad Monk shouts with laughter from morning till night, Howe never stops giggling, and Stevarse minns about like a peacock on heat. According to the Brothers, whose business it is to look on the bright side of things anyway, the TUC and the Labour Party are tearing themselves to bits, and all we have to do is to sit back and count our winnings. Boris, I must confess, is very sceptical, and in my own experience, he's the only one who knows.

Do thank your friend in the construction business for the crate of Pimm's. I'm keeping it for our proposed meeting at this location.

Yours aye,

DENIS

10 Downing Street
Whitehall

20 June 1980

Dear Bill,
I wonder how Daphne would feel about me coming to stay at Old Moorings for a few days? I feel a brief recuperation out of the front line might be to everyone's advantage, especially if the two of us can get in a few rounds of golf and generally refuel the tanks. Anyway, have a think about it – always assuming that Daphne's state of health can stand the strain – and let me know.

M., I must confess, has been pretty fraught of late, ever since the big Eurosummit, and even little Peter Carrington, out of whose arse the sun is normally deemed to shine like a beacon on Jubilee Night, has been sent to the doghouse. Personally I haven't followed all the matches in the league table to date — not, as you know, Bill, having much time for the foreigner in whatever shape or form — but according to Boris the Boss's plan was basically sound: i.e. veto the French farm price rises, throw your weight around, and in the end Brother Froggie will come to heel on the Contributions.

Accordingly, Tweedledum and Tweedledee, i.e. Walker and Carrington, twinkle off to Brussels with firm instructions to stand firm and resist all brands of continental flattery, free bottles of pop, evenings out at the Folies Bergeres and so forth. Instead of which, as Boris discovered before any of the rest of us on his short-wave wireless, the Twins caved in at an early stage, agreed to some botched-up compromise deal and caught the first train back to London.

As sheer bad luck would have it, Bill, I happened to be mooching around the Boardroom when the two of them were called in the following morning. All a-beam, hair glinting brightly in the sun, clearly thinking they'd done rather well for themselves. One glance at the Proprietor's face should have convinced them of their error. I knew from experience that a Force Eighter was on its way, and seeing for a change that I was not to be its victim hovered in the wings, pouring myself a sharpener in anticipation of a damn good show of fireworks.

My God, Bill, they certainly got it fair and square amidships! Did they think that M. had been to Dublin and points west, gone fourteen rounds with Giscard and Schmidt, put up with being vilified in the Froggie Prints as Madame Non, just in order to have the rug pulled from under her by a couple of cretins with a joint mental age of six? Why did she have to do all the work, could she never trust anyone to do the simplest thing if she didn't personally supervise? (This harangue being familiar, I should add, to yours truly, and making me feel sympathy even with a thoroughly obnoxious little HMG like Walker.)

To begin with Peter Carrington looked a bit hot around the gills, polished his glasses, and I thought might be going to take his punishment lying down. But just as I was about to step in and suggest sharpeners all round, his aristocratic poise suddenly deserted him. 'Listen to me, you boring old bag' (ipsissima verba, Bill, as the lawyers would say). 'If you think that Walker and I are going to spend the best years of our lives sitting up all night in Strasbourg with earphones strapped to our bloody heads in a roomful of Belgians haggling about the price of beetroot, you've got another think coming. Remember Rhodesia! I don't know whether you happen to have heard, but I have been hailed as the greatest Foreign Secretary this country has had since Palmerston. You're not talking to third-rate lobby fodder like Stevarse or Heseltine! Thank God I managed to inject a bit of class into your miserable bunch of suburban wankers. Well, that's it. I resign!'

With that, the immaculately dressed little fellow hurled his briefcase into the air, ultimately to be fielded by Eric, and strode from the room, leaving Walker somewhat uncertain what iron to play next. Under cover of opening the door for Lord C., I withdrew to the attic and pulled up the ladder.

According to Boris's latest information, some kind of peace has been patched up, but the Boss has still got a very nasty light in her eye and I have been keeping the lowest of possible profiles at breakfast behind the *Daily Telegraph*.

I don't know if I told you, Bill, but ever since we got in there's a very odd little East End barrow-boy figure who lurks from time to time on the fringes of things here. Apparently he owns the *Daily Star*. He's constantly on the phone to Cosgrove or the Saatchi Brothers to find out what the Party Line is on this, that and the other and he strikes me, Bill, as an arse-crawler of the first water. Besides which – I don't know if you ever see it at the barber's – the paper he puts out is absolute Corporals' Mess stuff.

Well, Bill, you can imagine the shock to the system, given the prevailing mood of tension and despair, to be told that the same Cockney whelk-peddler, whose name incidentally is Matthews, is to be dignified with the ermine. To tell you the truth, Bill, I was so taken aback that before I knew what I was saying I told M. she might as well have given a peerage to Maurice Picarda's accountant – I can't remember his name but you know the one I mean, pencil moustache, trilby hat, padded shoulders, spent some years at Her Majesty's expense at Wormwood Scrubs. Crikey, Bill, straight through the club-house window with that one. You will now understand the reason for plea for asylum as outlined in para 1.

Yours in purdah,

DENIS

10 Downing Street
Whitehall

4 July 1980

Dear Bill,

I must say I did enjoy our little shindig here at Number Ten during M's summiting business in Venice. While the cat's away the mice will play, what? I was exceedingly glad not to have to trail along on that particular outing. I made enquiries and apparently the whole place is built on a lot of islands, so there's no golf course. Also, with all that dirty water sloshing about and the Eyeties emptying their gerries out of the window I'm told the pong is something shocking at this time of the year, besides which, as you know, that prize ass Carter was there, holding hands with his wife and exhibiting his grisly little daughter to the photographers. (Alberto Saatchi, who is my source, or it may have been Luigi, tells me that our American friends' latest wheeze is to dig up some old film star to take over. I think his name is Charlton Heston but I wouldn't be too sure. Really, Bill, it does seem a bit absurd! M. has her faults, God knows, but we would all think it pretty odd if they wheeled in Frankie Howerd as a substitute. Don't you think?)

I'm glad to say that by the time the Boss flew back, Boris had the place roughly shipshape. The various nasty stains the Major left by flicking butter pats at the ceiling in the Cabinet Room barely notice, and you'd never guess that the old boy in the oil painting in the hall had had that moustache painted on him by Squiffy. M. did raise the question of the lavatory cistern being pulled away from the wall – that *was* Maurice Picarda, wasn't it? – but I blamed the terrible thunderstorms and painted a lurid picture of damn near being struck by lightning while behaunched. I could tell she didn't believe it for a moment, but there was no come-back.

At the time I didn't entirely understand the cause of Picarda's somewhat lachrymose condition. However, we had a long heart-to-heart last night, and things haven't been going too well for the poor old sod. You know his garage business blew up some months ago? Well, after that he hung about in Gozo for a bit until the coast was clear, and on his return started a small business selling some kind of solar heating equipment to our friends in the Gulf. I couldn't quite follow his sales patter on the phone, but apparently you have to attach some sort of umbrella contraption made of cooking foil to the chimney, plug it into the Serviwarm and Bob's your uncle: heating bills slashed and so forth. According to Maurice it couldn't possibly have gone wrong: conserving mineral fuels, boosting the export drive, precisely the kind of thing the Monk is always droning on about. Blow me, Bill, two weeks ago the bank manager starts bouncing his cheques. Not surprising, I suppose, when you think he was paying fifteen per cent on a couple of million. Ugly talk about bankruptcy, Maurice not absolutely certain in his own mind as to whether he'd been discharged after the last lot, so can you wonder, in the circs, if the chap takes a lotion or two too many to dull the heartache?

I took it upon myself to raise the matter with Howe when he was mooching about in his brothel creepers outside the Boss's den, waiting for the green light to come on. Apparently, as you have seen in the gutter press, they've got some big pow-wow this week at which they're meant to be deciding what the hell they're up to, and about time too in my opinion. Anyway, buttonhole Howe, what about Picarda? Small business, always been one for initiative and enterprise ever since he started selling spare parts to the Army during the war, solar heating damn fine wheeze, good and faithful Tory, what's gone wrong? I don't know if I've mentioned it before, Bill, but Howe seems a bit slow on the uptake to me, like a lot of these lawyer johnnies, and for a long time he didn't seem to haul in what I was talking about. Hummed and hahed, scratched his bum, I helped myself to a sharpener, and he eventually condescended, no green light being forthcoming, to give Counsel's Opinion. Number One: overall target to bring inflation within manageable limits by the mid-nineties. Number Two: in order to achieve this, you do something called cutting the money supply. This is the bit I have never understood and, strictly between ourselves, Bill, I don't think Howe does either. The idea all stems from some little Californian guru called Milton Shulman. In the process, Howe vouchsafed, a whole lot of people — by this I presume he meant Picarda — are going to get their fingers burned. No U-turns, no going back, into the Valley of Death, etc. I was about to take issue with this on the grounds of basic sanity when the green light flickered and he sponged away across the polished floor clutching his briefcase with a somewhat haunted mien.

A propos your summer golfing proposal at the Royal and Ancient. I am going to do my damnedest to make up the foursome you propose but the Boss is already muttering darkly about traipsing off on her annual pilgrimage to stay with that awful old bird with the red face who owns the Isle of Muck. I honestly don't think I can stand it again after last year, and if the worst comes to the worst I'll try the slipped disc and appalling agony ploy. However, Saatchi and Saatchi are racking their brains about how to cash in on the Queen Mum's eightieth birthday racket, so the R&A may have to go by the board in favour of standing about outside Balmoral sipping the Duke's somewhat parsimonious tinctures. What a ghastly prospect!

Yours in the doldrums,

DENIS

10 Downing Street
Whitehall

18 July 1980

Dear Bill,

I don't know whether I've ever expatiated in our correspondence on this Prior bird. Red face, on the plump side, runs a farm somewhere near Colchester apparently. I always get on very well with him. He's not a golfer, but he likes a snort and he usually has time to chew the fat with yours truly, which is more than you can say for the Mad Monk or some of the other creeps we have through here. There was a bit of a rumpus last week, as you may have seen in the *Telegraph*, when he made the very reasonable suggestion that some of the unemployed layabouts you see hanging about outside the betting shop in any High Street could usefully be set to work washing sheets and cleaning out the bogs in the hospitals.

Honestly, Bill, you'd think he'd proposed compulsory castration for the entire proletariat. (Incidentally quite a good wheeze, but not an automatic passport to electoral success!) All the Labour yobbees up in arms, Tony Benn whistling like a steam kettle and wild talk of Forced Labour Camps. The trouble with the Socialists is that they're totally out of touch. The Major was telling me only the other day about a club near Folkestone where the greens are absolutely cluttered up with unemployed skinheads and punks playing on weekdays when the Members want to use the course. Picking up fifty quid a week on the dole and the green fees still peanuts in clubs like that, there's not a thing to stop them. What is worse, the Major says you can't get near the bar for the buggers lining up to order lemonade. So full marks to old Prior for trying to thin them out.

What puzzles me though, Bill, is where M. stands on Farmer Jim. He came round the other night about half past seven I should think. I was fairly well tanked up, having spent a fruitful afternoon watching the English Classic at Sutton Coldfield on the box, and was practising a few putts in the hall with my little indoor contraption from Lillywhites – did I ever show it you? – Boris retrieving the odd wild shot. In breezed Prior, a bulky file under his arm, weirdly enough quite chipper at the prospect of meeting the Boss. All the same, I proffered a sharpener and we fell to talking about how you can't get a decent Cox's Orange Pippin nowadays for love or money and all thanks to Johnny Frog flooding the market with Golden Disgustings. Prior had accepted the other half and the time was passing very agreeably, everything tickety-boo, when the Boss flies out of her study looking as if raw meat alone will satisfy her.

'Now then, Jim, we've got no time to waste. We were elected on Union Reform and the Party isn't going to wear this cosmetic stuff you're proposing on the secondary pickets. Goodness me, we're all tired of leather-jacketed bully boys standing about outside factories full of perfectly happy people who want to do a decent day's work for a decent day's pay' — I could see Prior's eyes glazing over at this point, which didn't go unnoticed — 'and making their lives an absolute misery.' 'Quite so, Mrs Thatcher,' was our rubicund chum's rejoinder, 'but remember what happened to friend Heath.'

I think I've told you before, Bill, that the red rag effect of any mention of Old Sailorboy Ted is pretty predictable. Prior realised what he had done, and we both pulled our sou'westers down over our ears, patiently waiting for the storm to abate. Much of what

M. said was personally offensive and very familiar to anyone who knew the form, and I think Prior had probably heard it all in Cabinet anyway. He hummed and hahed a bit, sipped his poison, nodded several times and finally, when there came a brief lull, handed the glass to me, looked at his watch and said that was all right then and M. could leave it with him. The Boss watched him go with rattlesnake eyes, looking not unlike the Chief Dalek about to exterminate and destroy. She then retired to her study to ruminate in solitary and didn't speak to one for several days.

I hesitate, as you know Bill, to put my oar in when it could only lead to further acrimony, but do you remember the drama at Burmah over the bridge school in the paint shop? Pegleg Ferguson stepped out of line on that one and was promptly given his cards by the Chairman. Then they brought in old Posner, as you recall, which wasn't a very happy choice, but that's another story. The peculiar thing about this set-up is that Prior has stepped further out of line than Pegleg ever dreamed of doing. The Boss slates him even on the telly when he must, all things being equal, occasionally be watching, but they still keep him on. There's no talk at all of telling him to get on his bike. Pretty odd. It did just cross my mind that she might be a bit scared of him. She couldn't be, could she? Boris thinks it's all a cunning ploy to keep both sides happy but, as you know, these politicos are a closed book to me. One sometimes wonders how they'd manage if they had shareholders breathing down their necks.

A propos the Isle of Muck. According to Boris's sources, which are usually impeccable, there's not much hope of a reprieve. Which buggers up the Royal and Ancient. Also the Queen Mother hurdle remains to be cleared. Our holiday plans, in other words, highly classified, at least as far as I'm concerned. I do wish someone would tell me occasionally what the hell was going on. Bloody awful weather, what? I suppose Daphne's charity couldn't fly us out to some trouble spot in the tropics for a bit of peace?

Try and keep me briefed.

Yours aye,

DENIS

10 Downing Street
Whitehall

1 August 1980

Dear Bill,
Forgive me for not coming to the phone the other morning but I

was somewhat glued to the unfolding panorama of the British Open at Muirfield. Do you remember the time we played there? I think it was with that funny little moneylender friend of Maurice Picarda's. (Someone told me the other day that he was now President of the World Bank, which I must say I find pretty hard to believe.) If memory serves he was taken short around the ninth or tenth and very much upset some lady golfers in the adjoining copse. Happy days, what? I kept remembering it every time the cameras showed that particular little nook on the TV.

Apparently there's been a bit of a hoo-hah over the latest unemployment figures and some of the Left Wing johnnies have been getting very excited down at the Talking Shop. Wild talk about the Thirties and how miserable it all was. As I said to Boris, the stuff you hear nowadays is baloney for the most part. You and I were around then, Bill, and I thought we had a pretty good time of it, all things considered. Plenty of golf and parties, booze at seven and six a bottle, no servant problem, the lower orders used to call you Sir, everything tickety-boo. And if Chamberlain hadn't been such a damn fool upsetting poor old Hitler, I dare say the party would still be in full swing. However, that's all champers under the bridge.

M. seems to be keeping her head through it all very gallantly, I must say. I wouldn't like to have to stand up in that frightful bad breath they have down there struggling to make myself heard above the brawling of those Labour yobbos. Do you ever listen to it on the wireless? It's just like feeding time at the gorilla house the way they carry on, our lot not much better than the others. What I said to Boris is it's all letting off steam, really. If you go and stand outside the building itself, everybody's going about their business in a perfectly ordinary manner, not much thought given to two million unemployed, only real problem all those ghastly sweaty tourists laden down with orange haversacks trying to pull a fast one on the decent hard-working members of the British Hoteliers Association.

The other point the Labour buggers don't seem able to haul in is that being on the dole nowadays is by no means the romantic lark it was before the war. The Major was telling me only the other day about some Irish navvy who lives in a big house in a village near his brother's place in Wiltshire, picks up a hundred and sixty quid a week at the Post Office at some special supplementary rate or other, collects vintage cars, and when he goes on holiday to Tenerife they send it down to him by airmail. Even allowing for the Major's love of a tall story, it makes you think.

I mentioned the above to M. over a dish of tay following the shindig in the House, adding the other, to me, crucial point that in fact, if you look around, there are bags of jobs going begging. It's just that people nowadays are too damn choosy to take them on. Sticky, I know for a fact, has been advertising for weeks outside his local newsagent for someone to come and mow his lawn and muck out his daughter's ponies once a week, offering 75p an hour — well above the ordinary rate — and the only person to come forward was the wrong colour for the job, in Mrs Sticky's eyes at least.

Well, if M's policies are going to shake down a few idle sods into useful service to the community like mowing Sticky's lawn, then more power to her arm is all I can say.

Meanwhile the Monk appears to have wiped the froth from round his lips and come up with something quite sensible for a change. I refer to putting a bomb under the GPO. High time somebody did something, even if it's pretty cock-eyed like most of the Monk's schemes. According to Boris, all it amounts to is that if you want to buy a Donald Duck telephone set at the Army and Navy Very Expensive Gift Department, HMG will no longer stand in your way. Quite honestly, Bill, I never knew they did. Young Mark had  one in his repulsive flat for years where you have to lift up a girl's skirt to dial the number. I distinctly remember telling him whatever you do, don't let M. see that, but I'd no idea it was against the law.

The other thing is delivering letters. Maurice Picarda was on in a great state of excitement as soon as it was announced, and he's setting up what sounds a very lucrative wheeze involving two ex-Borstal boys in his care on souped-up Japanese motorbikes, and he reckons that for a fiver a shot he can guarantee same-day delivery anywhere within half a mile of Shepherd's Bush, where he is at present hanging out pending his latest bankruptcy proceedings. He thinks it may cause a bit of upward movement in the GPO's regular rates, but that's their own fault for being so incompetent. Those GPO sods have had it coming to them for years. If I've had one crossed line in the last month I must have had a hundred.

By the by, what about our chaps winning all those gold medals in Moscow? I drank to that, I don't mind telling you, and a pretty stiffish one, too. M. pointedly refused to join in the jollity, and even stopped Peter Carrington sending a wire to our lucky gong-wallahs. I said surely the best way to show the Russian Bear what we think about Afghanistan is to swim, throw things, and hop skip and jump better than they can. The fact is of course that we can't, not being stuffed with steroids and pep-up pills, but at least we can have a try.

Yours in high spirits,

DENIS

15 August 1980

Dear Bill,

What price the enclosed snap from Bonnie Balmoral? I always thought wearing a kilt was a pretty daft idea, but they do save time in the Gents.

A pretty grisly outing all in all, Bill, as I foresaw. We arrived at the station, M. not having addressed a word to me since we left King's Cross, despite efforts on my part to establish cordial relations: delightful landscape, number of tunnels, cathedrals visible en route, etc. All to no avail. In the end I retired to the buffet and lined up a few British Rail miniatures which I quaffed with a very nice cove called MacLehose who sells Fairisle jumpers to the Japs. A fund of good tales, and a real wrench when he got off at Dundee, or somewhere of that sort — I can never tell those towns apart.

Anyway. Whisked off in one of the Royal limos to Balmoral. God, Bill, what a dump! I don't know whether you remember that loony-bin near Esher where the Major's father spent his final years, but very much the same kind of atmosphere. Long corridors, antlers all over the place, arctic even in mid-summer, a lot of burly old lags standing about in the local fancy dress ready to bite your leg off if you step out of line, and a three mile trek to the bog.

The House Party consisted of various Royals, several antique specimens of the aristocracy and, to cap it all, my least favourite sky-pilot, Runcie (and wife). By lunchtime on the Saturday my spirits were on the floor, snorts not being available in any great abundance, and it being my clear impression that the D of E, Queen Mum and Princess M. must have some  secret supply, or at least a few bottles cooling somewhere offstage. I found no other explanation for their air of relaxed geniality and their being able to listen without any violent anguish to Runcie's views on embroidery. After lunch I was about to slope off to find a quiet corner for a kip, when M. snarled very firmly in my ear that HM was due to attend the Auchtermuchty Highland Games that afternoon and would take it in very bad part if I didn't turn out and 'enter into the spirit of things'. It was at this point that we all had to put on kilts.

The limos were duly brought out of the museum, and conceive of my delight when I found myself crushed into the back of a 1925 Daimler between Mrs Runcie and an overweight coon, some kind of ambassador or other from one of those African countries who had come for the lift. On arrival at Auchtermuchty we were greeted by the citizenry waving their flags, and took our places on a rather rickety tumbril draped in patriotic colours. Having sat through the Tory Conference at Blackpool I thought I could take anything, but after four hours of watching hideous women leaping up and down in kilts to the eerie wail of the bagpipes, Highland cattle being prodded by various grog-blossomed derelicts in tam o'shanters, and the usual Scots Porridge Oats stuff with the local Charles Atlas types dropping telegraph poles, my only consolation was to imagine one such being dropped very heavily on Mrs Runcie by my good self.

At about half past six the entire population lined up to sing a thirty-verse part-song in honour of the Queen Mum's four-score years. My God, Bill, you've got to hand it to her. Four weeks of that routine and I'd be in the drying-out unit. Seven o'clock came and went, local dental work still on display, spine-chilling discords and a cold wind getting up. Seven-thirty, refreshments in marquee. Hopes dashed to discover refreshments in question consist of fancy cakes and tea, provided by ample-bosomed ladies of the WVS. D of E very decently sidles up. 'You realise I have to do this every bloody year, Thatcher, so you can count yourself lucky.' Princess M. leaning against a tent pole looking rather flushed, but still keeping her end up. M. herself getting on like a house on fire with one of the Charles Atlas brigade in a vest.

Dinner back at the Waxworks a pretty bleak business. We sat down about eight, I should think. All the local gentry winkled out of their castles to make up the strength, self by another overwhelming stroke of good luck stuck between two blue-rinse specimens, dentures and jewellery all a-glitter, heirlooms strung about their scrawny necks and much talk about grouse-shooting, milk yields and Highland adultery. Booze as ever administered in doses barely visible to the naked eye in cut-glass goblets made in the shape of thistles. At long last the ladies withdraw and the D of E enquires in ringing tones, 'Come along Thatcher, what about one of your Clubroom tales, what?' Much laughter and thumping on table from assembled morons, fairly keen on taking the piss, I got the impression.

Meanwhile in the drawing room, roughly the size of Euston Station and just about as comfortable, Mrs Runcie had been prevailed upon without too much effort to play something classical. Nobody took a blind bit of notice, and fortunately it was barely audible above the roar of conversation. I was within a whisker of getting away behind a curtain unobserved when one of the blue-rinses grabbed me by the wrist and said it was time for

Scrabble (apparently HM's idea of after-dinner fun). I don't know if you've ever played it, Bill, but it's like making up a crossword without any clues. Fawning and congratulations every time HM managed a three-letter word, lot of mockery when yours truly came unstuck on the spelling, and luckily the whole torment brought to an end when a brace of corgis came galloping in and overturned the board. The evening concluded with a bottle of quite decent stuff being opened and passed around in thimblefuls, after which the Queen Mum pinned me against the wall and almost cheered me up for a moment with a frightfully good story about the late Duke of Gloucester having to play golf with Haile Selassie and the Queen of Tonga at the time of the Coronation and them getting lost.

I thought last year's session on the Isle of Muck couldn't have been worse. Alas, not so. Next year, D.V., Benidorm.

Yours in extremis,

DENIS

10 Downing Street
Whitehall

29 August 1980

Dear Bill,

I imagine word has reached you of our little Dieppe raid. As you know, the Major had been on at me for some time to join him and Picarda on a day off the leash, the plan being for a trip across the Channel on the ferry, a slap-up beano at one of those big French watering-holes — five courses and fifty-seven varieties of booze, followed by a bracing eighteen holes at the nearby links run by a very decent expatriate accountant chum of Picarda's. After which, tinctures were envisaged prior to a real God Almighty blowout at a four-star establishment where they cook everything in alcohol, ending up with a tour of the waterfront nightspots, casino etc, and back home on the dawn hovercraft. Not a bad itinerary, I think you'll agree, Bill, and my only slight qualm was that your absence in tropical zones would mean that you could only be with us in spirit. Many a slip, however, twixt cup and lip, best laid plans etc.

M. had taken three days off at some damnfool health hydro at Virginia Water — a total waste of money if you ask me but Fatty Soames said he shed three stones there in a week and Saatchis have been leaning on her to do something about her chins — so the coast was clear. I drove the Humber down to Folkestone, taking on board the Major and little Picarda at the Flag & Anchor, and after a bracing snort or twain contre le mal de mer we drove the old bus onto the Sealink Ferry. Usual rather tripperish crowd on board, but we managed to commandeer a quiet corner of the bar on B Deck, and we were soon putting the world to rights with the help of an impressive army of miniatures.

At some point — I can't remember when, but we were certainly well out to sea — we found ourselves joined by a rather crusty old bugger from Roehampton who claimed he had been at school with me, though I couldn't for the life of me put a name to him. I find it pretty hard to put a name to anyone, quite honestly Bill, nowadays. Do you find that, as you get older? Eric, the priggish little twerp, says it's the drink but according to our GP, whose name funnily enough I can't remember either, about three billion brain cells burn off every year in any normal person after the age of nineteen. Anyway, this cove Mackevoy, or it may have been Patterson, had some kind of log stove business near Wokingham that was making a fortune, and he and Picarda immediately got on like a house on fire.

Time flew by and before we knew it the ship lurched violently to one side as all the ghastly trippers rushed to the rail to catch their first glimpse of La Belle France. We old codgers had seen it all before and decided to stay below. I thought something was up from the tone of the voices upstairs. The ship seemed to be stationary for rather a long time, and various incomprehensible announcements were made over the tannoy. Eventually the Major suggested we pop up on deck for a shufty.

I had always been under the impression, Bill, that one of the few things to be said in favour of our Gallic neighbours across the water was that they kept the lower orders in their place. From time to time the workers get a bit restless during the hot weather and start winkling out the cobblestones with a view to using them as offensive weapons, whereupon the Riot Police know exactly what to do and do it pretty damn quick. None of that Blair Peach nonsense over there. Well, all I can say is that that appears to be a thing of the past.

From where we stood on the deck you could quite clearly see the quayside awash with tiny black figures in berets and three days' growth of beard, behaving like bloody hooligans and not a gendarme in sight. As I said to old whatever his name was, the log-burner wallah, Grunwick all over again. Banners waving about, chanting of idiotic slogans in their incomprehensible lingo, and meanwhile progress of SS *Sibelius* effectively blocked by a barrage of little bateaux roped together, and weighed down to the gunwales with more gesticulating Frogs, all yelling the odds about the price of Golden Delicious, or something else dear to their hearts.

The Major, to do him credit, took in the situation at a glance. No time to be wasted. Up the little steps to the bridge and a sharp word with Captain Olafsson, a shifty cove with a beard who looked to be the worse for drink, telling him to do his duty as a

Norwegian and go full steam ahead through the fishing boats and get us to the restaurant before our table was given away to the natives. All to no avail, Bill. Grin grin from little Olafsson, 'of course, gentlemen', next thing we know four burly matelots appear from nowhere and usher us below with no great ceremony. Another half hour elapses, a bit of parley-voo through the megaphone, one or two of the more spirited trippers lob the odd beer bottle at the Frog, fire is returned with airgun pellets and the Captain does a smart about-turn back to Folkestone. The Major, who by now is in a very nasty mood — the bar unaccountably having run dry — insists once ashore on buttonholing a bloke in the ticket office and asks for our money back. Thingummybob, the log-burner, does his best to restrain him before the police arrive, and we spend a very miserable evening in a horrible little pub down by the docks with a very loud jukebox, being sneered at by a gang of punks on their way to set fire to the pier.

I tell you, Bill, that's the last time I have any truck with Abroad. Sticky said it was just as bad going by air. He and Polly had to spend four hours sitting on the runway at Benidorm in a temperature of 106 degrees, screaming babies being sick all over them, and all because a couple of Spanish oiks with table tennis bats wanted a longer teabreak. I told M. when she got back from her hydro, looking pretty tetchy I must say, that this old country of ours may be a bugger's muddle but at least you can speak the language. Do tell, Bill, how did you manage in Martinique?

　　Yours agog,

　　DENIS

10 Downing Street
Whitehall

12 September 1980

Dear Bill,

The more I see from this end of things the less I understand. I don't know whether the Major has been on to you about his chum Sharples who runs a biro factory near Chislehurst — you met him I think at that champagne beano given by the Oddfellows in Pershore — I dimly remember a cove with a ginger moustache drifting about rather the worse for wear, indeed I think he may have been our host. Any rate, the news is that the bloody bank has foreclosed and it looks like Carey Street. The point the Major made, and very emotionally, over the phone late the other night was that it was all our fault. If the kind of people who put M. in are going to the wall, what's it all about? To be quite frank, I

absolutely agree.

I did in fact raise the matter with the Boss on the way back in the helicopter from our godawful trip to the Outer Darkness. The official reply, as far as I could gather above the roar of the rotors as we passed over Wick, was that if people priced themselves out of a job they'd only got themselves to blame. When I risked going on to point out that Sharples made his pile out of a handful of darkies, none of whom ever got more than thirty quid a week if they were lucky, I was told that there were bound to be some innocent casualties in the war against inflation.

It always comes back to this notion of the money supply which, for the life of me, I find extraordinarily difficult to grasp. Ever since we got in, according to little Howe, the plan has been to cut the money supply. But there it was in the pilot's copy of the *Daily Telegraph*, Money Supply on the Up and Up. No exchange controls, spondulicks flooding in from bloody everywhere. What worries me, Bill, is that I don't honestly think that our lot understands it either. Like Poland. I mean, they're all cock-a-hoop in this neck of the woods about the wonderful little unions and bully for them getting the right to strike. All exactly the kind of thing we're supposed to be one hundred per cent opposed to. I thought of raising this, too, but the firm line of M's mouth and the fact that she was busy making notes for a speech on the back of her sick bag made me think we'd probably had enough of politics for one day.

I don't know whether you've heard of a cove called Goldsmith, Bill — I think he was one of those rum customers who used to hang about Wilson, like that mackintosh chappie who is currently out on bail. They all got knighthoods and things out of that secretary woman of his. (I always felt sorry for the wife.) Anyway, blow me down if this Goldsmith, who runs a lot of off-licences and cash-and-carry places up and down the country, hasn't thrown a great beano at the Savoy for some rag, as I gather, that they give away free in the supermarkets, and has the brazen effrontery to try and dignify the occasion by inviting M. to make major speech on state of the nation! To put the tin hat on it, M. has said yes. I lay the whole thing at the door of our friends Saatchi and Saatchi, who'll do anything for the odd bob but, emboldened by a sharpener, I did say en passant to M. that she shouldn't touch this bloke with a bargepole. Scatty Longhurst, Sticky's broking friend, says there's been some malarkey about share dealing and, although I've learned from painful experience never to believe a word Scatty says, a lot of very decent blokes apparently did get their fingers badly burned a year or two ago. Anyway, bib and tucker and limo at the door for Wednesday night, whole thing promises to be a pretty good shambles and more anon.

What else shall I tell you? Oh yes. I always said I had a pretty good nose for a rotter, Bill. You remember a week or so ago, I mentioned the little East End johnny who owns the *Daily Express* that M. for some inexplicable reason gave a peerage to? I said to Boris at the time he was a wrong 'un. Would you believe it? I was absolutely right. Last week tremendous rumpus, turns out this Whelks fellow, under cover of darkness, has paid a gang of hooligans to knock down that lovely old Firestone factory on the Great Western Road. We always used to pass it before the war on the way out to Sonning in Eddie Gorringe's drophead coupe. Those were the days, eh? Do you remember the night Sticky got locked in the khazi at the French Horn and we had to take the door off with your Number Five Iron? I think after that we were somewhat non grata with Mine Host. Sowerberry? Hampton? I can't remember his name, but I know he bought it during the Blitz, poor old bean.

I am going to do my damnedest to go AWOL on the Great Pow-Wow at Blackpool this year, so you might pencil in a tentative date for our little jaunt to Folkestone. Maurice Picarda has just managed to raise the wind to open a hotel and conference centre down there and I feel we ought to lend support.

Yours aye,

DENIS

GRAND METROPOLITAN HOTEL
BRIGHTON

10 October 1980

Dear Bill,

What a hell-hole this is, Bill! I remember it before the war, when it was full of fossilised old Indian Army specimens with their memsahibs dribbling out the twilight of Empire on the prom. Now it's been taken over by some jumped-up little Eyetie who's painted it all in assorted garish hues. Muzak in the bogs, carpet on the walls and leather-style banquettes. M. is absolutely in her element. If I had the choice, we'd be in the Pig & Whistle up by the station which is still run by a native — I think he said he was in the RAF with Percy Topplemore. He certainly had one of those handlebar moustache numbers — and at least the place hasn't been refurbished.

I did have a last ditch moment with the Boss as to whether I could be excused parade, especially as all I have to do is sit on the platform grinning like a Barbary Ape and throwing myself about clapping like a madman whenever anyone opens his mouth. Application refused. It turns out that those frightful little creeps the Saatchis have done a special report for the Boss proving that yours truly is now a major electoral asset, achieving the same score as Captain, the Wilsons' cat. Boris told me that Alberto and Luigi have even got together various unemployables to stop people in the street, show them a photograph of me and ask them who it is. All I can say, Bill, is I hope our scaly friends from Fleet Street don't get hold of that one, or I shan't be able to show my face at St George's ever again. Imagine the gales of laughter from the Battle of Britain boys.

As you would expect, M's lot were all very cock-a-hoop about the shambles at Blackpool last week. A propos, did you see Benn in action on the box at all? He put me in mind of that new friend of Margaret's with the German name who runs the supermarkets. Very much the look of poor old Tuppy Hetherington before his missus had to enlist the help of the men in white coats. I'll never forget the afternoon he shed his tweeds on the fairway, snapped all the Major's best clubs over his knee, and ran gibbering off into Guildford without a stitch on. Old Benn has much the same air about him. I can't believe he's a plausible alternative to Jim, but M. has very high hopes. The man they're scared of is the one with funny eyebrows that chap on the telly is always impersonating. The Major says he takes photographs of himself sitting in bedrooms, so I think there may be something pretty rum somewhere. The only one of their lot I ever liked was George Brown, and now he's on the wagon he's unbearable. Exactly what happened to Bomber MacLehose, if you remember. Went TT and is now the biggest bore in East Sussex.

The one M. starts foaming at the mouth at whenever she pops up on the gogglebox is the Shirley woman, who looks to me rather a good sort. But I can see M's point: one Wonder-woman is enough to be getting on with. M. keeps saying she's going to have to go to the hairdresser's before she can be taken seriously as a political rival.

Anyway, the logical upshot of all this, according to Boris, is that M's wets are in for a trouncing. Time to come out in our true colours, etc. Talking of which, you should see some of the people hanging about down here in Brighton. A lot of younger MPs are pretty good yobboes, as I suppose is inevitable nowadays, all accompanied by brassy tarts; the usual so-called Party Workers, i.e. garage proprietors, night club owners and the Maurice Picarda brigade, not to mention the Fleet Street reptiles having a field day, all reeling about blind drunk, sniggering in anticipation at the thought of one making some sort of gaffe. I have therefore spent a good deal of the time here in the Walt Disney Suite — which is, thank God, equipped with the one colour television set in the whole of Brighton that gets something other than the Conference — tuned in to Wentworth, and taking advantage of the very liberal trickle of snorterinos brought in by a succession of Maltese waiters.

I see there's something coming up in Estoril in November. I just might be able to shimmer out for a day or two without it being noticed, so it might be worth alerting Mrs Chancellor at the travel agency to see if she's got anything in the way of package cheapies.

Did you see the FO sent us out to Athens? All very badly blitzed still, and not a bunker in sight. Neither M. nor I had a blind idea why we were there.

Yours till the cows come home,

DENIS

10 Downing Street
Whitehall

24 October 1980

Dear Bill,
How extraordinary we should have run into each other at the Birmingham Motor Show! Did you decide to buy the Fiesta in the end? I could see Daphne was getting on like a house on fire with the salesman. They are jolly good little cars, if economy is the name of the game. Maurice P. swears by them. He used to drive one in his ballpoint days before the chemical toilet fiasco in the Gulf.

In view of our VIP status I couldn't really linger. Saatchis had given the Boss seven minutes and she was due to do her lap of honour in the new Metro just as you were embarking on your very interesting tale of life out East. Edwardes, the rather smarmy little South African johnny who runs Leylands, told me that they're cock-a-hoop about advance orders and claims 83mpg, which I find hard to believe. Also bags of room for a crate or two of the snorterinos, but, needless to say, those bloody shop-stewards haven't wasted a moment before torpedoing the whole bang shoot by embarking on a nationwide work to rule just because some idle bugger chooses to take a three hour teabreak. I keep telling the Boss one of these days they're going to have to pull the plug on that lot, Metro or no, and concede victory to the Nips. Poor old McIllvanney who bought it with Wingate's mob will be turning in his grave, but at least it'll teach those Moscow-subsidised vermin in the TUC a lesson or two.

Talking of the Congress, you probably saw that we had the smelly socks brigade round for tea and cakes a few days back. I told the Boss it would achieve precisely sod all, but Saatchis were keen on a bit of window dressing. What a shower, Bill! You or I wouldn't employ one of them as nightwatchman, let alone a caddy. Little Len Murray seems a decent enough chap, but between ourselves I don't think even he has the slightest idea of what's going on. The one who really gets up my nose is the Welsh cove with the whiny voice and glasses. Thinks he knows all the answers. Breezed into Number Ten, bold as brass, grinning like a Cheshire cat, and before I knew where I was the bugger had his arm round my shoulders and was blowing in my ear, enquiring whether we had anything stronger on the premises than a tea-bag. I don't know about you Bill, but I've always had my doubts about the Taffs, and Jenkins is a typical specimen of the breed. Anyway, the Boss took them all into the Cabinet Room, flanked by the Monk, Brother Howe and Farmer Prior, leaving yours truly to entertain the bloody chauffeurs in the pantry. Shocking tales they told. They don't mind hanging about outside the Ritz until half past three in the morning if it's a gent, but they're buggered if they're going to do it for the tribunes of the plebs.

The thing I can't understand, Bill, is that when we moved in M. made it pretty clear to those Union hobbledehoys that the days of wine and roses at Number Ten were over, but here we are going through the motions just like Wilson and Callaghan. Alberto Saatchi, the one with the moustache who smells of Parma violets and is always picking his teeth, promised me it wouldn't happen again. Apparently all that transpired when they got in there was that the Boss laid it on the line about two and a half million unemployed being all their fault. The Monk frothed at the mouth in sympathy, Howe sat there beaming like an owl, and no one else got a word in edgeways. As he was going out little Len Murray whispered in my ear that I had his deepest sympathy. Cheeky little monkey.

A propos the roughhouse on the other side, the general whisper at this end is that Healey has got it in the bag despite efforts to discredit him with his followers by effusive support from our lot. There's some doubt about the way the withered old party with the long white hair and the bottleglass specs will turn. Foot. Perfectly decent chap. I've bumped into him a couple of times at cocktail parties. Spends his time in  second-hand bookshops and walking around Hampstead Heath, but otherwise as normal as you or me. All the pinkoes think he's the bee's knees for some reason. But as I may have observed before, Bill, there's nowt so queer as folk in politics.

Do thank the Major for the duty-free; I'll try and have a word with Heseltine about his demolition difficulty but Boris tells me that Gothic Churches normally carry some sort of damnfool protection order.

Happy motoring.

Yours aye,

DENIS

10 Downing Street
Whitehall

21 November 1980

Dear Bill,

A few shocks and surprises since I last put p to p, though on the American Election front I could have told them all along that Reagan would leave Carter hacking about in the rough by the first hole. I may have mentioned this before, but I've always said there was something very rum about a chap of Carter's age going about holding hands with his wife in public, and obviously the Yanks as a whole thought the same.

All in all, the OAPs appear to have cleaned up. As you can imagine, the beleaguered garrison at this end are chuffed to naafi breaks about old Foot being wheeled in by the Reds. The fear always was that the big burly chap with the eyebrows would make mincemeat out of the Boss, be viewed as credible alternative by the electorate as Mad Monk piped us further and further up the garden path, etc. Somehow they don't see this happening with  the windswept old philosopher at the helm, especially now he's got one foot in plaster. Jolly bad luck, actually. That sort of thing can happen to anyone at half past eleven at night, witness the fate of Tubby Arkwright the time he did his Cresta Run down three flights of stairs after the Oddfellows' do at Maidstone and had his neck in traction for the best part of a year.

Personally, as I think I said before, I can't make old Foot out at all. Over a glass of sherry a perfectly decent bird, sort of batty old party you quite often see just when you're about to drive off tottering across the Right of Way muttering to himself. But get him on a soapbox and he does talk the most awful balls. I can only think it's intended to curry favour with all those long-haired Trots, because he comes from perfectly respectable West Country stock, brother in the Colonial Service who did splendid work riding round on a horse in Cyprus and cracking down on that mad sky-pilot with the funny hat and the beard. Boris for some reason thinks he's the best thing since sliced bread but I find myself utterly bewildered. He can't really think that he himself would have any sort of a life under the regime he proposes with the proles in charge.

As for the CBI shindig, I've been keeping my head down and stonewalling away whenever questioned. I used to see quite a lot of those chaps in Burmah days, and as drinking companions there's not a word to be said against them. Personally, though, I've always thought it was a mistake for us humble Boardroom buffers to get up on our hind legs in public, especially after three or four hours of knocking it back in the snug at these bally conferences. Incidentally, you notice how everyone, including our lot, picks on Brighton for their get-togethers — the thought uppermost in most of their minds, if you ask me, being a week away from the wife at the firm's expense and not having to drive home in the small hours after a number of Snortoes de Luxe.

You know my views on the interest rate, Bill, NatWest and so forth. As far as I can see, all the people who are squealing now are the ones who have been foolish enough to get into the red, spending money they haven't got, and it's a bit rich of cocky little Edwardes to start lecturing the Boss about how to set her house in order. By Christ, Bill, after all the blank cheques the Monk has handed over to keep those lazy goodfornothings at British bloody Leyland in colour tellies and cocktail cabinets crammed with booze, you'd think he'd have the decency to pipe down. As for that chap at Ford's, Beckett, I've never really thought much of their cars. You remember all the trouble you had with the Escort which broke down on the way to Plumpton that afternoon we had the cert?

However, that said, the Boss is plainly giving them as good as she gets. There was a knees-up here the other night in honour of the Queen Mum, bib and tucker, decorations will be worn, candelabra out of the bank, etc., extra catering staff from Stevarse's Rentaserf firm. Quite a jolly sort of beano as it turned out, with the old girl firing on all cylinders and coming out with a few very ripe stories — amazing at her age when you come to think of it, Bill — and blow me, who comes in at the coffee and cigars stage but that oily little monkey Heseltine, asking everyone for twenty-one quid in used notes. The Queen Mum clearly thought it was a scream and gave him a handsome tip, but you can imagine the consternation among some of our more po-faced members. M. explained to me afterwards that it was something Saatchis had thought up for the press, the idea being that if we're going to give the firemen a fiver on the end of a string we have to show that we're able to take a joke ourselves. Or something like that.

Meanwhile M. blazes on, unswerving and undaunted. What the Becketts of this world fail to understand is that it's all that fat idiot Heath's fault. Once he's stuck his ugly nose in there's not a hope in hell of the old girl performing a U-turn or anything else. I haven't ventured into the connubial chamber of late, but I form the clear impression a little wax model of our seafaring friend may be receiving some fairly intensive acupuncture treatment in the long dark hours.

I don't suppose there's any chance of a brief excursion to parts unknown? I always believe it's a good idea to make oneself as scarce as possible during the somewhat tense run-up to Yule. Brochure enclosed.

My best to you and yours,

DENIS

10 Downing Street
Whitehall

19 December 1980

Dear Bill,
I'm beginning to think that Christmas, bloody as it indubitably will be, may not come as such a bad thing after all. At least I should be able to manage a quiet day propping up the bar at the Waggonload of Monkeys in Great Missenden, and anything would be preferable to life at the Talking Shop at the moment, which is quite frankly hell on wheels.

You probably read about M's Mystery Tour to the Emerald Isles, about which there's been a good deal of idiotic speculation by the alcoholic wrecks in the Press Lobby. Having been on the trip, I am in a position for once to impart a few nuggets of fact, unlikely though these may seem at your end.

You know my views about our friends the Bogtrotters, Bill. Ever since we came in I've been urging the Boss to hack through the mooring ropes, cast the little buggers loose, green and orange, leave them to fend for themselves, tear each other limb from limb etc etc as is their traditional wont. As it is, a whole lot of our Income Tax is being syphoned off to maintain a military presence at the sharp end, having bricks thrown at them by a lot of curly-headed yobboes, paid for from cradle to grave by you and me, when they should be grappling with the Russian Bear.

I remember, when I was asked down to Deal by old General Wenham, his boy was back on leave and he said he'd rather be struggling through the mosquito-infested swamps of Borneo being picked off with poison darts than have to be cooped up in the Bogside, listening to that stupid prat Paisley blethering on ad nauseam. According to him, both sides are the most frightful clowns. The Prods, as they call them, aren't C of E at all, but some sort of Baptists who dress up in bowler hats every so often and march up and down with drum and fife making absolute arses of themselves, and all because of something Oliver Cromwell did to William the Conqueror in the year dot. I don't know about you, Bill, but I find it hard enough to remember what happened in the '39 show.

Anyway, latest flap concerns six of the RC lot who are in jug and have spent the last year or so smearing the wall with shit to get extra blankets, etc etc. Prison Governor, rather a daft-looking bloke with glasses, very reasonably told them to stop arsing about, no way to run a prison, not a zoo, etc. Now they're bent on starving themselves to death. I told Peter Carrington what I thought was the sensible thing to do, which was to shut up and let nature take its course, reductions always desirable at this time of cuts in Government expenditure, etc. Instead of which, Bill, Peter C. et al all worked themselves up into the most frightful lather: world press up in arms, foreign TV men snooping about, M's image in danger of taking a dent, etc. Some initiative in order.

Before you can say Jack Robinson, limos at the door, onto the Aer Lingus shuttle, Howe, Carrington, Atkins — he's our man in Ulster, totally out of his depth but not one to refuse a drink — Yours Truly allowed to come along for the ride, sitting in the Non-Smoking bay surrounded by what I took at first to be a bunch of unshaven thugs laden down with offensive hardware but who turned out to be our gallant lads in the SAS.

The idea, as it emerged, was a top level eyeball-to-eyeball conference in some four-star bordello near the airport with the Senior Leprechaun, a shifty little bugger by the name of Haughey, very reminiscent of that so-called gynaecologist who ran a clinic next door to Maurice Picarda's establishment during his Rubber Goods phase. O'Leary? No matter. M. inevitably taken in by the blarney within minutes. Arm round the shoulder, Jameson's in ample quantities, gales of laughter, risque anecdotes from Peter C., Howe misty-eyed recalling some obscure Irish relative of advanced years in Connemara, apparently a dab hand at the harp.

I tottered off at about half-one, having been bored almost to death by Atkins' tales of domestic misfortunes and deciding it was time for Bedfordshire. The following morning, imagine my surprise to find them still at it. Empty bottles as far as the eye can see, frightful fug, ashtrays overflowing, wet cigar ends, enough to make a man take the pledge. Cage opens, reptiles flood in, camera bags and reporters' notebooks at the ready. Little Haughey on his feet at once, announcing historical breakthrough, new way forward, epoch-making agreement, two great countries, etc. I could see Carrington and M. looking a bit askance, though clearly in no mood to focus. Turns out afterwards that somebody said something in the middle of the night with which they all agreed, but unfortunately in the light of day nobody for the life of them could remember what it was.

A propos your very kind enquiry. What I would really like is a new set of those Scandinavian woolly jobs from Lillywhites to keep my clubs warm. I should warn you, when you come to open my present, avoid doing so in the presence of Daphne. The Major bought it in Hamburg and I thought it might tickle your fancy.

Toodleoo for now,

DENIS

CHATEAU
ST. DENIS

1981
BOTTLED

10 Downing Street
Whitehall

January 1981

Dear Bill,

If the following narrative appears to be slightly incoherent, I can only offer by way of mitigation the very terrible toll taken by alcohol through the system over the ten days of festivities. If I had a twenty pound note for every snort forced on me since Christmas Eve I should be a very rich man indeed. Alas, any illusion of bonhomie or optimism thus produced has now evaporated in no uncertain manner and I am left with a splitting headache and a New Year resolution to cut down by at least a couple of bottles a day.

Things started coming unpicked, as far as I can recall, on Christmas Eve when we arrived at an icy Chequers to find that Mr Woo, the very capable Filipino caretaker put in by the National Trust, had broken his leg while bringing in the coke and had been taken to hospital in Aylesbury, where he was put in the Princess Alice Memorial Ward and not expected to be up and about much before Easter. This inevitably threw the Boss into a bit of a tiswas, and for a moment or two she seriously considered taking up the Carringtons' invitation to join them and their in-laws up the road. However, this was not to be, and M. was soon on the phone to her Cockney barrow-boy friend in the *Daily Express*, who also, it now transpires, runs that ghastly hotel underneath the Chiswick Flyover where the Major stayed the night the baggage handlers went on strike at Heathrow. Little Matthews instantly obliged, and by the time we'd opened a cardboard crate or two of snorts and managed to get the Calor Gas working, a swarthy menial in a white hat had arrived and was humping various pre-cooked delicacies out of a battered van and into the deep freeze. He seemed quite perky, and I was mildly disappointed when he knocked back the proffered snort and drove off into the night, narrowly missing the local carol-singers who were advancing up the drive, escorted by a posse of police armed to the teeth with machine-guns.

Luckily M. was still in a state of some euphoria on account of the Hunger Strikers running up the white flag. Personally, I had a sneaking feeling all along that as the whiff of Christmas Pudding and warm Guinness began to circulate along the corridors of H-Block the Paddies' nerve would begin to crack. However, such has been the mood in recent months that the slightest good news brings on a fit of euphoria all round, and I was beginning to hope that it might see us through the Sacred Festival without unpleasantness. As it turned out, this was not to be.

You may have gathered from the *Telegraph* that Joe Soap at the moment is wretched old Howe, the once-ebullient sporter of the brothel-creepers and the freshly shampooed quiff. It appears that he has to carry the can for the failure of this Money Supply thing to work properly, though as neither he nor the Boss understands a blind thing about it, this strikes me as a bit unfair. There are, as you will have heard on the grapevine, a host of Whitehall Sir Hector this's and Sir Herbert thats, plus the pinstripe and brolly brigade, all chewing the rug in the wings. Anyway, some time

before the Season of Goodwill, M. decided that the whole lot of them were deeply suspect, pinkoes, hobnobbers with Heath in the past, etc, and the only answer was to bring in a tame boffin hitherto hiding out as a tax exile in the US of A. As far as I can see, quite a decent bird, no different from the rest of her little band of eager beavers, except that he has a rather higher opinion of the Boss, which may explain why he is being paid the fifty thousand smackers.

However, Brother Howe had clearly got wind of the fact that he might be in for a reshuffle, and on Boxing Day — Christmas itself very quiet, both of us thank God having something cold on a tray in our respective rooms — jangle, jangle from the front door bell, enter Howe, puffing at stub of cigar, followed by talkative wife, both laden down with gifts, exuding bonhomie. Just happened to be passing on my way back to Town, taken liberty of dropping by, trust not inconvenient. No, no, not at all, what could be more delightful, kisses exchanged with talkative wife, Denis will get us something from the cellar. Meanwhile insincerity of the foregoing clearly indicated by frosty look from M., capable of freezing the balls off a snowman. H. not aware of this, however, always one to look on the bright side.

Yours truly, having lingered a while below decks to sample the Imperial Tokay laid down by old Macmillan — only decent thing he ever did — returns aloft to find M. still glacial, talkative wife examining pictures, Howe attempting to light new cigar at wrong end. Sherbets all round, comes a silence. Howe: 'What a pity about John Nott.' Boss: 'How do you mean, what a pity about John Nott?' Howe: 'I mean his getting mixed up in this Rossminster business. Sticky wicket.' Another awkward silence, broken by Lady H. embarking on long range weather forecast. It may have been the tinctures, but it took me a moment or two to twig what it was that Howe was on about, and then of course the penny dropped. Friend Nott, a bald geezer with glasses and a fishy look, generally tipped as obvious Substitute waiting in the Club-room in the event of any New Year Reshuffle. Answer, nobble Friend Nott by snide suggestions he had blotted his copybook on the Revenue front, and Brother Howe allowed to stay in Davis Cup team, he hopes.

M. refuses however to be drawn either into the fiscal misdemeanours or the meteorological stuff, and changes the subject rapidly to Fred Astaire and the BBC's Christmas package of old films, what a good impression Mike Yarwood had done of Michael Foot, etc. Bedraggled pair leave moments later still under impression their sortie has not been in vain. I put in a word for old Howe afterwards, pointing out that if anyone to be tossed to the wolves why not Heseltine or Stevarse, where real public enjoyment would be derived from the spectacle. M. however remaining tight-lipped retires to den.

Toodleoo for the nonce,

DENIS

10 Downing Street
Whitehall

16 January 1981

Dear Bill,

I expect you've all been having a jolly good chuckle about our Norman being given the heave-ho by the Boss. Personally I can't say I was over-distressed to see the back of the smarmy little bugger, although I must say it did come as a bit of a surprise, as M. has always given the impression the sun shines out of his arse, and even tolerated his so-called jokes, allowing him to refer to her as 'the blessed Margaret' etc. Well, he's certainly got his come-uppance now.

Everyone seems pretty mystified here about what actually lay behind Stevarse's fall from grace. I think it had a lot to do with the arrival of M's latest recruit to the staff, an American professor called Walters. I'd just got back from the Lillywhites' Sale — where who should I run into but the widow Tremlett, rather flushed and weaving her way into the Apres Ski department on the arm of some swarthy little Greek johnny in pebble spectacles and an astrakhan

82

overcoat — when the bell rang at Number Ten, and there was this cove on the doorstep, fresh from Heathrow with six or seven tartan suitcases on little wheels.

Needless to say, I hadn't the faintest idea who he was, and assumed him to be an emissary of that new President they've got in, Hopalong Cassidy or whatever his name is. Everyone else had gone out, so I showed him the spare room, gave him a towel and a piece of soap, and he began the lengthy task of hanging up his suits. Eventually he toddled down in a clean shirt, gleaming shoes etc, rubbing his hands and saying he wanted to get at it. I assumed he meant the drinks cabinet and ladled out a pretty lethal snorto de luxe, knowing the knack Americans have for putting it away, and poured myself a largish one to keep him company.

Emboldened by the amber fluid I broached the obvious topic — 'What brings you to our shores?' It soon transpires that this is the bean there's all the talk about to be taken on at fifty grand a year to sort things out. What strikes me as odd about these chaps, like that fat old geriatric Mr Macgregor the Monk brought in to close down British Steel at an even larger inducement, is that if they're so good at it why don't they stay in America? I was wondering whether I could formulate this in some tactful manner, and considering on balance it might be better avoided, when M. arrived, full of apologies, traffic, Whitehall absolutely chock-a-block, must be the Sales, and our American visitor began rubbing his hands again and asking when he could really get down to it in earnest.

I was just fetching some new litre bottles from the cellar when high-pitched cries and laughter from upstairs suggested that the meeting had been joined by a third party. Sure enough, it transpired that Stevarse had blown in with an enormous bouquet of flowers for the Boss from some visiting band of strolling ballet wooftahs at present throwing themselves about for the delectation of the locals at Sadlers Wells. Catching sight of the American, he became very arch. Sorry he hadn't brought him any flowers, hadn't realised he was so young, much better looking than in his photographs. I could see the Boss beginning to bridle at this line of talk, however our Papist friend seemed oblivious of the mood and plunged on. 'As long as you realise, my dear' — giving him a pat on one tartan-clad knee — 'you are only here as decoration, to add a bit of class to the Leaderene's entourage. Don't expect any help from us mere Cabinet Ministers, we are just a teeny bit busy what with one thing and another, and there are some of us who feel, strictly between ourselves, that all this Business Efficiency number is just a touch passé. I know you don't agree with me, Margaret' — here he leaned across and squeezed M's elbow in a disagreeably obsequious manner — 'you're so delightfully twinset and pearls in your old-fashioned suburban way.'

Wasn't there some bloke in Elizabethan days who was very thick with the Virgin Queen and eventually went too far, put his foot in it and got his head chopped off? I couldn't help being reminded of that scenario as I watched M's lip beginning to curl, and Stevarse rhapsodising on about how much free time our American guest was going to have and how they could go to Museums and Art Galleries together. The trouble with bachelors, Bill, is that they can never spot the storm cones being hoisted. 'Thank you, Norman,' the Boss eventually breathed. 'That will be all. The Professor and I have some serious work to get on with. I would be grateful if you would be outside my office tomorrow morning at half-past seven with your portfolio.'

Never a nice sight to see a fellow getting his cards, Bill. You remember at Burmah the occasion poor old Groggy Rossiter took one afternoon off too many and ran into Sir Hector walking through the ornamental fishpond holding his trousers? None of us had much time for him, but he did make a very pathetic sight calling in at the canteen to say his last farewells to the tea ladies. I found poor Stevarse sitting in the hall on the way down to breakfast, blubbing like a schoolboy and wiping his eyes with one of those big mauve hankies he always has floating out of his pocket, drenched inevitably in some repulsive French scent. As I said to him, it wasn't anything he'd done, merely that M. had worked herself up into a mood for human sacrifice and he just happened to be the ram caught in the thicket. He snivelled on about how he was now accused of leaking secrets, how dare she speak like that to a close friend of the Pope, and I later suggested to M. that she might drop him some sort of conciliatory line, no hard feelings etc. Not but what I'm pretty convinced she's storing up a bit of trouble for herself. If she thinks our friend Norman is now going to sit on the Back Benches preserving a dignified silence and muttering Hear Hear from time to time she is very much mistaken. Viz E. Heath, another lonely bachelor, who has no intention of burying the hatchet, except in one particular place. Say what you like about marriage, and both of us have said a good deal in our time, you do learn to forgive and forget. At least I do, even if she doesn't.

Ah me, we live in troublous times.

Yours till the cows come home,

DENIS

10 Downing Street
Whitehall

30 January 1981

Dear Bill,
Everyone cock-a-hoop at this end, as you can imagine, about the

cowboy chap taking over in the Americas. As you know, I've always had my reservations about Carter ever since he started that business of walking about hand-in-hand with his wife, which suggested to me that decay in the grey cells had set in, but the new bloke looks equally rum. His hair colour is very obviously out of a bottle and M. says he's really 83, so I wouldn't give him very long in the hot seat before he turns his toes up. He has the look about him of that chap behind the bar in the Wig & Compasses on the front at Deal the Major always swore wore makeup and who keeled over shortly after marrying a wife half his age. This Reagan chap has the same decrepit painted-up air, and I fear little Mr Bush will be asked to step in e'er long. However, the Boss thinks he's absolutely the bee's knees, saying all the same things that she says and deluging her with signed photographs of himself at an earlier epoch, wearing a white hat and sitting on a horse. Not but what we have been invited over to the US of A next month to go and kiss hands in the Oval Room. I imagine it will be pretty thick with other old film stars in wigs, with a generous sprinkling of the Mafia. Hardly my idea of a Winterbreak, Bill, but M's already slavering to climb aboard the Concorde.

Meanwhile, all eyes here are focussed on the other side. I know the Boss isn't doing too well at the moment with the pollsters, but we were all pretty chuffed to discover that poor old Foot is trailing behind with only 26% knowing who he is. I put it down to his broken leg and his popping in and out of hospital all the time. No one's going to have too much confidence in a chap who seems to operate on the end of a flex from the Geriatric Ward.

(By the by, do you follow the career at all of that chap Bosanquet who used to read out the news on the other channel? He seems to rival Maurice Picarda on the drink problem front, marked tendency to blackouts and sudden insensibility due to a surfeit of snorts. Nowadays however he has trained all the Press johnnies into saying that he suffers from epilepsy, a frightfully good wheeze which I mooted to Margaret might be worth falling back on from time to time in our own private life. E.g., on visits to the Opera, 'You must forgive Denis, he's been completely epileptic since teatime'. M. failed to comment, and obviously didn't think it was much of a joke.)

However that may be. With repeated collapse of Uncle Michael, Red hopes are now pinned on the Big Split. I think I may have mentioned a fat chap with glasses we met in Brussels once, very up with European high society and dropping names as if there was no tomorrow. Jenkins the name, though not to be confused with that oily little Welshman with the squeaky voice who seems to make such a good living out of the Unions. Jenkins, the Brussels one, has been hovering about for some months now waiting to sound the trumpet and rally the faithful, i.e. drawing-room liberals everywhere, plus the messy-looking woman that Margaret can't stand. Latest wheeze is that they gang up with the Liberals and do some kind of deal to pull the rug from under our friend from the geriatric ward, i.e. Old Grandpa Foot. (Quite a decent old cove, actually, as I may have said before. I see him hobbling down Whitehall from time to time, blind as a bat and always clutching a great pile of books, very like that Methodist sky-pilot who was run over in Tunbridge Wells at the end of the war.) I told the Boss over tinctures the other evening not to bank on the fat cat Jenkins getting his little bandwaggon off the ground, but she thinks given a fair wind it should put the kibosh on the Opposition for the next twenty-five years or so. The ability of everyone here to look on the bright side never ceases to amaze me.

Do you notice how the Monk keeps getting pelted with eggs? No matter where he goes, there's always some little bolshie lurking with a box of Standard Whites at the ready. Never happens to any of the others. I can't understand why he carries on. Oddly enough I ran into him the other night at an extraordinary gathering organised by Saatchis at which M. entertained the Professor Branestawms of our day, all of them encouraged to bring along their inventions. I pressed him on the egg question, did he mind constantly having to wipe the yolk out of his eye, etc? Gave me a very wild look. Obviously thought I was the barmy one. After that I got talking to some cove from Barnsley who'd dreamed up a contraption for making petrol out of alcohol. I rather steered him round by the end of the evening, I think, and he promised to go home and work on it. I'll let you know if he delivers anything drinkable.

Yours aye,

DENIS

10 Downing Street
Whitehall

13 February 1981

Dear Bill,
Poor old Maurice seems to have worked himself up into a shocking state about BL. I had to listen to him for an hour on the blower the other night, all through the International Golf, on the subject of his double-glazing enterprise, Picwarmth Ltd, and why it was in the hands of the Receiver. Why should Edwardes be bailed out and not him? Here we were, all being told to cut our fuel bills, Picwarmth to the rescue with some type of asbestos padding he got hold of after a big fire in Taiwan, ready to be installed by what he calls his highly-trained staff, which you or I know perfectly well is the same bunch of tearaway darkies he was

using when he was in ballpoint pens, solar heating and his dispatch service, and the Government allows him to go to the wall without so much as waving him goodbye. I didn't see the point in arguing the toss with the old boy as he was clearly in a very emotional state. Nor did I like to ask whether he was still with that fat woman from the Antique Supermarket, but there was certainly someone in the background giving him a bit of stick.

As a matter of fact I find myself pretty baffled by the Leyland caper. Our lot have always been saying that we've got to stand on our own feet, make our own way in the world, stop nannying the proles etc and now the Monk is giving a blank cheque to little Edwardes to blow on those workshy yobboes at Longbridge. If you ask me, as far as the Boss is concerned at least, it was all done by some pretty nimble PR chancers at the time of the Metro launch. Always make a pitch for the wife, these car salesmen. I remember the Major telling me it was the first rule in his book. So while I was shunted off for tinctures with a lot of silly women in leotards M. was slid in behind the wheel and encouraged to do a ton round the dirt track, photographer johnnies in attendance. When she came back she was exactly like someone who had been on the Big Dipper. Eyes gleaming, breathless, a lot of talk about shining new appliances, optional extras and eighty-three mpg, which I personally take with a pretty large pinch of salt. PR men in active negotiation with Saatchis, offering a hefty discount under the Cars for Stars scheme — you may remember that woman on the telly with the teeth got one.

You know the form, Bill. I remember you describing how Daphne set her heart on that Japanese Landrover with the eight-wheel drive and sunroof. Lot of flak, inevitably, but I managed to make the point that there are certain areas in which hubby knows best, that there was nothing wrong with the Rolls and if she wanted a runabout she always had the old Ford banger. In any case, just the kind of thing the press monkeys were bound to jump on. Peter Carrington, I must admit, was v. impressed. In his book I had steered the Boss out of what could have been a pretty sticky situation. Typically, ever since then, M. has had a soft spot for little Edwardes, and apparently the Monk has now done some sums on his pocket calculator and worked out that if they closed down the whole shebang as they intended the bill for supplementary benefits would come to more than what they're shelling out by way of largesse as it is. So there.

Meanwhile you might have thought that it would have stopped the Boss in her tracks. Not a bit of it. She is now firing on fifteen cylinders, enemies swatted like flies on all sides. It's a horrifying sight to see her eyes gleaming as she leaves Number Ten, ready for the afternoon scrap with poor old Foot — on the ropes already and clearly beginning to wish he'd stuck to antiquarian book-selling. (I was told the other day that it was his wife who put him up to it in the first place, which doesn't surprise me.) Ditto the smelly socks brigade. Little Len Murray dragged in again with his five point plan for putting things to rights, brutally savaged by the Boss and quickly dragged out of the cage by his friends waving chairs to create a diversion.

I suppose you've noticed. Front page of the *Telegraph*. This Roy Rogers character holding hands with his wife already. Just like Carter. At the age of seventy, I find that pretty obscene. I can't believe he'll last. However, more of that when we hit Washington.

I got your message about me picking up one of those American walkie-talkie telephones for the garden when I'm over there. Is there anything else you wanted on the leisure front? Saatchis are apparently providing us with some spending money.

Yours in the Lord,

DENIS

10 Downi

27 February 1981

Dear Bill,

I don't know whether you spotted this snap of yours truly in the *Telegraph* last week, but I enclose it for your delectation.

What happened was somewhat unfortunate. Do you remember that rather sharp little cove, Courtauld, who manages the gents' sportswear department at Lillywhites? I was in there the other day picking up some new togs, when up he bustles rubbing his hands no end and saying I might be interested in their new line in Apres Golf wear. Assistant summoned forward wearing tartan-lined Sherlock Holmes number, much favoured by the aristocracy, etc, prepared to make a very generous reduction. A glance in the full-length mirror was enough to convince me I'd clearly get the bird at Littlestone, but as it was a cold day and, if I am to be entirely frank, I may have imbibed a little too freely over luncheon at the RAC, a credit card changed hands and before I knew it my old dirty mac had been packed up in a suitcase and I was bowling off along Jermyn Street attracting wolf whistles from every side.

Needless to say, there were the usual Press Scum lurking in the bushes outside Number Ten, blaze of flashlights and I entered dazzled to encounter a straight left from M. What on earth did I think I was playing at? Look what happened to Wilson when he started modelling macs for the Estonian jailbird, take it off this minute, bloody fool, etc. So that was that. Courtauld was v. apologetic down at Lillywhites, offered me a credit note, but it didn't seem the same somehow so I blew it all on a row of stiff ones round the corner in the Ritz Bar.

I've been trying to keep out of the way as much as possible in view of what's been happening with the Miners. The Boss is in a prickly state at present and best left alone anyway. I began to smell a rat when little Pym got up on his hind legs. (Quite a decent bird who I think may have been at Eton with Sticky's elder brother, the one who was cashiered for that nasty business in Benghazi.) I've always found him very sound on keeping the lower orders in their place, hence my alarm when he gets up and begins spouting about adjustments and the need to bend with the wind. Apparently old Humpty-Dumpty Thorneycroft sounded off along the same lines. Next thing that happens, a perfectly sensible decision is taken to shut down twelve or so coal-mines in the Rhondda Valley where they've been losing money since the First World War. Whereupon the Taffys rise in rage, shut up shop before it's shut up for them, and light the braziers outside the gates.

I could see the Boss was beginning to show signs of panic but in view of the fact that the black-faced boyos had yet to receive the blessing of Uncle Joe Gormley I advised her to sit tight and await developments, ideally large brownie in hand.

The point I made, Bill, is that they could easily see off a full-scale revolt, huge mountains of coal having been piled up all over Wales for the simple reason they can't sell the stuff. The Major was telling me only the other day that he'd been down to that coal merchant friend of his in Swindon, and even with the ten per cent off for old times' sake a ton of smokeless briquettes still set the poor old boy back a hundred quid, and most of that was rock. No wonder, then, the miners have lit up the braziers, having to shift it somehow. (You must be thanking your lucky stars you

89

went over to the log-burner. Precious little chance of the lumberjacks coming out.)

Meanwhile, back at the seat of power, all would have been well, I surmise, if Peter Carrington had managed to keep his nerve. As I may have said before, he's a very decent little cove, but I had forgotten the fact that he went through all that ghastly business when he and Heath shut the country down four days a week, and he still wakes up in the middle of the night screaming at the thought of Joe Gormley. At the first sign of trouble he appears at the Talking Shop, pale at the gills. I must say, I award him high marks for guile, though. Straight in to the Boss, advising her to emulate her predecessor Heath. Stand up to the buggers. Heath very wise in many ways, history will vindicate him, could probably be persuaded to come round to Downing Street and lend a hand. As you well know, Bill, any mention of the seafaring bachelor is like a red rag to a bull, and Margaret's response was predictable enough. Little Howell, the Energy chap, was instantly whistled in and told to run up the white flag. Carrington grinning up his sleeve like a Cheshire Cat, and finally accepting my offer of a very large one.

Do you remember that poetry book we had at Mill Hill, Bill? There were some very good lines in it by someone or other to the effect that once you start paying out money to the Danes you'll never get rid of the buggers. I told Carrington this. What about the Sewage Wallahs? I said. They'll be on the rampage next. What are we supposed to do then: stop going to the lavatory? Carrington was very condescending, as much as saying in so many words I didn't understand what I was talking about, compromise was the name of the game and we had to show we'd got a human face, just like that woman with the bad haircut they've all got their knickers in a twist about.

We're just off to the Land of the Free to see Old Hopalong. I still can't get used to the idea of him being in the White House. Imagine if Kenny Moore had got the Boss's job, you'd think it pretty rum, wouldn't you, Bill?

So long, my friend, and may the Good Lord take a liking to you.

Yours,

DENIS

10 Downing Street
Whitehall

13 March 1981

Dear Bill,

I hope you got the duty-free Bourbon. I asked one of Carrington's lackeys to drop it off at the Club. Unfortunately the Walkie-Talkie Telephone you wanted for Daphne was re-routed to Seattle owing to a baggage mix-up, but it may turn up in the fullness of time. I would have done more about it, but I am still somewhat under the weather thanks to jet-lag et al.

I can't remember whether you've ever crossed the Big Pond, Bill, but the thing that strikes you from a cultural point of view is their extraordinary drinking habits. The first night we got there — as you know, it's earlier when you arrive than when you take off, and I couldn't entirely make out whether it was yesterday or tomorrow back home, but not to worry — we drove to the White House all spruced up in bib and tucker on the stroke of seven. Greeted by the most godawful fanfare from *Call Me Madam* played by a lot of Marines in ill-fitting uniforms with their hats slipping over their ears. The Major had warned me not to expect too much on the drill and turn-out front when it came to ceremonial. Old Hopalong standing at the top of the steps, as I feared holding hands with the First Lady — but I was damned if I was going to follow suit. We were then ushered into a darkened room full of very old film stars, some of whom I vaguely recognised from the black and white talkie days.

I had just been introduced to that rather nice old bean who plays golf and used to do a double act with Bing Crosby before he turned his toes up, when a big black man in some sort of mediaeval costume eased forward with a trayful of long-stemmed goblets and asked me whether I would prefer a Shot Bulldog or a Copacabana Fizz. I could see with my practised eye that there were obviously no bona fide snorts to hand so I took pot luck with what I surmised to be a bit of everything poured into a glass and covered with grated coconut. Absolutely lethal, at least after half a dozen or so. The trouble is, you see, that having got you there at tea-time, Brother Yank doesn't believe in getting his nose into the trough much before 10pm, by which time one and all are absolutely pie-eyed.

No wonder when it came to the speeches they were a touch over the top. Hopalong kicked off with the most ballsaching encomium of the Bulldog Breed, apparently under the impression that Winston Churchill was still alive, and comparing the Boss to Boadicea standing up to the Trots. (The news of the miners' cave-in didn't seem to have penetrated to their neck of the woods, which was probably just as well under the circs.) M. then sprang to her feet, eyes blazing in the candle-light, telling Hopalong that he was the best thing since sliced bread and that should he feel like nuking the Ayatollah or any of the other Middle Eastern monkeys we would be delighted to place the entire Royal Air Force at his disposal. I could see poor little Carrington going white about the gills and burying his head in his hands, but this could have been the effect of the Bulldogs.

By the time the Boss had finished it was six in the morning by my watch, and I was looking forward to a spot of Bedfordshire. However it was not to be. Tables cleared by more gigantic Uncle Toms in fancy dress, cigarettes lit, and the Mafia man with the toupee was wheeled on to sing his Hundred Best Tunes. At this point the Hollywood geriatrics began to show signs of life, and Hopalong led Margaret onto the dancefloor for a smooch. I was aware that eyes were turning in my direction and it eventually dawned on me that I was expected to do my bit with the First Lady. I can't say I enjoyed it, but we did a couple of circuits without either of us falling over. I tried to explain how the Queen wasn't really in charge, as they all seem to think, but the old girl clearly wasn't concentrating and conversation rather dried up after that.

The next day there was a return match at the British Embassy, with the same cast, and I was sorry to see that our chaps, presumably out of deference to the natives, were proffering the same kind of poisonous rubbish in the way of booze — tomato sauce mixed with brandy and grated chocolate, I think it was. Same speeches, M. comparing Hopalong to Abraham Lincoln, Hopalong proposing toast to King George VI, Mafia man wheeled out to sing identical selection, and the same nausea on the dancefloor to wind things up, except that Reagan on this occasion was being followed round in the Slow Waltz by his medico carrying a little black bag. I must say, Bill, he does look very rum. His hair is a funny kind of orange colour, make-up half an inch thick coming off on his collar, very like one of those figures in the Waxworks. When he speaks it's really uncanny. I formed the impression he has very little idea of what's going on. The only time he spoke to me he seemed to think I was Peter Carrington.

We meet I think on the night of the 12th for the Inner Wheel do at Tunbridge Wells. I have alerted Fatty Farmer who is providing beds.

Have a nice day,

DENIS

10 Downing Street
Whitehall

27 March 1981

Dear Bill,

Lot of rumpus as you may have seen this week about another weirdo in the FO being caught with his trousers down. I don't know what it is about the Foreign Office, but it does seem to attract the dirty raincoat brigade in very large numbers. Makes you wonder when they get down to any work. Do you remember that retired Nautical Attache who lived down the road from the Major? Used to come into the Saloon Bar as regular as clockwork on the stroke of six in a floor-length evening gown and a hat with flowers on, expecting to be called Vera. Now, I gather, he's a disc-jockey in Bangkok. I am beginning to look at Carrington in a new light.

You may have thought the Boss had got her back to the wall with all this shindig over the Budget. Not a bit of it. Apparently the Wets kicked up a stink about not being told in advance about the 20p on petrol but I don't see why they didn't look in the papers and read it there like everyone else. Not but what it wasn't a fairly stormy session. I always think I'm fairly well sound-proofed wrapped around a bottle of Gordon's up here in the attic, but the Proprietorial tones penetrated as clear as a bell. I think old Farmer Prior got the worst of it, closely followed by Gilmour. I don't know if you've seen him on TV at all, a streaky version of little Carrington with a face like a cemetery on a wet afternoon and a wife who is the spitting image of Margaret, which can't be much consolation to him when he toddles home at night after a thumping from the Boss.

M's repeated argument, on a point of house-keeping, is that they can't go on borrowing money, what would the neighbours think, etc? I can't quite understand the logic of this. Bill, I  don't know whether you've seen the adverts in the *Telegraph* for National Savings, but they are now offering something like 14% tax-free, and I've been seriously thinking of shifting my little nest-egg from Brother Furniss at the NatWest. Though having seen a bit of the way these characters go on I am hesitant to trust them with my own money, and Furniss does keep a very decent bottle of Amontillado in the safe, which you won't get from the Giro. My argument, however, is that if that isn't borrowing, what is?

One point is they all now admit that this money supply thing they've been on about ever since they got in is a total non-starter. The idea was that if you brought down the money supply, whatever that means, inflation would come down as well. Now, even despite their efforts, inflation has come down a bit but the money supply has gone up. I asked little Howe, busy though he obviously was, whether he could perhaps enlighten me. He was very huffy and told me to go and ask that American chap with the tartan suitcases, Walters. Pressed, however, and trapped in a corner of M's sitting-room, he burbled on a bit about how everything was going to bottom out soon, and it was all going according to plan, but that it was sometimes difficult to understand what the hell the civil servants thought they were doing.

If you ask me, the 20p petrol wheeze was all a plot dreamed up by the Boss in cahoots with her little friend Edwardes. You remember they gave her the old soap when she went up to Birmingham for the Metro launch at the Motor Show, 93 miles a gallon and all that caper. I have absolutely nothing concrete to go on, but I strongly suspect that we are now all supposed to throw up our hands in horror at 150p a gallon, cash in our old bangers, leave the Rolls to rust in the garage, etc, and invest in one of their ghastly little sardine boxes. M. keeps going on to me about how we should fly the flag and how I would find it ideal, clubs in the back, etc, mentioning various shades from Lilac to Autumn Gold, but I am resisting it and, anyway, what's 20p these days? The doorman at the Ritz literally spat at Maurice Picarda last week for giving him a five-pound note.

Yours in hope,

DENIS

10 Downing Street
Whitehall

10 April 1981

Dear Bill,

What about Hopalong getting hit in the shoulder, just like all his old films? I gather it was done by some nutcase who thought he was in a Western. I suppose in a country like America, given their drinking habits, most of the time they have no idea whether it's real or on television anyway. No wonder they all go round the bend and start shooting each other at the drop of a hat. Margaret sent a telegram of condolence but hasn't had a reply yet. There's a feeling at this end that the old boy may in fact be in worse shape than they're letting on. After all, he is seventy and you remember how long Archie Wellbeloved took to get over it when he shot himself through the foot whilst trying to rid the church of sparrows during Evensong.

Talking of Archie, I gave him a ring the other night to ask his advice about who they should have as the new Bishop of London. Margaret had got her knickers in a tremendous twist about Runcie trying to bring in yet another of his various stooges and I told her to leave it to me. Archie, who may be pretty senile but still has his ear to the ground, came up with this fellow from Truro who, he assures me, is very sound on women priests and cracking down on our gay friends, of whom, if you ask me, there is a pretty fair sprinkling in ecclesiastical circles. I passed this on to the Boss, and you will be glad to hear it has gone through, despite considerable tantrums and slamming down of the receiver at Buck House on account of Truro once having administered a public wigging to Princess Margaret when she was carrying on with that nancy-boy pop singer.

Meanwhile they're all over the moon here about the new ructions on the other side. Just when poor old Foot thought he was in for a week or two of peace and quiet now that Jenkins and his little crew have set sail in the good ship Social Democrat, up pops Benn in the middle of the night, eyes rotating like Catherine Wheels, and announces he is going to oust Healey from the Number Two spot. My own view, considering the lateness of the hour and the emotional stability of the subject, was that Benn had had a few in the Members' Bar and was sounding off as many of us do in the small hours following the ingestion of more than the usual skinful. In our case, Bill, we forget about it altogether next morning, and no harm done. It turned out, however, that Benn had total recall and meant every word of it. I must say, my heart goes out to poor old Foot. He must be beginning to regret ever embarking on such a wretched old age. As I may have said before, I think it was his wife who put him up to it. There he could have been still, wandering about on Hampstead Heath, taking the dog for a walk, browsing through his second-hand bookshops, not a care in the world: instead he must be up at the crack of dawn, hardly time for a shit and a shave, and straight into battle with Benn or the Boss. What a life!

However, what's sauce to the goose does something or other to the gander, and M. is happy as a grig about the Benn affair, predicting fifty years of glorious rule, golden jubilee celebrations etc and the Winston treatment when it finally comes to the wooden box.

I have rented a little place on Sandwich Bay for Easter. Any chance of making up a foursome for a stroll round Royal St

George's? M. promises me she will definitely be in Brussels, hammering out the fish.

Take care.

Yours until the cows come home, and by the way, how is Daphne?

DENIS

KHAZI HILTON
RIYADDH s. ARABIA

24 April 1981

Dear Bill,

Crikey! What a Godforsaken dump this is. Sand as far as the eye can see, wogs swarming about as if they owned the place, all the women wearing black dust-sheets, and not a snort in sight. If you want one, you have to ring the British Embassy and it's sent round in a locked van with motorcycle escort. Luckily Carrington warned me about the form, and I rigged up a kind of false golf-bag with a few sawn-off ping-irons visible at the top and all the rest suitably cushioned bottle space. I got a pretty odd look from the Chief Wog's frisker at the airport, an ex-Wingco in the RAF, who said: 'If it's golf you're after you've come to the wrong shop, old fruit.' I said we were stopping off in Grand Canary on the way home. Apparently if they catch you at it you're strapped over a barrel in the marketplace and given fifty lashes so I am being extremely circumspect.

India, or it may have been Pakistan, was an absolute washout. You may wonder why we keep traipsing off to these far-flung corners of the globe. I certainly do. It's all the fault of the Foreign Office as far as I can see. Margaret clearly hasn't a blind idea what she's doing, but there's always a bevy of Whitehall johnnies with briefcases waiting at the airport, bumsucking away at the locals in the most shameless manner, trying to flog them all kinds of ball-bearings, tractors, guns and that kind of thing, with Margaret just being the cherry on the cake.

I knew she wouldn't take to that Gandhi woman. She never really warmed to Golda Meir either. She can't forgive either of them for getting there first. As we got out of the aeroplane at Benares or Calcutta or wherever it was, it was like stepping into the Hot Room at the old Turkish Bath in Jermyn Street, and within seconds my drip-dry was soaking wet. The Boss had made a big effort, some little number run up by Tropicana of Piccadilly, but was clearly beginning to wilt within seconds, whereas Mother India was breezing about in a long floaty number with nothing

96

much underneath, looking as cool as a cucumber in a pair of Chanel sunglasses. Advantage Mrs G.

By the by, Bill, it's very confusing about her being called Mrs Gandhi. I asked her about her father, assuming, as you would have done, that he was the little spindly fellow in the loincloth who was always lying down on a bed of nails in the path of oncoming trains. Not a bit of it. She told me in a rather huffy way that her old man was Pundit Nero, the one who used to wear a pillbox hat with a rose in his buttonhole and was so thick with Mountbatten's good lady. Jolly confusing, what?

The banquet was very much what you would expect, a touch of the old Raj, curry and turbans, only enlivened by a frightful shouting match between M. and the Gandhi woman, both at it like a pair of fishwives. All the Indians are up in arms about Whitelaw's latest scheme to stem the immigrant tide. On that leg of the trip the drink laws still hadn't begun to bite, and owing to jetlag I may have been over-enthusiastic about putting my oar in. I told our dusky hostess that in view of recent events in Brixton we just couldn't afford to let in a whole lot more of her compatriots. All industrious, charming little fellows, etc, but put them in South London and in no time at all they'd be bunging bricks at the Constabulary like some country coconut shy. Not that I can say I blame them.

Whereupon, Bill, solids hit the punkah. Gandhi woman rises to her feet, eyes blazing, pointing out that all her mob are quiet as mice, running newspaper shops and colonising Bradford. Brixton lot an inferior breed altogether, mad as coots, high on drugs, etc, wouldn't let them into her sub-continent in a million years, etc.

Back at the Maharajah Hilton, the Boss v. critical of my intervention, telephone calls made to British Consul, yours truly packed off on two-day sightseeing tour of the Himalayas. Actually not a bad time at all. My escort was an old chum of the Major's, chotah pegs for White Sahib very much in evidence, and my memories somewhat confused.

Here we are, however, in Wogland. My God, Bill, it's no exaggeration to say that it's literally the arsehole of the universe. No wonder poor old Picarda came unstuck when he flew out here on his chemical toilet caper. The Chief Wog, King Khaled by name, is a funny little bird in dark glasses and one of those dishcloths. M. and I poled up to the Palace only to discover the old boy had popped out to see one of his relatives having his arm chopped off for fornication, and when he got back he refused to talk to M. on the grounds that she was a woman.

We had strict instructions from Peter Carrington on no account to offend them this time, as they could cut off the supply of Four-Star at the drop of a hat. I was therefore sent in to haggle with His Nibs. The FO bloke in tow, not the brightest of sparks, did most of the talking and spent a good half hour trying to interest the King in the idea of a Gulf Force. From what I could gather, this was to consist of one old RAF Hercules on standby at

Gatwick in case of Russian attack anywhere in the Middle East. Old Sheepseyes sat there pretty impassively, said nothing at all, and in the end we buggered off. M. very displeased, who did we think we were, etc? I pointed out that at least we hadn't given offence as far as I could tell, and that with any luck the oil would continue to flow.

I looked into the possibility of double-glazing for Maurice's sake, but as none of the houses have any windows I think it may be a bit of a non-starter.

See you back in Civilisation.

Yours aye,

DENIS

10 Downing Street
Whitehall

1 May 1981

Dear Bill,

There are times sitting upstairs when I get a bit gloomy about the way things are going. The best they can say nowadays is that it's all bottoming out, or alternatively flattening out, which means in layman's language that things couldn't possibly be worse and therefore are bound to get better.

The only gleam on the horizon has been the Major's greenhouses. I don't know if I've told you, but the old boy has been on to me for some time, usually ringing up very late at night and in an emotional condition, protesting about the cost of heating lettuces. His thinking is that no one will buy his greenhouses if the overheads are going to go straight through the ceiling the moment they turn on the juice.

I put his point of view to little Howe as he was getting into his overcoat the other morning. (Damn funny weather we've been having — Maurice Picarda woke up in a snowdrift outside the Cat & Hamster and thought he was having the DTs.) As they have this rebellion on their hands from the backwoodsmen I found a sympathetic ear. The Major's argument was that the other Euros subsidise the Small Radish Farmer with cheap Derv whilst the Men of Kent have to pay through the nose and go to the wall, result death of the British Radish Industry. Howe hummed and hahed for a bit, but I could see it was soaking in. Anyway, they've now agreed to chop 10p off their original 20p on diesel, although the mark-up on Four-Star remains the same. I don't personally see what they're all so steamed up about, 20p nowadays being about tuppence three-farthings in real money, but the MPs are a funny lot, they all feel obliged to let off steam from time to time, as does our friend the Major, and I suppose it's worth it to keep him quiet.

Meanwhile they're all fastening their seat belts and waiting for the balloon to go up yet again over Ulster. The usual scenario — chaps starving themselves to death, hooligans roving the streets, Paisley trying to garner a few votes on the sidelines with his cretinous parrot cries as usual, Boss and Whitelaw doing their two wise monkeys number over no surrender to the men of violence. I may have said this before, Bill, but quite frankly there's only one thing to do and that's for us to get the hell out of Ireland and leave the little monkeys to pelt each other with droppings in perpetuity. I have repeated this formula, ad nauseam I may say, to Ol' Oyster Eyes, but the trouble would appear to be that they signed some damnfool piece of paper a few years ago promising the Prods there would be no twitching of the rug, leaving in the lurch, etc. I said to Whitelaw this Government had torn up enough pieces of paper of that kind to fill a Corporation Rubbish Tip, so why hang about? As with the White Trash in Rhodesia, when it comes to selling people of that ilk down the river a short sharp shock is probably healthier in the long run. Gloomy shaking of the head, impression conveyed yours truly talking through hat as ever. Whitelaw knows perfectly well that I represent the voice of sanity, but he can't bring himself to face it.

On a more serious note, Maurice and I had not a bad day out at Worplesdon on Thursday and bump-ed into old Scatty Longmuir with that girlfriend of his who used to be some very big noise in the ATS. She got a bit tiddly at the Merry Mermaid and we had to rig up some sort of stretcher out of my Sherlock Holmes overcoat to lug her out into the carpark where she slept it off in the back of Scatty's Japanese Landrover. Scatty has really cashed in over the last week or so with this boom in the City, and was ordering doubles like a man possessed. I did what I could to introduce a note of realism with one or  two anecdotes about the Monk, but he wouldn't hear a word of it. Margaret was a wonderful woman, say what you like about this country but we could still drink the rest of the world under the table any day of the week. As we were breaking up there seem-ed to be some move afoot to hire a chara and come up to Town for the Royal Wedding. Number Ten an ideal base camp. I only hope that in the morning they won't have remembered anything about it.

Ah well, sun is over the yard arm, so down to work.

Yours aye,

DENIS

10 Downing Street
Whitehall

8 May 1981

Dear Bill,

Bit of a turn-up about old Giscard, what? Losing the election, I mean. I met him once or twice at the Common Market get-togethers, and he always struck me as a prize greaser. In my experience any Frog in office for more than a couple of years starts to think he's Napoleon or Louis the Whatever It Was, at which point the lower orders winkle out the cobblestones and create havoc. Then they bring in someone new and all go back to sipping their evil-smelling liqueurs in their pavement cafes. At which point the whole process begins all over again.

The funny thing was that nobody here knew the first thing about this Mitterand cove, and Carrington had to send out for a copy of *Paris Match* so they'd recognise him when they have to meet him. In the meantime Herr Schidt caught the first shuttle over to RAF Benson and was soon closeted with M. in the Gladstone Room plotting the Frog's downfall on the grounds that he's a Leftie. Personally, as you know, Bill, I don't trust any of them further than I can throw them, but M. loves all the toing and froing and the argy-bargy about the price of fish. I have refrained from pointing out to her that there may be some lesson to be learned from the tumbril treatment being meted out to old Giscard, though I like to think that with yours truly in the wings exercising a restraining influence this scenario may be avoided.

Trouble is, so long as old Worzel Gummidge remains nominally in charge of Transport House, M. very naturally feels she's got Downing Street on a long lease. Even their modest successes in the Local Elections have only led to further feuding, hair-pulling, nose-thumbing, etc, and I gather that relations between Brothers Foot and Benn have now degenerated to total non-speaks. Though I must say, Bill, barmy though he is, old Wedgie of the Whirling Eyes does occasionally hole in one, viz his scheme for getting the hell out of Ulster a.s.a.p. I don't know whether he got the idea through the odd political by-ways from yours truly, but I have observed over the years that lunatics do have moments of clarity. Do you remember when the Major's father had to be incarcerated at Esher wearing that funny life-jacket with the ribbons at the back, he still managed to pick out the first three in the St Leger when the rest of us lost our shirts.

I managed to escape from Colditz for a sharpener or twain with the Major at the RAC Club on Tuesday. He had come up to sell some old lengths of garden hose at Sotheby's, and we ran into Sticky Wilkinson, who is now working there as their expert on Japanese Ceramics, would you believe it? Sticky and the Major went very much off the deep end about the Hunger Strikers, but I did offer one ray of hope, which is that in my experience when the Proprietor puts her foot down in a big way at the Bar of World Opinion, stressing that there will be no last-minute reprieves, U-Turns, etc, it is quite often a sign that she is on the verge of going about, though of course this is never admitted afterwards.

I remember something of the kind happening with Daphne when she refused to have that Antiques woman of Picarda's in the house ever again after the incident at the Flower Festival, and then, blow me, there they were two weeks later closeted in the snug at the Goat & Compasses, swapping dirty limericks, shrieking with laughter, and thick as thieves over a couple of large ones. I seem to recall Maurice got a snap of them, albeit rather blurred.

Apparently there are some Jap reject clubs on offer at Lillywhites. If Daphne persists in her New York trip, you could hop on the Bluebell Line and we could get together over a spot of lunch at the Club.

Yours as ever,

DENIS

10 Downing Street
Whitehall

22 May 1981

Dear Bill,
Terrible weather we've been having! Boris says it's caused by the US Space Shuttle. You probably heard about my disastrous little outing with the Major and his new friend from the North. I don't know if you've met him yet, but he's called Bagley and runs a fish farm somewhere outside Newcastle. We got down to Worplesdon at opening time, to find the course completely waterlogged and the Club Secretary in his waders behind the bar v. apologetic, cellar flooded, no booze but he had got this new Space Invaders machine in, would we like to try our luck free of charge? Not much of a consolation, you might think, Bill, but the Major had fortunately come equipped for emergencies with a crate of Auld

MacTavish Highland Dew tucked away in the boot of his Jag, and after a snort or twain I got rather gripped by the machine. Have you seen one in your peregrinations? You put in fifty p. and suddenly the screen is filled with rank upon rank of nasty little foreign jobs advancing on a broad front. Then you press the tit and blow them up. It doesn't sound much, but it's  damn clever the way they do it, and by three o'clock in the afternoon I was really beginning to get the hang of things. By that time however the Major and his friend were getting a bit peckish and persuaded me to join them at a local hostelry just down the road called the Golden Bucket. They didn't seem particularly pleased when Mine Host told us that the kitchen was shut and slammed the door on Bagley's fingers when he tried to use the phone to place a bet on the 3.45 at Haydock Park.

We then drove into Bagshot. I'd forgotten what a dump that place is, Bill. All bypasses and Shopping Centres, not an afternoon drinking club in sight. In the end we had to make do with what are called Club Sandwiches at some ghastly Playboy Hotel. £4.99 for two bits of dried toast, a handful of crisps, an old bit of turkey and an olive on a stick. However, as luck would have it, they had another Space Invaders machine of slightly different design, this time with little orange lawnmowers wobbling in from outer space and very satisfactory sound effects when they blew up. The Major said he didn't want to play because it reminded him of the time he had to go into that clinic at Cheltenham with Delirium Tremens. Rain still bucketing down, Bagley getting legless on Southern Comfort, so we decided to drop in on Maurice Picarda's brother, who breeds Dobermanns outside Dorking. By this time Bagley had seized the wheel. As you know, Bill, map-reading has always been my forte, but the Major like a bloody fool insisted on holding the book upside down, swearing he knew the way, and ticking Bagley off about not overtaking. Old Bill fell in behind just as we were going past Guildford Cathedral and from then on it was like American television.

When they finally ran us off the road, Bagley made the serious error in my view of breathing in Mr Plod's face and asking him did he realise who he'd got in the front seat, and that we were already late for a vital rencontre with the Boss. Absolutely fatal, Bill. Much ironical banter from the Force, comrade Bagley frog-marched off to the Station to give a sample, the Major and myself bundled into the back seat of the Panda with no great civility. On arrival at the nick I was delighted to see that they had one of the Space Invader machines, which had apparently fallen off the back of a lorry, this time with submarines which blew up with a puff of green smoke. And so I passed the time quite agreeably while Bagley was roughed up in the cells in the usual manner. We finally got out with a severe caution at midnight — I think the Major had made some contribution to the Christmas Fund — and travelled back hard arse in a very slow train to Charing Cross.

Ah me, plans now afoot for the Wedding. I think I have a scheme for avoiding it altogether. Poor old barmy Fothergill is mad keen to go, and I thought given a pair of my specs and the Sherlock Holmes coat he might well pass undetected.

Yours till then,

DENIS

10 Downing Street
Whitehall

5 June 1981

Dear Bill,

I was very upset to hear about your failing to make your date at the RAC with Maurice last Tuesday due to the traffic jams. I don't know if you realised that the whole snarl-up was caused by the arrival of the Chief Wog and his retinue of wives, slaves, eunuchs etc. If you had, I imagine you would have been even more hopping mad than you were. Carrington, poor little sod, was in a state of blue funk as the C.W. has a way of taking umbrage at the drop of a hat, and as you may remember there was no end of a hooha a couple of years back when he took exception to something on Nationwide. Ever since then the FO have been pursuing what you and I would call a brown tongue policy vis a vis our friends in the black tents, crafty little buggers that they are.

I myself was on an eight-line whip from the Boss about not putting my foot in it, no reference to members being amputated for fornication, stay off booze etc. Hence my mild surprise, once the evil-smelling tide had surged in to Number Ten for the official pow-wow, robes billowing and dishcloths awry, to be taken on one side by one of their number, obviously some relative of Old Sheepseyes himself — a wizened little geezer with silver teeth who introduced himself as Prince Big Ben Arafat or something of that sort. (Just imagine, Bill, if the Duke of Edinburgh was allowed to have as many wives as he liked, wherever you went you'd be stumbling over Princelings on both sides of the bar in any village hostelry.) I couldn't make out what he was saying at first, and was about to summon the interpreter, when the word 'snifter' clearly emerged from the otherwise unintelligible harangue, closely followed by 'snort' and 'gorblimey'.

The Boss was deep in parleyvoo with His Eminence, but Boris, who has some experience of Russian involvement in the Middle East, quickly assessed the situation and beckoned us through to his little pantry where I was somewhat surprised to see several teapots already laid out. There was soon quite a party in progress, with the Sons of the Desert knocking back Boris's powerful snorterinos out of English bone china as to the manner born. Boris himself meanwhile emphasised on behalf of the Government Margaret's deep sense of shock and outrage at Mr Begin's latest brainstorm in Iraq. I couldn't quite make this out, because when M. and Carrington were chewing it over during breakfast they both agreed that it was high time someone gave the Iraqi a bloody nose, serve him damn well right. However I held my peace.

An expedition to the Playboy Club had just been proposed by one of the Sheiks, when the Boss clearly realised the Royal Entourage had thinned out a bit, and swept in like Matron at a midnight feast, clapping her hands and shooing them through into the Blue Conference Room for the usual nausea and exchange of official speeches. At dinner I myself was clamped between two very orthodox ones, who were sipping rancid goat's milk and clearing their throats a good deal. As you know Bill, if people neither drink nor play golf I always find the going rather hard, but if you remember Sidi Birani as I do, it is a bit humiliating to see the tables so entirely turned, British bankers cap in hand to Brother Wog for a few million for the price of a snort etc.

The weird thing about it, Bill, as I tried to explain to Carrington, is that this little local difficulty the Boss has got herself into over the Falling Pound etc. as far as I can see is all the fault of the Chief Wog doing what we asked him for a change. Keep down the price of oil, we cry, little fellow does so, whole economy topples. Economics has never been my strong suit, as you know, Bill, but Boris explained it to me as he was mopping up after the visit. If they keep down the price of oil, our trickle from the North Sea goes down too, whereupon all the sharks and money-lenders to whom we are in hock immediately close in, grab everything there is to be grabbed and bugger off to America, where Hopalong is making conditions particularly nice for them. Pound sinks, inflation up, Boss left chewing fingernails through the slow watches of the night.

Barmy Fothergill is chuffed to Naafibreaks about being sent along to the Wedding in my stead, so keep your fingers crossed for a night on the tiles.

DENIS

19 June 1981

Dear Bill,

I don't know if you've been watching the tennis. I find it all a bit depressing. You settle down with a snort in your hand on a sunny afternoon, expecting to hear nothing but the thwock of ball on gut, the occasional cry of the umpire and the rustle of applause as you drift away into a deep sleep, and all you get is one or other of these superbrats effing and blinding at the authorities like Question Time in the House of Commons. Admittedly all those linesmen are geriatrics. Squiffy's brother did it for years and years, died in harness, and was, I think, still upright in his little chair for several hours before they discovered he'd passed on. But none of that excuses intemperance from the young. Besides which it now emerges that most of the women are ferocious lezzies, and that no young girl is safe in the showers. All of which rather takes the gloss off the whole caboodle. Thank heavens the world of golf is not infested with perverts. (Though it has to be said that from time to time life down at Worplesdon gets pretty hairy when the ex-Battle of Britain ace Banger Perkins blows his top and starts thrashing the caddies with his niblick.)

Back at the Bunker, the casual observer might surmise that the old girl's hair would be falling out by now, fingernails gnawed to the knuckle, future viewed with despair. Not so. Constant pop of champagne corks, flushed faces and cackles of lunatic laughter. As you may have seen, she summoned all her Wets in for a dressing-down a week or so ago. I collared Carrington on the way out, beckoning him into the Snug with a bottle of Old Grand-dad, to which I happen to know he is not averse, and received a very amusing account of how things had fallen out.

To begin with, the Monk, who was looking pale, made a solemn announcement that he couldn't be at the next meeting because he had to go into 'hospital'. Needless to say, much sniggering up sleeves, assumed by all and sundry 'hospital' = funny farm, crunch come at last, etc. Sensing this, Sir Keith added a rider to the effect that he had in fact ruptured him-

self — no laughing matter I can tell you after my own experiment in waterskiing in 1954 — but there was a good deal of tittering, noseblowing, eyewiping, etc, before the Boss moved them on to Any Further Business. Once again the revolt of the Wets, which had been built up as another Battle of the Bulge, failed to materialise, Farmer Prior making a few half-hearted remarks about the need to help school-leavers, for which he was savaged by M. and told he hadn't got a monopoly on concern and compassion. Then they were all ordered to go away and think up some more cuts, at which there was a groan, scraping of chairs, and that was that . . .

Next thing was that M. had to go down to the Circus Maximus to do battle with old Worzelus Gummidgus, the white-locked champion of the Plebs who, armed with the new unemployment figures, clearly scented blood. According to Doris, who was in the Distinguished Strangers Gallery, Worzel did his usual knockabout turn, roars of ribaldry from the Smelly Socks Brigade, much coming and going from the bar, cries of Resign! etc, whereupon the Boss weighed in like Queen Boudicca of yore, scimitars flashing at the hubcaps, and cut them all to ribbons. Poor old Worzel was soundly reprimanded for making jokes about a tragedy over which she had no control, and the old boy staggered off into the night muttering under his breath.

I caught sight of him the other day, at a reception given for Mr Yamaha, Leader of the Nips, and he looked to me very much below par. I think they all hoped that once Benn had been carried off to the Intensive Care Unit with straws in his hair he would be out of action for the duration. Now he's bouncing back with eyes rotating even faster than before and giving them all pause for thought. Incidentally, according to Dr O'Moynihan, pains in the legs are the result of drinking too much tea. Which only goes to show, Bill, that all Eric my bodyguard says about how snorts burn out the brain cells is all absolute cock, and you're far worse off knocking back the Typhoo with the Yobs like poor old Wedgie B. Needless to say, a lot of the Trots are now firmly convinced that the CIA shot a poisoned dart into his bum through a furled umbrella as he was coming out of the Public Library, but if they did, more power to their elbow and one can only pray that they will persevere in their efforts.

Meanwhile in Warrington, old Fatcat Jenkins is fighting a lone battle for the SDP. The *Telegraph* seems to have taken quite a shine to him, and, hoping to pour oil on the troublous tide, I took the liberty of opining at breakfast that he might well do us a bit of good up in the Northern Darkness by buggering up the Reds. To my surprise, I got my head bitten off in no uncertain manner. We live, I was told, in a two-party state, Worzel not such a bad chap, no need for opportunists to come into Croydon North-West and overturn the applecart.

Au reservoir,

    Yrs,

DENIS

10 Downing Street
Whitehall

3 July 1981

Dear Bill,

Is that little bungalow at Bells Yew Green still on the market? With things as they are, I have been thinking more and more of going to ground, at least until the present riot season blows itself out. I don't know how things have been down in your neck of the woods, but up here every yob and skinhead who can find his way out of his own front door unassisted has been roaming the streets lobbing bricks at the Constabulary and setting fire to the supermarkets. We're all being told to say that there's nothing racial about it, but you can't help noticing the odd coon in amongst them. Needless to say, the I Told You So Brigade has not been slow off the mark. Enoch, for whom I had a certain amount of time at one point, has been going round muttering about the Coming Apocalypse. What everyone conveniently forgets about Old Catseyes, or so Fatty Soames tells me, is that he was responsible for admitting the Minstrels in such numbers in the first place when he was Minister of Health and short of bods to swab down the Out-patients and keep the Tubes running on time. And, quite honestly, Bill, a very good job they do. I remember when poor old Maurice cracked his head open playing Torpedoes with the Battle of Britain contingent — his life was saved by a buxom Barbadian nurse called Winifred, with whom he ended up the staunchest of chums.

Meanwhile our Sailorboy Friend with the blue rinse has clearly sensed that the time has come for a coup. He was off sick for a long time, I don't know if you saw, something to do with his glands, medico apparently told him if he didn't stop signing books he was a goner. He has now come bouncing back, looking bronzed and fit, raring for a final shoot-out with M. First whiff of a Molotov Cocktail and out he pounces on the Jimmy Young Show, blaming the troubles in Toxteth, Moss Side and any other Side you care to mention on the Boss. If it wasn't for her, says our leathery-faced organist, there would be no unemployment, inflation would be down to zero, land flowing with milk and honey. All of which may be true, Bill, but it's a bit strong coming from an old stumblebum like Heath who brought the whole damn country grinding to a

halt. You may remember that afternoon when all the lights went out in the Flamingo Club. But enough said.

Whitelaw to my mind is completely out of his depth. Place going up in flames all about him, and all he can suggest is that parents should be held responsible for the fifty p into the swear box the beaks are doling out by way of fines. A fat lot of good that will do. If you remember, Bill, in the old days, when the mob went on the rampage in our Protectorates, the routine was all laid down in black and white in Company Orders under Duties in Aid of the Civil Power. Select ringleader, one warning through the megaphone, and, if that failed, let fly at said ringleader with every weapon in the armory. Instead of which poor old Willie can only burble on about reinforcing their truncheons and putting blotting paper inside their helmets. I must say, Bill, if you or I was a copper lying in hospital with a fractured skull the sight of Old Oystereyes looming up at the end of the bed bringing words of comfort and joy from the Boss would not necessarily do all that much for one's morale.

Oh, I almost forgot. That frightful ass Lord Margolis or whatever he's called has ensnared the Boss for another summer jaunt to mow down the grouse on the Isle of Muck. Do you think that crooked osteopath of Sticky's in St John's Wood could furnish me with some kind of chitty diagnosing terminal Hammer Toes or something of that nature? The Boss probably won't swallow it, but these are desperate days and it might be worth a try.

Yours under the weather,

DENIS

10 Downing Street
Whitehall

17 July 1981

Dear Bill,

Ah me. The best laid plans of mice and men, as the Major's mother used to say, always get ballsed up in the end. You remember my little wheeze to shunt poor old Barmy Fothergill into my slot at the Royal Wedding? Blow me if the rotten sod doesn't disappear into the Intensive Care with yet another liver attack two days before the shindig, God rot his socks, leaving yours truly with no alternative but to go down to Moss Bros and get fitted out with the grey topper and spats. As usual it proved impossible to find a native to run a tape measure over one. As you know, I have a profound aversion to any darkie or Iranian student fumbling up and down one's trouser leg. Anyway, after two hours waiting with a crowd of sambos, chinks and every other of the 57 varieties hiring medals by the barrowload for the great day, I finally got palmed off with a suit four sizes too small and a hat that slipped down over the ears every time I cleared my throat.

Got back to the Talking Shop to find all hell had been let loose on account of the King of Spain chucking at the last minute. All because the Happy Couple, it transpires, had been routed through Gib by the FO as part of their Mediterranean Cruise. Always a pleasure to see Carrington caught with his trousers down. Obviously none of his merry band of Pinkos and Bertie Wooftahs had thought twice about it and he's now being pissed on from a great height by HRH, not to mention the reptilian chorus from the Gutter Press. As I told Carrington, who was in the process of being carpeted by the Boss, what on earth did it matter if there was one King the less in the front pew, and anyway why should C and D have all their plans changed by some little waiter figure on the Costa Brava when the apes had been on the Rock for thousands of years and are determined to remain British come what may?

After this, old cemetery-face Gilmour was wheeled on in the House to repeat my sentiments. You could tell his heart wasn't in it, Bill. He is, as you know, dripping Wet, and no doubt wants to give away every scrap of Empire the remains to any tinpot potentate that asks for it.

The Boss has come back full of beans from her little summit jaunt to Ottawa. Did you see them on the TV, Bill? Driving round in golf carts. I thought it looked bloody silly. Probably something Saatchis had thought up. The whole scenario outlined to Margaret before take-off was that the Euros should form a solid phalanx and tell Hopalong in no uncertain manner where he got off as far as Interest Rates were concerned. However, according to Boris, who went along, M. broke ranks and went completely overboard for the old screen idol, dewy-eyed assurances, sun shone out of his arse, best thing since sliced bread, etc, exact re-run of our last disastrous visit to Washington when we had to drink all those awful Bullfrogs and Rimshots or whatever they call their fancy snorts.

They're still a bit windy, by the way, about the Fat Cat Jenkins nearly pulling it off up at Warrington. I had to sit up with the Boss to see the results on the telly and that funny little Canadian cove who's always brought on with his pendulum got quite carried away, predicting that if this sort of thing went on at the next election M's lot would be reduced to a party of one. (He didn't say who, but my guess would be Enoch.) Boss went pretty white at that, and I had to toddle off to the sherbet cupboard and administer a stiff brownie and water before the old light returned to her eyes. Since then, the Wets have been setting up even more of a caterwauling than usual, calling for U-Turns on every front if all is not to be lost, and the Proprietor had to go down and read the

Riot Act to the 1922 Committee, telling them that if they'd followed her this far up shit creek it's a long way to walk back and trying to cheer them up with the news that Benn was back from hospital and once again kicking the stuffing out of old Worzel.

My account of the nuptials must wait for my next screed, Boris having just opened what looks like a very acceptable consignment of Damson Vodka from the Kremlin.

Chin chin, old fruit, and Dosvidanye.

Whoops,

DENIS

10 Downing Street
Whitehall

31 July 1981

Dear Bill,

I'm sorry I missed you in all the confusion after the Nuptials. I had assumed that once we got out of St Paul's I'd be free to join you for a few celebratory tinctures in the Cat & Hamster, but not a bit of it. I was immediately shanghaied back to the Talking Shop to pass around the peanuts for every conceivable coon and dervish in creation, not to mention Mrs Hopalong, who was obviously pretty miffed at being put in Row H, while that other film star woman Grace Kelly who married the Casino fellow was right up at the front.

I don't know if you saw the ceremony on the box, Bill? All very well, no doubt, slumped at home, snort in hand, but from where I was sitting it was like being inside one of the Major's Japanese greenhouses. Frightful stench of scent, cameras poking out of every bunch of flowers, that prize ass Runcie mincing about in a silver reachmedown like something out of Dr Who, and then, to cap it all, up gets this dusky songstress from Down Under in a multicoloured tablecloth and air hostess's hat, and warbles on for bloody hours. Poor old Spencer looked a bit groggy. It was obviously touch and go whether he'd keel over bang in the middle of it like that very fat waiter did when the Major's mother was giving her song recital in Aid of the Pit Ponies.

Anyway, the Captains and the Kings have now departed, thank God, except for one poor coon who had his whole bloody country pulled from under him during the celebrations. Margaret very decently offered the SAS, in the form of two balaclava bruisers from the Prince's Gate show, to pop over there on a scheduled flight and release one of his wives who had been kidnapped. I detected a rather wistful look on the little fellow's face when he was given the glad tidings that all was well again.

Back at home a bit of excitement has blown up over the question of reshuffling Humpty Dumpty. M. had just put a cloth over the parrots' cage and was hoping to slip away for a few days of P and Q in the West Country when old Thorneycroft, God rot his socks, pops up again and starts sounding off about poor little Howe, cheered on by Brother Pym.

It all began when Howe, hoping to rally the rabble, announced yet again that the worst was over, light at the end of the tunnel, everything bottoming out all over the place etc. Old Humpty, as you may know, has a finger in various pies, including Sir Charles Whatsisname, the little wop with the moustache who runs the hotel chain, and they're all very worried about what the slump is doing to their profits. Humpty's tail fairly vigorously twisted in boardroom, sets up inevitable caterwauling, seeing his pension schemes jeopardised by the Boss's madcap capers.

Anyway, it didn't go down at all well with M. This isn't the first time Old Humpty's stepped out of line. Howe's talkative wife on the blower morning noon and night saying Geoffrey's been made to look a BF etc, and the word now is that Humpty is up for the one-way ticket to Siberia, possibly accompanied by Brother Pym, explanation to the faithful to suggest senility, insanity, etc. After all, he is 72, and has never struck me as being all there at the best of times. There's always a chap like that in every boardroom, burbling away into the blotting paper with no one taking a blind bit of notice.

That slimy little creep Heseltine seems to be riding high up in Liverpool. Picarda got very excited when he saw him chauffeuring a lot of fat cats round the black spots, offering them cheap sites and generous incentives. Could I put in a word for Picwarmth? He could guarantee jobs for at least half a dozen young darkies in unpaid apprentice situations making double glazing units, given suitable subsidies from HMG. I went so far as to ring up the oily little blighter on behalf of our mutual friend, only to be told that the PR exercise had finished at midnight the night before, and that anyway the Big City mob had got it all sewn up, and that this was no place for cowboys and spivs, clearly a reference to our friend. I don't mind telling you I returned the compliment on Maurice's behalf with knobs on. Give me Humpty Dumpty any day if the alternative is young Gingernuts.

Yours till the sun shines,

DENIS

14 August 1981

Dear Bill,

I hope you got my p.c. from Bude. Rather an old joke, but I liked the surgeon's face. A look of old Groggy Rossiter about him, I thought. The weather was pretty decent on the whole, but I must say I never thought I'd heave a sigh of relief to be back at the Talking Shop.

The real nigger in the woodpile was little Peter Carrington, who managed somehow to impress tactfully on the Boss that if she didn't put her feet up and have a 'real rest' she'd be following the Monk into the Bin. Hence the quiet Cornish venue, out-of-the-way bungalow, billed as being within minutes of the beach. (True, were one at the controls of Concorde.)

Boss had also decided, on the advice of the Saatchi Bros, to immerse herself in culture. You can imagine how my heart leapt to see that she had packed a fat book, called The Brothers Kamarazov, by one of those foreign birds. A good solid two thousand pages, I estimated, should allow yours truly a few days out on the links plus the odd evening off sampling the local scrumpy. All boded well on Day One. 8am, reptiles admitted for photo call, M. and I driven down to beach for surprise encounter with some old bag from Margaret's past. I refused to roll my trousers up or put a handkerchief on my head as requested by one of the guttersnipes. After that they buggered off and we were dropped back at the Bothy and left to our own devices.

Set up the deckchair for M. on the lawn, canvas stool to accommodate Prime Ministerial legs, rug in case of clouding over later in the day, Brothers Whatdyoumacallit open at page 1, step into golfing pumps and hightail it up the tracks to adjacent Clubhouse, where who should I find ensconced behind the *D. Tel.* but Harry Collis-  Browne, the Major's friend from Folkestone, who made a mint out of rubber inflatables and then retired with his secretary to Godalming. Not a bad hat, by any means, and a fund of anecdote and reminiscence. All the drinks on him, not allowed to put my hand in my pocket, keen fan of the Boss, she should have Humpty Dumpty strung up by his thumbs, couldn't understand why the police weren't issued with sten guns, i.e. absolutely one of us.

Following our liquid lunch, he agreed to totter round the greens with me, and after a somewhat erratic start we produced some very remarkable golf. Somewhere about the fifteenth, Collis-Browne was just rooting about in a thicket for some temporarily lost balls when a merry 'Coo-ee' brought us to our senses in no uncertain manner. I looked up, and there was the Boss, sensible shoes and hair tossed in the wind, striding across the sward knocking the tops off the dandelions with a knobbly walking stick. Hauled C-B out of the gorse bush by his braces and effected an introduction, but the old boy was a bit tongue-tied. M. said to carry on, she didn't want to spoil our fun, etc, but C-B now very much off his stroke and broke three clubs before we decided to call it a day.

Boss undeterred. Suggests a pot of tea for three at Clubhouse. C-B's face falls several hundred feet, assuming a somewhat Gilmour-like mien, cove behind the bar taps side of his nose, whole scene a bit like one of those drawings they used to have before the war in *Punch* where the chap lights his cigar before the Archbishop of Canterbury. Frightfully good. Didn't Sticky W. used to have a coloured print of it in the bog? Be that as it may, we were soon grouped round a pot of well-stewed Tetley Teabags and some rather soggy toast, listening to M's resumé of the Brothers K. It turned out she had devoured it at a gulp and was now redecorating the bungalow. Brothers K. apparently a let-down, not a patch on Murder Up The Nile.

Rather disastrously, old Collis-B. began to nod off during M's opening salvoes, but I explained that he'd been badly shot up at Dunkirk and was subject to fits. M. swallowed this one. Why didn't we walk into Polperro along the cliffs? With more geographical knowledge at my disposal I might have told her, but off we set. Boss leading the way, scrawny gorse underfoot, no discernible path, wind up to gale force, sky purples over, Boss bright of eye as ever, wasn't it bracing? Three and a half hours later we encounter bewildered rustic. Turns out we are heading in wrong direction. Recover breath sufficiently to enquire whether any hostelry within reach. No, says B.R. but Golf Club over brow of hill. Discover old C-B just coming to, and ready for the first snort of the evening, clearly convinced that the Boss is some kind of spectre. Return to bungalow and spend remainder of weekend re-roofing shed, digging garden, moving rockery and installing D-I-Y double glazing which arrived unexpectedly courtesy of Picwarmth. All the bits turned out to be the wrong size, and we learnt today that owners of bungalow have placed matter in hands of their solicitor.

M. is now warming up for reshuffle, one scheme under consideration being to send Prior over to Northern Ireland, on the principle that if he can't stand up to the Reds let him have a crack at standing up to the IRA. Just the sort of idea you'd expect from Saatchi and Saatchi. Humpty Dumpty is definitely for the chop, having well and truly cooked his goose, and rumours are rife that some unpleasantness is in store for Fatty S. of Rhodesia fame, though what he may have done to blot his copy-book I cannot for the life of me imagine. Burning the candle at both ends again I can only assume. They're obviously going to have to find someone to sit in the Chairman's seat. I suppose you wouldn't be interested? Not over-taxing and some perks. Or perhaps that stockbroker fellow from Ferring who always pops up on the board of Maurice's companies. Lord or Bart or something. Looks good on the writing paper, inspires confidence etc. And by God, could we do with it.

Yours till Hell freezes over, i.e. any minute,

DENIS

10 Downing Street
Whitehall

11 September 1981

Dear Bill,

As you will have seen from the Press, I made quite a little killing at the betting shop on the Massacre of the Wets. Old Cemetery Face Gilmour was given short shrift, likewise Fatty S. and poor old Carlisle, who between you and me had been hitting it a bit of late — and who can blame him?

The Boss is cock-a-hoop about her points victory over Old Farmer Prior. I thought he was pushing his luck a bit, blabbing to the reptiles about what he would or would not do in the line of duty. On no account was he going to be driven into exile on the Bogside, rather resign and go back to growing mangel worzels. Sure enough there was one hell of a scrap at breakfast, and I saw Prior coming out red in the face and puffing, saying he'd never been so insulted in all his life, how had I managed it all these years, I must be a wreck, etc. He then asked if he could use the phone in Boris's office, and B. very kindly played it through to me on the tape afterwards. The party at the other end, as I soon realised, was our seafaring friend E. Heath, speaking from a Gym & Health Sauna somewhere in Marylebone. The Farmer started off in a mood of high dudgeon, and lost no time in reviling the Boss. This obviously music to E. Heath's ears, 'splendid, splendid', Pinko P. could sit next to him on the back benches, they could have regular health food lunches to coordinate their plans, orchestrate opposition etc. At this I detected a slight cooling in Prior's rebellious tone. Heath presses on: Prior must realise of course that as the Senior Dissident, he Heath will of course take the chair at any discussions, but Prior could obviously come in under Stevarse, what fun, Norman so amusing, etc. What about dinner tonight, the three of them, to celebrate? The sound of backtracking now became deafening, Farmer P. began to mutter about no definite conclusion, offer of Northern Ireland job real challenge to patriotic duty, difficult task, Willie Whitelaw playing up historical perspective, and sure enough, later that day the Boss came in with a mad gleam in her eye to announce that Jim had seen the light and was even now buckling on his bullet-proof underwear en route for Belfast. But, as I may have said before, if a man can't stand up to Len Murray, what hope in hell has he when confronted with that mad bugger Paisley?

A propos the Workers by Hand and Brain, M. has now wheeled out some snotty little ex-airline pilot called Tebbit to wield the big stick. He started off well enough, telling all and sundry to bloody well pull their socks up and work harder. Needless to say, some wag pointed out that if they hadn't got any work in the first place how the hell could they do it any harder? Personally I thought that was a bit cheap, and anyway, when a new chap comes in, albeit up through the ranks, you should give him a moment or two to collect himself before pulling his trousers down.

My main concern at present, as you may have gathered from the media, is extricating myself from a very tricky situation with the Boss. Do you remember that friend of Maurice's who had a scheme to build pre-fab housing estates in the Lake District? Monty Greenstone, I think his name was, rather a shifty little cove with vicuna coat and sideburns. A few months back now, he and Maurice took me out to lunch at the RAC. Would I be consultant in exchange for a generous consignment of firewater — nothing through the books, obviously — to a little construction firm they were starting up to develop the National Parks? Here was all this land, going to rack and ruin, nothing but a handful of sheep, what better than a few motels, fast food shops, chalet-style executive second homes to liven things up a bit?

After a goodly number of scoops and stickies, the prospect began to look very rosy, whereupon the Greenstone bird stroked his moustache a bit, and said there was a minor snag. Planning wallahs dragging their heels over the Snowdonia Leisure Complex, Welsh Nat yobbos playing silly buggers, while share-holders' capital unfruitfully tied up. Next thing I knew G and P were back at No 10, making inroads into Boris's secret cache of pre-Revolutionary Vodka, and hammering something out on the Olivetti to which Yours Truly was duly required to append his monicker. I have no clear recollection of what it was, but something or other to the Minister responsible telling him to give the Planning Mob a boot up the arse, pull their fingers out and get weaving.

Naturally I thought no more about it at the time: Greenstone bloke stuffed it away in his crocodile combination-lock briefcase, more camaraderie and embracing and the two of them drove off in their Porsche, watched with a knowing eye by the Constable on duty.

Now some mischief-maker has burgled the file, fed the letter to the reptiles, and I am once again well and truly in the doghouse. Declaration of all my business interests to be handed in to Boss's study by 8am, plus a signed assurance that in future official stationery will not be used by my friends or acquaintances to promote their dubious enterprises: this all accompanied by invidious comparisons to Wilson's secretary woman and her slagheaps. So I advise you, for a start, when you've finished reading this to put it to the usual use.

Yours up to here,

DENIS

The Don Bradman
International Hotel
Adelaide Road
Melbourne

9 October 1981

Dear Bill,

I don't know if you've ever been Down Under, but it's a bit like Esher used to be before the war. Nothing much happens, but a goodly number of snorts disappear down the hatch every night and the bar stays open till breakfast time. Of course, being the other side of the world geographically everything's the wrong way round, so that we're awake when you're asleep, and I think it's spring here, rather than whatever's going on up your end. A cove I met in the little bar last night even told me that the bath-water goes out back to front and we both went up to M's bathroom to experiment. Unfortunately, when we got there, neither of us could remember which way it went out in England. M. came in in her curlers and that put a stop to our researches pretty pronto.

As you've probably read in the *Telegraph*, we're all fore-gathered for the Commonweath Conference. Personally I thought the whole business had been wound up years ago, but not a bit of it. All the Coons, the Gandhi woman, little fellows who've obviously never had a suit on in their lives from places you only hear about if you collect stamps: there's nothing they like more, it seems, than having a week-long get-together to talk about the old days, just like the Major with his Service Corps chums booking that hotel every year in Taunton and getting blotto for days on end.

I was on parade at the opening shindig when they all sat down

116

in a semi-circle with their flags for the Group Photo, one of those camera contraptions that goes round in a circle worked by clockwork, and the chairman, an Indian johnny, had hardly burbled his way through his speech of welcome when, blow me, up pops one of the Coons and begins berating little Muldoon from New Zealand for letting the Springboks do their Tour. Coons all Hear-Hearing away like a pack of monkeys, which really got my goat, Bill, I don't mind telling you. It was on the tip of my tongue to just ask them straight out what right they had to pick on a few inoffensive Kiwis punting the oval ball about with Friend Boer when there were literally millions upon millions of innocent people working in the salt mines of Siberia for cocking a snook at old Brezhnev. However, I caught the glint in M's eye and held my peace.

After that we were all invited aboard HM's floating gin palace, which she very sensibly had taken the precaution of mooring just off the point, well supplied with all fifty-seven varieties of plonk. At this, things did loosen up for a bit, and the Duke and I managed to lug Muldoon out of it for a while for iced tinctures in the B-Deck Saloon. It turned out we had a mutual friend in Arblaster, who used to ref for a while in the West Country, and apparently has now gone very badly to seed in Singapore.

Like me, Muldoon couldn't quite make out what the whole caper was in aid of, but the Duke explained that it went back to Queen Victoria. He himself had suggested over and over again that they should wind the whole thing up, particularly after we'd joined the Euro Business and weren't buying any more New Zealand Mutton Chops. But the Coons wouldn't hear of it, and nor would his Missus. The talk was obviously all piss and wind, but HM got a real kick out of sitting on the throne while the Paramount Chiefs kissed her feet and gave her monkeyskin handbags and ivory toothpicks, particularly that little Nyerere. These feelings were entirely reciprocated by the Fuzzy-wuzzies, even those who are hand in glove with Moscow and Peking. The Duke's a very wise old bean, and his theory is that his better half is regarded as some kind of Ju Ju object. You've got to remember, he says, that most of these chaps are tribal chiefs at heart, even though they wear shiny shoes and read books by Lenin.

I learnt from my airmail copy of the *Telegraph* that you are all getting steamed up again about Interest Rates, Howe taking a lot of stick on the mortgage front, CBI wallahs foaming at the mouth, M. bankrupting the country etc. All I can say is that from down here, by the pool, where I have spent the remainder of this balls-aching cavalcade, it all seems a very very long way away. However, I did notice in the small print that the NatWest deposit rate has shot up again very satisfactorily, which, even taking the taxman into account, must be good news for all of us. As I told the Boss at a beach barbecue we had to attend with the tall cove who at present lords it over the convict hordes, it's only the ne'erdowells like Maurice P. who run up debts at the bank who have anything to complain about. The Wise Virgins, like you and me and the Major, with our little nest-eggs, are very much in the old girl's debt and must support her policies up to the hilt. And what ever old Worzel may have said in Brighton, little Benn seems to be doing a splendid job.

Talking of Maurice, I did my best to help during our mercifully brief stopover at Bahrain Airport. I was meant to pass on a parcel of lagging material with a view to shifting some of his surplus from the warehouse at Deal onto the unsuspecting Sons of the Desert. Alas, my contact had been arrested only moments before, and I was just in time to see him being bundled unceremoniously into a waiting paddywagon.

Any chance of your joining me to spread the load of misery at Blackpool?

Yours in hope,

DENIS

10 Downing Street
Whitehall

23 October 1981

Dear Bill,

I don't know whether you've ever been to Blackpool — I have a dim inkling we discussed this before — but it really is the most ghastly dump. I can't understand why they choose it. It takes absolutely hours to get to from anywhere, then when you finally make it there's nothing but mile upon mile of Bingo Saloons, Space Invaders, sticky rock shops and Chinese Takeaways, and the plebs from Manchester and the Potteries gawping about on the Prom, all too ready to poke fun at their betters.

This year, Saatchis had booked us into the Barcelona Country Club, right out in the sticks, formerly the seat of some local mill-owner, and now run by a Mr and Mrs Len Wallop with a taste for piped music, plastic flowers, tropical fish let into the wall, and a few back numbers of *Lancashire Country Life* scattered about like they are at the dentist's. The snag, as I discovered on footing it downstairs for a recce on arrival, was the Health Juice Bar. Mr Len, it transpired, after hitting it fairly heavily out East, had come within a whisker of extinction in 1953 and signed the Pledge. Mrs Len verified this story with copious anecdotes of how much better he felt, and would you think he was only 76?

As good fortune would have it, I collided in an upper corridor with our Home Secretary, looking very down in the mouth about this state of affairs, and ere long a Special Branch van had backed up to his window, and helmeted officers were ferrying in assorted crates for discreet storage behind the sofa in Whitelaw's sitting room. Thus we were both able to fortify ourselves after breakfast each morning for the long ordeal beneath the burning lights.

All eyes, needless to say, were on old Sailorboy Ted when he bustled up to hold forth on the second day. The Press reptiles, as you may have seen, had worked up a phoney crisis with a lot of excitable talk about Teddy Benn and the Big Split, Boss at any moment about to be toppled, backbench rumblings and all the usual palaver. Fortunately you've only got to take one look at Heath to realise he couldn't topple a blancmange off a plate. He always reminds me of that old bachelor party who used to run the Company Flat for Burmah in Ennismore Gardens. You remember we all used to speculate about what he got up to in his spare time with no definite proof of his proclivities being furnished, even by Harris the company driver. You used to sneer at me for saying this, but it was always my opinion that he was one of life's non-combatants, who are, if truth be told, thicker on the ground than a perusal of Page Three of the *Daily Telegraph* would lead you to believe. The same, I suspect, is true of our Lost Leader.

As soon as he stepped up on the podium and little Parkinson banged down the egg-timer, I could see from my vantage point that the troops were preparing themselves for twenty minutes under the parapet. A few brave souls weathered the flood of boredom to shout this and that, but even they were ground down by the Yachtsman's remorseless recitative. Three people, presumably former cabin crew aboard the Morning Cloud, rose to their feet at the conclusion to try and prise the assembled burghers off their arses, but if ever there was a lost cause, Bill, that was it. I was put painfully in mind of the time the Major got the bird, essaying his George Formby impersonation at the Rotary Outing to Wendover.

Not a difficult act to follow, you might think, Bill, and you would be right. Little Howe, glasses gleaming and fresh from the hairdressers, got a few good laughs from reading out some gems of early Heath, excavated from the archives by one of his eager beavers at the Treasury – 'No Going Back', 'Inflation Top Priority', 'Must Pay Our Way', i.e. all the same old balls the Boss has been trotting out ever since she emerged at the top of the heap. In brief, E. Heath hoist with his own whatever it is you get hoisted with.

After that, lesser fry like Cemetery Face and Stevarse were mere cats' meat. However I did tell the Boss to keep a wary eye on Tarzan. Ever since he went off on his famous slum-crawl in Liverpool, pressing the flesh with all those discontented coons and street corner skinheads who've never done a day's work in their lives and wouldn't recognise a job if they saw one, I have had the clear impression that our Ginger has been looking for an opening to come in on the inside and pip M. to the post in the final furlong, hence his extensive bet-hedging and bleating on about One Nation, which is pretty ripe coming from him.

You've probably seen that the work-shy yobbos at BL are once again up to their seasonal pranks. I told the Boss that now surely we can come out of the closet and close the whole thing down once and for all. Here we are, allegedly in power and pledged to strangle every lame duck in sight, and we are pumping a million pounds a minute into the Longbridge Christmas piss-up fund, all to no avail. For good measure I passed on to M. the sad story of Maurice Picarda's Metro. According to his lady-friend it ground to a halt in the fast lane of the M1 just North of the Watford Gap, and when he finally got a breakdown truck out from Hemel Hempstead, all four wheels fell off, the gear lever came away in his hand, and when he got out to show it to the mechanic the whole thing blew up and caught fire. Typically of Maurice, he had failed to take out any insurance but I didn't tell the Boss that bit.

Any chance of a day trip down to Huntercombe before the clocks go back? I bought some new togs in Australia and I am quite keen to try them out in the bar.

Yours in perpetuity,

DENIS

10 Downing Street
Whitehall

6 November 1981

Dear Bill,

Thank you for your condolences on my being dropped from the squad for the Autumn Summit Break to Mexico but, quite honestly, after being left standing about all over Australia I was very glad to have a few days on my ownsome. I'd been meaning to have a blitz on the Den for months. Boris has been helping me to clear out the empties that have been gathering dust under the bed and behind the Wisdens, and I made a parcel of old clothes and broken golf clubs for Mrs Prosser's Jumble down in Kent in aid of her brain-damaged jockeys, in which I included various bribes and mementoes that Maurice had sent me from time to time, like that ghastly platinum desk lamp made in the shape of three ladies eating a lollipop, for which Mrs P. seemed duly grateful.

I understand the Mexican jaunt was the usual hell on wheels, though the Boss obviously enjoyed herself no end. Plenty of hot air both inside and outside the chamber, old Hopalong flying in to deliver his thoughts on helping the Third World, or the South as it is now called – the kind of thing Heath's always banging away about. M. and Carrington made a bravish stab at telling the assembled Coons and Commies to pull their socks up, but from what I gathered the message was considerably watered down from my original draft. As you know, I was out East only this year, being wined and dined by the Gandhi woman, and you don't need to look much beyond the airport perimeter to realise that the natives in those parts have no desire whatsoever to get off their arses and go to the office – let alone the lavatory, from the state of the streets. A lot of them are so bone idle they prefer to lie down and die on the pavement rather than make the effort of clocking in at the Labour Exchange. So what on earth – and this was my spiel to little Carrington before he left – is the point of people like Maurice going out there and trying to get them interested in making double-glazing units? As to the Africans, you remember Wilkinson's experience trying to build that flyover in Khartoum. And how can we be expected to shell out millions of pounds to the sun-tanned ragamuffins when we're rapidly disappearing down the drain ourselves passes my imagination. But it's no good expecting sense from politicos like Carrington. They like going off on these freebies and confabs in sunny climes just to get away from it all.

You have to hand it to the Boss, she flew back cool as a cucumber, despite earthquakes and the foreign food, eager to climb into the ring for a vicious ten rounds with poor old Worzel, who once again got whirled about, lost his specs, had his head thumped on the floor and a couple of fingers up his nostrils from Brer Enoch for good measure. Even Margaret's Wets raised a feeble cheer as the Old Philosopher's dentures hit the light, but despite the general glee they're all, if you ask me, pretty windy about the Alliance people, who put up some hopeless little runt with a beard in Croydon North West and swept the board. Now the woman with the untidy hair who gets Margaret's goat is off giant-killing in Manchester, planning to demolish a 19,000 Tory majority before breakfast, and the thought of any female competition in the Talking Shop is obviously fraying the proprietorial nerves more than somewhat, though my view, which I have often expressed to the Boss, is that until she can come to grips with her hair she can't be treated as a serious political threat.

Yours in the rough,

DENIS

10 Downing Street
Whitehall

20 November 1981

Dear Bill,
I sometimes think Margaret leads a charmed life. Did you see old Worzel on the Church Parade at the Cenotaph? I was stationed in

a rear rank with some minor royalty, coons' wives, British Legion Cadet Corps etc and a few miscellaneous body-guards, but I still got a pretty good view of events up front. I'm not usually one to shed a manly tear at these capers, but having fortified myself against the cold with a stiff sharpener or twain before setting out, I found the effect of the brass band and the long greatcoats very moving, and  couldn't help thinking of old chums like Tuppy Hornblower who bought it during the last lot. (I know he had a stroke playing silly buggers in the Mess at a Guest Night with the RASC but in my book that counts as Active Service if anything does.)

Picture the scene, Bill. Sun streaming down Whitehall, a few last brown leaves scratching along the pavement, assembled Royalty, M., little Steel etc all standing rigidly to attention, the note of the bugle dies away, the great bell tolls and a solemn silence falls over the Heart of the Empire. At moments like this you feel that everything is not in vain. Then, blow me – Worzel, who has already attracted a good many black looks from the Royal Box by turning up in a silly tie and some kind of German donkey jacket out of a Millet's sale, begins to fidget, pick his nose and scratch his arse as if waiting for the Number 11 bus. When it comes to the wreath-laying he shambles up in his brothel creepers and plonks it down like a poor old codger putting the empties out and totters back to resume his monkeyhouse act at the Proprietor's shoulder. As if this wasn't enough, he then keeps his mouth firmly shut during 'Oh God Our Help In Ages Past' on the grounds that he's a paid-up non-believer and professional God-botherer and doesn't believe a word of it. Not that that stops him singing the Red Flag in Blackpool. I could see the D of E going purple in the face, and all the Top Brass looked to be building up for a visit to the cardiac unit.

I expected Margaret, when we got indoors, would be fit to be tied, but not a bit of it. Old girl cock-a-hoop, large stickies all round. Peter Carrington being stuffy about it – Worzel had failed his medical for the '39 show, frightful little pen-pusher etc – but Boss cuts him short, pointing out the whole thing has been on the telly, Worzel must have been losing votes like air out of a burst tyre. I couldn't help feeling a bit sorry for poor old Foot all the same. I was reminded of the time that fellow Ginger Withers turned up at the Burmah Christmas Lunch wearing a dinner jacket when it said Informal on the card and we all threw bread rolls at him just to drive the point home. Personally I blame the wife in Worzel's case. She put him up for the job in the first place, and she should see to it that he is properly accoutred for all occasions and knows where he's meant to be going, like the Boss does with yours truly.

How long he can stand it in the hot seat I really can't imagine. They were all hoping that after the Blackpool showdown the Mad Tea-Drinker Benn, he of the permanently revolving eyes, would now come to heel. Not a bit of it. Last week apparently there was some debate down at the Talking Shop about North Sea Gas, the official Labour Rep spools out the Party Line, up pops Benn like a Jack-in-the-Box, quivering with excitement, foam flecking his lips, and announces that when he comes to power the whole of the North Sea will be sequestered, not a penny compensation paid to the shareholders, and all foreign oil men publicly strung up by the thumbs in Parliament Square. Worzel blows fuse and is assisted from Chamber.

So long as this goes on, Saatchi's view is that M. is as safe as houses, though there is the snag of the SDP. You know my views about the Woman with the Hair, but I do rather take my hat off to the Owen cove. Did you see him trying to strangle that Student yobbo at Sussex University? Some awful little Trot slinging rotten vegetables at him and clearly something snapped. Not that I have any sympathy with Owen personally, who is clearly some kind of smarmy, jumped-up Houseman, but it was high time someone struck a blow at all those workshy monkeys sponging off their Student Grants and smoking dope all day at our expense when they could be working on the roads. A propos, you see that little wooftah Livingstone has had his balls given a pretty good tweak in the High Court by old Gaffer Denning. That'll teach him to try and bring down the Tube Fares. So all in all things are going our way, I'd say.

Do you fancy the enclosed freebie weekend in Bloemfontein? Booze all the way, some kind of casino being opened by the Major's Battle of Britain chum who got nicked for the VAT fiddle, and I'm told a very good little course.

Yours in hope,

DENIS

10 Downing Street
Whitehall

4 December 1981

Dear Bill,

I don't know whether it's percolated to your neck of the woods, but the Boss's lot took a terrible hammering up on Merseyside. The tousle-haired temptress swept in like a white tornado, the only comfort being that Worzel's man lost his deposit. I can't understand what they see in the Williams woman, not to mention that smarmy little GP or the fat cat from Brussels with the speech impediment. If ever there was a set of hopeless hand-job merchants those are they.

And yet perfectly sane human beings appear to have fallen under their spell. Harken to what follows. On the Night of the Crosby Long Knives, scenting the wrath to come – the Boss sitting up late in front of three television sets, valium jar at her elbow – I thought it prudent to make myself scarceish, and accepted a phone invite from Maurice to join him and a few friends whooping it up in an American's flat in Paddington.

I arrived, self-driven, to find our old friend wearing a shiny new suit, dispensing largish snorts to a motley gang of hangers-on, the usual car-salesmen, laundromat proprietors and their ladies, all quite jolly, and Maurice, I observed with relief, noticeably abstemious, apparently being taken in hand by a large divorcee from the Personnel Department at the Army & Navy Stores.

Our American host did not seem to be present, slosh was available in ample doses, and the Personnel lady weaving her way through the throng replenishing our glasses in a very under-standing way. I found myself talking to a very amusing little woman who teaches Yoga at a health farm somewhere out near Tring, and we were getting on like a house on fire with her showing me the basic holds when Maurice suddenly took his shoe off and hammered on the sideboard to call us all to order. For one ghastly moment I thought he was going to announce his engagement like he did that time in Rye. Then I saw he had a wad of brightly coloured handouts, and naturally assumed we were all about to be given the Picwarmth Hard Sell and touched for a few thou apiece with the usual spiel about twenty percent off to shareholders if we placed a firm order before Christmas.

Not a bit of it Bill. Would you believe our friend has seen the light? 'The old two-party system has had its day, a time to break the mould, no Tory seat ever safe again, only hope for small businesses, generous grants, firm belief in profitability, we all need reflating, M. Picarda hoping to stand for Sevenoaks in the SDP interest.' Well, Bill, you could have knocked me down with a barn door, especially as by this stage I was not altogether steady on my feet. A moment later various television screens leapt to life, Mrs Crosby was seen bindling about looking cheery, and in due course, in the small hours, the Lord Mayor or whoever he was read out the score to wild cheering, at which point Maurice's seedy friends went absolutely bananas, some kind of supermarket fizzy drink was produced, and Maurice made another speech, somewhat less coherent than the first.

Having had my arm twisted for a fat contribution to party funds, I was not in the best of moods as I piloted the Rolls back to the sanctuary of Downing Street, only to find some joker had plastered the roof with damnfool stickers for the SDP. As I tiptoed up the wooden hill I could hear the Boss picking over the pieces with poor old Whitelaw, who was looking very flushed and weepy and had obviously given up the idea of staying sober.

If you ask me, this all bodes v. ill for the Boss, and U-Turns are clearly not being excluded from the scenario. They've all been in the Talking Shop trying to cobble something up in the way of a sop, without, I may say, much success. The latest news is that any minute now Brother Howe will shuffle into the Lion's Den and announce yet another dose of salts by way of Christmas cheer, i.e. higher TV licences, more on false teeth and glasses, cuts in the dole and a short sharp shock for the long-haired student yobbos and their bank managers. This last absolutely makes sense to me, though needless to say the smart arses up and down Whitehall will continue to live out the evenings of their idle lives on generous index-linked pensions, e.g. that friend of Daph's sister at Esher, Sir Whatsisname, the one who dresses up in women's clothes.

This latest package has been cooked up by two of Margaret's new backroom boys, a shifty little lawyer called Brittan and his smarmy little sidekick with bouffant hair name of Lawson, a former reptile, chiefly notorious a few years back for landing a whopping mortgage. A couple of sharks, if you ask me, very reminiscent of those two street Arabs who used to cook the

125

books for Maurice when he was running his Afternoon Drinking Club in Hendon. As for Friend Tebbit, the less said the better. The idea that our Norman would strike fear into the hearts of Len Murray and the Smelly Socks Brigade is quite laughable, and what our lot says about him behind his back doesn't bear repeating.

By the by, not a word to a soul, but the only pleasure the Boss has had all week was over poor old Fatty Prior getting roughed up at the Funeral by the Animal Paisley and his Heavy Mob. A propos, have you spotted the odd-looking fuzzy-haired Gyppo figure who trails along in Prior's wake, grinning like a golliwog? The Major's theory is that he is some sort of poet on the run from the House of Lords, but I can't believe even Margaret would be as foolish as that. Still, it's a rum old world.

Could you do your usual re the Yuletide Hooch from the Cash 'n' Carry? On four crates the saving is really quite dramatic.

Yours in anticipation,

DENIS

10 Downing Street
Whitehall

18 December 1981

Dear Bill,

I don't know whether the Major has rung you with the news of his Scott of the Antarctic expedition last week. We'd arranged to meet at the Club at ten for pre-lunch snorts, and at five past twelve he staggered in, snow on his boots and badly frostbitten. It was only after four large brownies that he felt minded to unfold his tale.

Apparently he left Eastbourne, where he had been staying with Mrs Frobisher, on the seven-fifteen, and just after East Croydon they ground to a halt in drifts some half an inch deep, known to British Rail as Adverse Weather Conditions. An hour later they were still there, windows steaming up, tempers v. frayed, no one around to say what was going on, the Pakistani Conductor having locked himself in the lavatory for fear of reprisals. Fortunately the Major had a bottle in his overnight bag and, finally, emboldened by a stiffish swig or twain, he decided to climb down on the line and walk, accompanied by a couple of other stalwarts from BP.

It appears they had miscalculated somewhat in imagining they were just outside Victoria, and after an hour's steady trudge over the snow-covered sleepers, they met a man from the Railways who said they had paralysed the entire system. At this the Major saw red, and the old boy has now got to present himself before the beak at Wandsworth sometime in the new year.

He asked me if I could put in a word with Sir Peter Parker, but after what happened last time I put in a word on behalf of an old  friend I am somewhat chary of repeating the experience. Anyway I told him that Parker was far too busy whizzing up and down on his Flying Banana from London to Glasgow with charred toasted sandwiches flying about his ears and perfectly good plonk going to waste by the crateload, smashed to smithereens every time they go round a bend.

Meanwhile, pre-Christmas Tension is building up nicely, and I took the liberty of suggesting it might be the main plank in the Major's defence when he comes to Court. M. has a miniature rebellion on her hands, with Cemetery Face and his little band of Wets frothing at the mouth about the dole money being cut, when it seems to me to be the most sensible thing they've done for a long time. Here we have, Bill, three million or so workshy yobbos sitting at home watching The Two Ronnies, cigars and tawny port to hand at the expense of hardworking chaps like you and me, what better than a blast of cold air, a short sharp shock from Brother Howe to get them up off their arses and bindling about looking for odd jobs like mowing the Major's lawn? But Old Cemetery Face lives in a world of his own, quite out of touch with ordinary people. Ditto our Sailorboy friend, who has also been huffing and puffing, keeping a weather eye open for any bandwagon he can conceivably clamber on that will restore him to supreme power.

Also getting stick, I am pleased to say, is that ghastly streak of piss David Howell, who has deemed it politic to throw open our country lanes to bigger and better juggernauts, thereby incurring the wrath of the Home Counties Brigade, who find it impossible to close an eye in their thatched Tudor mansions for fear some metal-encased fragment of the butter mountain should remove the granny annexe. You remember what happened that night poor old Podmore bought it while painting a message of good cheer outside his Uckfield love nest!

Worzel's travails, as you may have surmised from a cursory view of the *Daily Telegraph*, are also still far from over. Fresh from falling down an organ shaft en route to address the faithful, he decided to wreak vengeance on a cruel world by lashing out at an innocent little Australian Gayboy whose only offence was that he had been selected to stand in the Labour interest for some bombsite or other south of the Thames. Predictably, every Trot in creation has come crawling out of his Moscow-subsidised rat-hole baying for blood, Benn has shed his straitjacket and returned to the fray, eyes ablaze and threatening to fight like a tomcat in the cause of free speech for all. Naturally the Boss is laying down Port in consequence, and has taken to doing press-ups in Hyde Park in preparation for the next twenty years in office.

On a gloomier front, I must decline your kind invite for Boxing Day snorts, as we shall be doing the usual Chequers routine, fledgelings returning to the nest, etc. Mark is proposing this year to delight us with his latest flame, a busty divorcee from Yorkshire who runs a home-made jewellery outfit somewhere near Kettering, you know the type, sheepskin and a Jag and too much lipstick. I anticipate that the central heating will be on the blink as per usual, and we are experimenting this year with a Bolivian couple recommended by the Carringtons. All in all a melancholy vista, I think you will agree.

Forgive the Christmas Card. It's meant to be M. and self in August at the Saatchis' behest, hence my somewhat roseate features.

Yours six feet under,

DENIS

128

CHATEAU
ST. DENIS

1982

BOTTLED

CHEQUERS

Dear Bill,

Should this ever reach you, very best wishes to you and Daphne for 1982. The only good news is that your very thoughtful crates from the Cash and Carry got through before the big freeze up. I agree with you about the Glen Fiji Triple Strength. When I downed my first gulp I thought the top of my head would come off. Pow! After the sixth or seventh one got the hang of it. But God, Bill, has it been needed!

Margaret had the damnfool idea that she would bring the car down and work off a bit of her aggression on the M40. The little weather bloke with the moustache forecasted a mild night with a slow thaw heading in from the West turning to warm rain on high ground. Boris bundled the prezzies, turkey, crackers and various seasonal freebies from British Industry, the Wog Embassies etc into the boot of the Rolls, I climbed into the passenger seat well swathed in rugs and hip flask at the ready, and away we purred.

We hit our first minor snag just north of Paddington, where a juggernaut had jack-knifed across the flyover and there was a tailback of some one and a half miles. Snow was falling heavily, A.A. on the radio advising everyone to stay at home, coon teenagers strolling up and down the jam thumping on the roof and shouting abuse. Consolation from the Boss to the effect that things are much worse than this in Poland. Boris says no. According to him, Solidarity blowing up the coalmines, Trots and agitators teeming under every bed, Walesa the worst type of Scargill figure, this General Jabberwocky only doing his patriotic duty, all in all valuable object lesson for the Boss and she should be on her guard for a coup probably led by Mad Mike Hoare at the end of Janaury.

As so often with Boris, I couldn't help feeling there might be a grain of truth in his analysis. I was talking to Furniss at the NatWest over a pre-Christmas snorto de luxe, and he tells me that they've been lending the Polaks bloody billions over the last few years, all on the assumption that if the solids hit the fan, brother Russky would toddle in and foot the bill. Not so. Deep gloom at head office. Only hope now for getting their pound of flesh pinned on the good General and his dynamic style of leadership. I told Furniss I didn't think it would work for a moment, knowing the workers, but when you think Bill, that our hard-earned deposits are being poured down some bottomless hole in the ground in Silesia it really makes you wonder what it's all about.

Meanwhile, inch by inch, we headed into Darkest Bucks, hypothermia cases stumbling about in the snow flailing their arms, verges laden with abandoned cars, and arrived at Chequers at 4.30a.m. to find that Mr Wu, while loyally trying to clear the drive, had fallen over once again and been taken to Stoke Mandeville. The promised Indonesian couple engineered by the Carringtons had apparently had a flaming row with their last employers in Hampstead and were now in custody pending extradition. This left Yours Truly to act as Major Domo, cum Head Cook and Bottlewasher over the festive tide.

Before doing anything I decided that a sharpener would not come amiss. However, when I spun the kitchen tap to dilute the aforementioned Fiji, nothing came out. Margaret now in a huff retired to the freezing bedroom to bury herself under a mound of blankets, leaving me to polish off crate and discover the whereabouts of tank. I can't remember whether you've ever been down to our company accommodation here at Chequers but the upstairs part is an absolute rabbit-warren. Everything you expect to be a room is a cupboard and vice versa. Luckily Boris seemed to know his way about, and was able after a couple of hours to report that he had unfrozen the tank, and that one tap in the gun room was now producing rusty water. Raising our glasses to celebrate this little success, we were immediately plunged into terrible darkness.

I will pass over subsequent events Margaret having been in very high spirits throughout, insisting that it is all good practice for the Total War on the Miners, now billed as our New Year attraction. Boris left some hours ago a la Captain Oates, feeling he'd be less of a drain on the dwindling booze supplies. The only consolation is that the little perisher Mark didn't get through with his bit of stuff from Yorks. Tell the boys I went down bottle in hand.

Yours,

DENIS

10 Downing Street
Whitehall

15 January 1982

Dear Bill,
When are you off to Barbados, you lucky bugger? I do hope you manage to get away: you remember Batty Dugdale, one of the Burmah reps in the South West? I bumped into him in the Club the other morning, very much the worse for wear after three days

at snowbound Luton with his Missus and the grandchildren, waiting for a package Jumbo to whip them off to South Africa and sanity, all to no avail. I never liked the look of that Laker chap. Has a lot to answer for, in my view, encouraging the great unwashed to take to the airways, thus buggering it up for the rest of us.

We are all sitting here on tenterhooks, waiting to see which way the Miners will jump. Unofficially, the word is not a penny more than nine per cent, M. prepared to fight to the last OAP etc, and the same for Mr Buckton's little band of Bolshies. (The effects of the rail strike are in any case irrelevant as the whole bang shoot has frozen up due to the lack of hot water bottles to lay over the points.) In fact, if you ask me, the Boss is all of a tremble, dreading a showdown with King Arthur. Last year, you may remember, they all caved in at the first squeak from Brother Gormley, who was furthermore quite a decent little NCO. This time, with the wild-eyed Red from Barnsley calling the tune, I have a feeling you won't see Margaret's arse for dust.

We all had a good laugh at Worzel's Peace In Our Time stuff at the end of their Special Conference. Do you remember that episode in the history books where a poor dithering old king was bullied out to Runnymede to put his monicker to some kind of Bill of Rights by various burly Barons? Apparently much the same took place at Bishop Stortford: poor old Worzel dragged in in chains by the Union jackasses and told there would be no more cash until he and Benn kissed and made up in public. Everyone managed to keep a straight face, and the reptiles were dispatched to proclaim peace in banner headlines in all the Tory newspapers. Meanwhile, Saatchis appear to have been active in the ranks of the SDP. Maurice got a poison-pen letter, presumably emanating from their office, warning him to keep away from Sevenoaks or the Liberals would let his tyres down, but the old boy is still determined to stand, and has put himself forward as Shadow Spokesman for Market Gardening.

No chance now of the day out to Huntercombe with the Major and Sticky. Apparently they both came a cropper tobogganing down from the Clubhouse and Wilkinson is now laid up with his back.

Give my regards to Curly the Barman at the Noel Coward Rooms should you ever reach the Island in the Sun.

Yours in cold storage,

DENIS

10 Downing Street
Whitehall

29 January 1982

Dear Bill,
Thank you for your condolences on the safe return of the son and
h from his Sahara car rally. Honestly, what a prize twerp! I
washed my hands of the little blighter years ago, and when the
Boss told me he was intending to drive across the desert with
some fancy French bint he'd picked up in the pits, my response
was that he could go to hell in a handcart for all I cared..Next
thing I know, M. is hammering on my door at some unearthly
hour to say she has just heard on the Jimmy Young Show that the
little bugger has been missing for four days and what was I going
to do about it? Answer, turn over and go back to sleep. Cue for
maternal hysteria, call myself a man, etc, why yours truly always
so pathetic in a crisis? Eventually I found my glasses and
endeavoured to pour a bit of oil on the troubled H20, arguing that
a) a bad penny usually turns up in the end and b) that being
inexperienced in these matters he had probably driven off on one
of the B-roads in search of a quiet layby to try a bit of hanky-
panky with la belle froggette. Need I tell you that this last analysis
went down like a cup of cold sick, waterworks turned on, hanky
out, male sex maligned, wailing and gnashing of teeth, all
culminating in yours truly agreeing to jump on the first Laker
standby to Timbuctoo in search of Prodigal Son.

Later: Proprietor now back on course, heading for showdown
with the CBI, DT hurtles down to Gatwick, soon steadying the
nerves with a largish brownie at thirty thousand feet, rudely
jostled by reptiles, all treating the whole thing like a day trip to
Boulogne, air blue with smutty anecdotes.

Touch down desert airstrip, local time 11.30p.m., a real dump
if ever I saw one called Tamanrasset. (I had a dim memory that
poor old Podmore bought it somewhere near there while serving
with the Rats, but no matter.) Usual wog nonsense about no
snorts, some smarmy little FO cove whispering out of the corner
of his mouth about special arrangements at the Tam Hilton, and
off we drive. Reptiles have beat us to it, and are soon drinking the
place dry. Would you believe it, ten quid for a single? Obviously
mine Host, Ali Baba, had seen them coming, and was asking a
hundred quid a go for his Telex. It turned out that no one had the
faintest clue the so-called race was even on. It had all been
organised, if that is the word, out of a little office in Paris by a
bunch of cowboys as a publicity stunt. In these times of high
unemployment however an army of motorcycles, delivery vans,
articulated trucks and every conceivable type of wheeled vehicle

had set off from Marseilles to pit their wits against the hostile environment while the vultures circled overhead, scenting a bit of free grub.

Given such a bunch of hopeless layabouts at the wheel Mark was not the only one to have come to grief along the way, and in the meantime, thanks to the Boss hoisting storm cones, the entire Algerian airforce in the shape of three helicopters and an old Hercules was grinding through the sky overhead, in constant danger of collision with the squadron of French Mirages put up by Mitterand who seems to have taken a strange shine to the Boss. (Very decent of him, en passant, considering the man's a raving Red who has, you may remember, several times tried to arrest the NatWest's representative in Paris for issuing private cheque-books.)

I was sitting comfortably enough ensconced in the Lounge enjoying the patronage of the *Daily Telegraph* Motoring Correspondent when one of these pilot johnnies breezed in for a quick one and said would I like to go aloft in his kite for a shuftie at the terrain? Moments later we were bucketing about in the inky blackness, friend wog shouting back incomprehensible references to flickering lights beneath, and it crossed my mind that given a fair wind the Boss might soon have to send out another search party to bring in yours truly.

When we eventually returned, empty-handed, to the Bar, bugger me if young Mark isn't sitting there with a carefully nurtured growth of beard, drawling away to the reptiles, affecting great unconcern about the whole episode, and clearly seeing himself as the hero of the hour. At the first possible juncture I took the blighter to one side and gave him a pretty largish piece of my mind. Did he realise that the air forces of the entire Free World had been out trying to find him and his bit of French fluff for the last seventy two hours? That his mother was on the very brink of a breakdown? That I myself had had to come out to this Godforsaken oasis and would no doubt shortly be expected to partake of sheepseyes with the wog powers that be, and all because he refused to take a job like any other young man of his wealth and background? Absolutely no response. Sulky look, not his fault if parental brigade overreacts, he and Mamselle Fifi perfectly happy sitting in the desert waiting for the local A.A. man to turn up.

The rest, I imagine, is history. Flash-bulbs popping all the way back to Chequers. Unquestionably the worst moment of the whole episode, when Saatchis had invited every reptile in the business down for a photo call on the lawn, and it was suggested I should put my arm round the little sniveller as a sign of delirious happiness at the reunion. I drew the line at this despite a withering look from M., and broke away at the earliest moment to recover my equilibrium in the Waggonload of Monkeys.

How would you feel about two days in the Seychelles at the beginning of February? I met a little man in the Club the other day called Davis who said he could fix it up.

Yours in anticipation,

DENIS

10 Downing Street
Whitehall

12 February 1982

Dear Bill,

What about this train strike, eh? Thank God for Mr Buckton and his merry band of Reds say I. As you've probably gathered from the shower of PCs flooding through your letterbox, Maurice P., the Major and I have been having a whale of a time at the Club. Of course the Major could perfectly well have driven up and down in his new Merc, but he told the wife that it was out of the question and he would have to stay three nights in town. I offered to put him up here but the Boss put her foot down, recalling previous occasions, smashed china, nocturnal singing, burned carpets etc. Maurice P. was on to some similar wheeze to get away from his Antique Hypermarket Woman, and spun a yarn about a three day SDP conference, which apparently she swallowed h, l and s. So they took a double room in the Ladies' Annexe.

I went round there on Wednesday night for a snort and there was a very good crowd assembled in the Snooker Room. Do you remember the log-burner chap from Wokingham we met on the boat? He was there, scattering twenty pound notes in all directions. Also a very entertaining little man with a squint, called Redhead, who organises cheapies from Luton Airport and said the next time we went to Portugal together he could certainly oblige with fifteen days all in for £87.25. Amazing when you come to think that the single in the same direction is twice that.

About nine-ish, things were getting fairly unbuttoned, Maurice P. offering his Russian Dance on the snooker table and the Redhead cove suggested a foray into Soho to a little downstairs joint for an entertainment entitled Paul Raymond's Festival of Uncensored Pagan Sin. Off we went. Usual racket about Life Membership, obligatory bottle of flat champagne for fifty quid, familiar depressing line up of clap cases jerking about in jackboots. Redhead, by now molto paralytico, began to shout various suggestions from the stalls and we were asked to leave by a pair of blue-chinned bruisers with Italian accents. All good fun, I think you'll agree, and as long as Parker stands firm I think we can bank on a repeat next week. Perhaps you might join us.

Back at Bleak House little Pym has blotted his copybook with all and sundry. I read the gist of what he had said in the evening paper, and formed the opinion it was very sound stuff. Gloomy times ahead, workshy buggers had better get used to the idea that there is no crock of gold waiting for them at the Pig and Whistle, everybody buckle to, get their heads down, and be damn grateful for their bread and dripping sandwiches. M. was opening the windows when I got back, and for want of anything better to say, I let fall words to the effect that Brother Pym seemed to have sounded the right note, must be music to her ears, clearly a good sort, very decent, plainly one of us, and not too stuck up like little Peter C. To my amazement I received a double-gamma burst from both eyes, and poor Pym was condemned in absentia to be strung up by the thumbs. When the dust had settled, Boris explained that the Icecreamio Twins from Saatchis had been in a few days previously, little Howe had brought his briefcase, and they'd cooked up some scheme for winning the election in 84, Luigi Saatchi urging that the talk from henceforth be all 'ultrapositive' and based on 'a good news hype' – bloody silly the way these admen go on – gentle take-off into miniboom, bulbs coming up, evenings getting longer, all the usual nonsense. Saatchis then took their money and buggered off. Pym not being privy to this wheeze, or so he claims, had thus incurred the proprietorial wrath, though if you ask me, Bill, she doesn't trust Pym much further than she can throw him and thinks he may be after her job. There was then the usual ritual dance: M. taxed by Worzel, leaps to feet in defence of Francis P., then scurries off to brief the reptiles, off the record of course, that she is hopping mad, Pym in doghouse etc. I shall never understand it.

If you ask me the Boss has got it all wrong. I don't know whether you remember when Maurice P. got into hot water with his chemical toilets workforce, i.e. those moronic darkies, all threatening to walk out. Maurice P. eschews encouraging words, spells out the grim message, moronic darkies all burst into tears and agree to take a pay cut. Of course the whole bang shoot fell in the water three days later so it didn't make a blind bit of difference, but my point is pretty clear I think.

So Brother Laker bites the dust. Good riddance in my view. I may have said this before, Bill, but it is high time the Hoi Polloi were booted out of airports, cluttering up as they do the entrance to the VIP lounge and littering the place with beercans.

Sorry you missed the Lillywhites Sale. I got a pair of those moonboots for when the snow comes back and a left-handed squash racket. Might come in useful one of these days, and very much reduced.

See you anon,
Yours aye,

DENIS

10 Downing Street
Whitehall

26 February 1982

Dear Bill,

Would you believe it? Some snotty-nosed Leftie MP had the gall to ask Margaret whether she would be picking up the tab for my little excursion to the Sahara last month, and now I get a bill from the Tamanrasset Hilton for £1893.95 including bar drinks and room service, which I am expected to pay. I knew the little Ali Baba chap was watering the gin and adding a pretty good mark-up, but assumed the Foreign Office would shell out come the day of reckoning. I have written to Mark asking for a contribution, but the day I get a penny back from that little skunk will be the day I sign the Pledge. Still, hats off to old Mitterand for paying the Mirage and helicopter fares.

So, our little midweek beanoes at the Club would seem to be at an end, that bloody fool Parker having caved in and given Buckton his three per cent with all the trimmings. What a prize prick, Bill! I have a feeling he used to be something in sugar with that dreadul man who lived near Henley, and I know there was some shemozzle about him driving a Rolls under poor old Callaghan, but I told the Boss she should give him his cards pronto and bring in some less smarmy type who might be prepared to smack Buckton between the eyes and sort the whole thing out once and for all.

I can't understand – can you – all this sentimental tosh about the Laker man. I've said this before, and I'll probably say it again, but he has a lot to answer for in my view, cluttering up the departure lounges with the great unwashed, making it very difficult to get to the toilet on long-haul flights, and impossible to reach the bar for a drink when you arrive. Boss, on the other hand, has to don dark glasses to shield her eyes, such is the blaze of light beaming forth from Sir Frederick's arsehole. 'Good old Laker! Spirit of free enterprise, taking on the bully boys of Nationalised Industry, cutting the fares, pushing back the frontiers etc. etc.' After a bellyfull of this night after night I ventured to ask if she felt like that why didn't she step in and bale him out? Instant four megaton blast, exit DT with shirt tail smouldering. Anyway, the latest on the Laker Front, as you've probably gathered from the *Telegraph* is that Sir F has been fished out of the sewage by that Tiny Rowland cove. He seemed to me when I met him at the Guildhall rather a good sort, but the Major told me in confidence he is ninety nine per cent certain that he's a Kraut, his real name is Scharnhorst or something like that, and he may well have been Rommel's ADC in North Africa. Does that smell right to you? Anyway M. approves on the grounds that any enemy of E. Heath is a friend of hers.

So what else is new? Little Howe ponces in and out with increasing regularity to show Margaret his sums for next month's Day of Doom. Boris tried to break the combination lock on his briefcase while he was in the gents but it was fitted with some kind of buzzer device and Howe came flying out with his trousers round his ankles. There is a lot of talk though about bumping up the price of petrol yet  again. It's a mystery to me, Bill. They've been banging on for years about the price of oil being the nigger in the woodpile, responsible for inflation and all our other woes, and the moment it starts coming down they throw up their hands in horror and start banging on the Purchase Tax. Fairly safe to assume that the Southern Comfort will be through the ceiling once again, ditto the Medium Tar, so could you do your usual re the Cash and Carry, and I'll get Maurice to send one of his darkies down with a pickup truck.

Yours up to here,

DENIS

10 Downing Street
Whitehall

26 March 1982

Dear Bill,

Gripping days, what? We're all on tenterhooks here to see how Fatso Jenkins fares up in Glasgow. Saatchis, as you know, had written him off, but despite his girth and general shortage of wind, at the time of writing the old cove does seem to be making a last-minute dash for the tape.

God knows, our side have done their damnedest, and Howe's budget has been hailed on all sides as the first streaks of a new dawn, although quite honestly, Bill, it looks to me about as inky as inky black can get. I did a few sums on the talking calculator that Sticky brought back from Hong Kong, and I estimate that my own **weekly** expenditure on the very barest essentials, to wit snorts, gaspers and juice for the Rolls, has risen by 103% recurring.

The black sheep of the week, I fear, is poor old Oyster Eyes. With every day that passes, more and more opprobrium is heaped upon his balding head. Boris blames the current rocketing in the crime figures on Margaret's unemployment policies, but that seems to me pretty good leftist drivel. I felt rather sorry for old Whitelaw, and ferried him down to Worples-

don in the Rolls the other afternoon, trying to spell out the views of the ordinary chap in the street. Was it any wonder, I opined over a large brownie in the Club before we set out into the March gale, that more and more criminals were at large in the community, accommodation no longer being available at any of Her Majesty's Prisons. Here was a gloriously simple way of killing two birds with one stone: scrap all these wishy washy apprentice schemes for mopping up the unemployed youth, and set them to work building prisons up and down the land. Toxteth, Merseyside, Brixton. Whitelaw said there was one there already, but no matter. I pressed him to another large one and ploughed on. But as usual whenever I put forward a constructive suggestion, the old boy stood there with a glazed look, obviously thinking I was barking mad. Just as we were driving off from the first tee some bleeper thing went off in his pocket and his minder hurried him away to a waiting staff car, leaving DT trying to make up a foursome with the Battle of Britain mob.

No wonder the hangers and floggers are feeling pretty frustrated. I've a lot of sympathy with them, as you know. A good hanging never hurt anyone in my book, but what hope have they got with Oyster Eyes dithering about on the one hand, and the pissy-arsed little Euros on the other? If you can't even give some whipper-snapper in the fourth form six of the best without getting written approval from a lot of do-gooding Dutch bureaucrats, what hope of bringing back the noose, or flogging a bit of sense into Johnny Mugger? I line up with Enoch on this one, i.e. no jabbering Walloon or crop-headed Hun is going to tell us how to run the good ship SS Britain.

Talking of the Foreigner, I was pretty pissed off when you failed to turn up to the Club last week for lunch with Picarda's Danish Industrialist. Maurice had been there for a good couple of hours in my estimation, and the Dane, who I think I told you has invented a machine for recycling old copies of the *Daily Telegraph* for use as building bricks, had arrived the day before by mistake, and had been drinking ever since. Nice enough, and obviously full of jokes, but somewhat handicapped by not speaking a word of English. Maurice did his best with a word or two of German, and lunch was not by any means disagreeable, though the Head Waiter came over a couple of times to ask us to keep the noise down a bit for some bishops at the other end of the restaurant. About half way through, Jorg, as he asked me to call him, insisted on us toasting each other from a stone bottle containing some kind of colourless Danish sticky made from damsons, which Maurice and I found absolutely top-hole. If I could remember the name I'd order a crate of it, but I do recall a crown on the label and a black man playing a banjo, so I'd probably recognise it if I saw it again. Jorg then delved in his brief case and produced a sheet of coloured brochures showing smiling Danish housewives compressing the local equivalent of the *Daily Telegraph* and lots of little bricks ripening in the sun with views of the fjords thrown in for good measure. Maurice was absolutely bowled over by it all, and has agreed to set up a British subsidiary, Pickbrick. The long and the short of it is that I should take a pretty healthy slice of the equity with a seat on the board to follow. I must say I am seriously tempted by the idea, if only for the pleasure of seeing little Furniss's face when I tell him what he can do with his deposit account.

Hope you all had a good day at the Gold Cup. I lost a Monkey.

Yrs as per usual,

DENIS

10 Downing Street
Whitehall

9 April 1982

Dear Bill,

I'm beginning to think I may have misjudged little Peter Carrington. When we first came in I took rather a shine to him: gent of the old school, not averse to the odd snorterino, the inevitable bit of side one expects from the Etonian brigade, but quite prepared to stand up to the Boss and trade blow for blow, unlike some of the other spineless creeps one sees slithering about the premises. Now I am beginning to hae me doots, as old McGargle would have put it.

I suppose the fact is that two or three years in politics, plus jet lag, having to talk to the Boss, booze round the clock etc. would drive anybody barmy. Be that as it may, you've probably heard on the wireless that there's some kind of rumpus blown up down in the South Atlantic, where there are a few inbred settlers left behind by various whalers over the years clinging to outcrops of guano-spattered rock, along with the odd sheep, reindeer and unhinged boffin. A state of affairs that has continued perfectly amicably for many centuries, until the excitable gauchos from el pampas across the water suddenly go bananas, letting off pistols, ole ole, and cry all this is ours now. Though why they should want to take charge of these half-witted sheep-shaggers beats me.

When the balloon went up, the Boss got very excited, and pressed the intercom for P.C. pdq. Red faces at the F.O. P.C. it would appear A.W.O.L. buggering about on the Golan Heights trying to persuade Brother Begin to make room in the Promised Land for a couple of million dispossessed Wogs, an exercise about as pointless as trying to persuade Maurice or the Major to sign the Pledge. Why, you might enquire, would Carrington be thus engaged, apart that is, from the urge to enjoy a little Winterbreak among the olive groves? The answer of course is the Foreign Office's quite obscenely bumsucking attitude to the bearded sons of the desert on whose good will, we are told, our whole economy rests.

The real prick, I may say, is another Eton greaser called Hurd, who on this occasion was left minding the shop. He has also, according to Boris, just got spliced to some typist who is half his age, i.e. a D.O.M. to boot. Round he pops notwithstanding, to explain his master's absence at this time of crisis. I am glad to say the Boss administered a microwave attack that shrivelled him to cinders, and Carrington was told to abandon the skullcap routine and get his arse back to Whitehall where the safety of the sheep-shaggers hung perilously in the balance. Next thing — announcement on Jimmy Young Show that the invasion fleet has landed — balloon goes up: Parliament recalled for Saturday morning emergency session: high feeling the order of the day; even old Worzel waving the flag; many old buffers to whom Falkland Islands is just a name in the stamp album burst into tears. Long and the short of it is a slow motion replay of the Prince's Gate show; give Brother Gaucho a bloody nose and little Nott haring about like a blue-arsed fly with the prospect of having to walk the plank at the end of the day if there's any kind of balls up.

Did you see Dougie Bader on *This Is Your Life*? I don't mind telling you I was blubbing like a baby and got through two bottles of your cash 'n carry hooch before the programme ended. Ah me, those were the days.

Is our Bank Holiday outing still on?

DENIS

P.S. Carrington has now done the decent thing. Clearly my words have had some effect.

10 Downing Street
Whitehall

23 April 1982

Dear Bill,

I was very moved by your patriotic demonstration outside Number Ten the other evening. I hope you didn't think I was being stand-offish not coming out, but I always know when the Major is in one of his argumentative moods, and hearing Maurice in such good voice in Rule Britannia, I deemed it best to acknowledge the ovation from an upper window. The Boss, entre nous, however chipper she may have appeared on the gogglebox, was not in the best frame of mind to receive spontaneous assurances of grass-roots support, even from such sober citizens as your good selves. I am sure you will understand.

I must say Hopalong has behaved like a prize twat over this one, and M. has made it pretty clear that the invitation to address the H of C may have to be drastically modified. Fancy sending over such an utter duffer as old Haig! I could tell from the moment I saw him blinking in the flashlights wearing that absurd tweed hat that the man wasn't all there up top, quite apart from the jetlag problem, and the various servicing requirements dictated by his clockwork heart pacer. Little Pym steered him into the manoeuvres room, and I did my best to make him feel at home with one of those American drinks with a bit of everything in, including tomato sauce and grated chocolate on top. He drank this at a draught, seemed rather perkier, and asked for another. His team of medicos, the Cardiac Brigade, five rather gloomy sawbones in black, looked somewhat askance, but I nonetheless obliged on humanitarian grounds, knowing he was in for a four hour bout with the Proprietor. I then withdrew to watch the snooker on the BBC.

From what I could hear through the door he rumbled on for a bit about the weather, but soon the Boss's shrill blast rose to hurricane level, harsh words were to be heard and what the FO wallahs call a full and frank exchange of views was clearly in progress. Being well fortified against these tempests, I think I may have nodded off, and the next thing I knew I was being hauled out to say goodbye for the benefit of the reptiles. Haig looked pretty badly mauled, and muttered something into the arclights about constructive new ideas, while Pym and the Boss looked on with acid gaze. Afterwards, while he was waiting for the taxi to take him back to the Air Terminal, Haig, assuming I think that I was Peter Carrington, R.I.P., suddenly focused on me, threw an arm round my shoulders, saying he couldn't understand why we'd taken against the Argies, nicest bunch of bastards he'd

142

run up against in a long time, damn sound on Communism, a lot in common with the Boss when it came to knocking the shit out of old Brezhnev. I thought this mildly rum at the time, since according to Pym the Russkies are lining up with the Gauchos, but Pym might have got this wrong as he's after all new to the job. On reflection, however, it struck me, that Haig, absolute dunderhead though he may be, might after all have a point. Do you remember Batty Dugdale's funny uncle, Septimus, Arthur, some name like that? Run out of town with the Revenue men hot on his tail in the late forties, as I recall, set up in Argentina with a fancy ranch, breeding steers in a very big way to go into the Oxo Cubes. According to Batty who's been out there on and off over the years, Sidney or whatever he's called, the uncle, has a very agreeable style of life. No servant problem, tinctures on the verandah, extremely civilised existence, and so what if a blind eye is being turned to old Bormann and a few senile members of the Hitler Youth hiding out in the hills? We've sheltered some pretty odd people over here in our time. Look at the Tariq Ali man for instance. Not to mention Karl Marx holing up all those years in the British Museum when he was wanted by Interpol.

I'll tell you one very peculiar thing about it, Bill, and that is the Top Brass. I don't know whether you remember that rather pimply faced little subaltern who used to make up a four from time to time at Sandwich, can't remember his name, anyway, he's now C in C Combined Forces, and he was very chatty when M and I trailed round with Nott to raise morale. I asked him who was actually in charge of the Fleet, the Nelson figure, shouting Fire Number One down the megaphone. It transpires it's not like that any more. Apparently there's this top secret hut near Virginia Water somewhere, with all the brass sitting round with Space Invader machines, waiting to press the tit at long distance. Just like Cape Canaveral when people go to the Moon: the Boffins do all the work, matelots only there to line up on deck and appeal to the cheering crowds, PR work, planting flags etc. It all sounds jolly odd to me, but as you're always saying, I'm just an old buffer, half plastered most of the time, but that's neither here nor there.

Where will it all end, you ask? On this point, the Saatchis are remarkably sanguine. In their view it'll be either (a) triumph, Argies pull down their blue and white rag and skulk back into their holes, or (b) total cock-up by our lot, national disaster. But this, they say, is just as good as (a) as far as M's popularity goes, British always keen on leaders in defeat, Gordon of Khartoum, Captain Scott, Dunkirk, Dieppe Raid. I asked them what happened if it just went on and on and on, with the Fleet sailing round in circles, Argies playing sillybuggers, Haig whizzing back and forth until like the legendary Oozlum Bird he vanishes up his own orifice? They obviously hadn't thought of that scenario, and looked pretty shifty.

Most extraordinary thing about it is Old Worzel's attitude. All those years stumbling about on the Aldermaston march, picking his nose at the Cenotaph, and now here he is, waving the flag and Up the Boss. I'm beginning to think that he may after all be one of us. When things have quietened down a bit perhaps we could ask the old boy out for a lunch at the RAC. What say you?

Yours for the duration,

DENIS

10 Downing Street
Whitehall

7 May 1982

Dear Bill,

I don't know how the Falklands situation looks from your end, but things are certainly pretty hairy here in the Bunker. I think last time I put p. to p. old Haig was still whizzing to and fro on his mission of peace and reconciliation and seemed set to do so for some considerable time to come. Shortly after that however, the old boy rather flaked out, describing the Argies as a bunch of brainless thugs, and was henceforth somewhat persona non grata in the corridors of power. Then little Pym took off in the Concorde to try and sort things out. As far as I could gather he got a pretty good flea in his ear from the Yanks, and was told that Hopalong was far too busy having his wrinkles lifted to bother with his so-called oldest ally.

If this whole episode has demonstrated one thing, Bill, it is that all those years of sucking up to the likes of Hopalong and the chap before whatever his name was who used to walk round holding hands with his wife have been a blind waste of time. I've always held the view that the U.S. were pretty good eighth raters when it came to a scrap, no doubt due to their disgusting drinking habits and having a glass of water put in front of them every time they sit down. As for Hopalong, you know my view: they would think it jolly weird if we had Donald Sinden being Prime Minister instead of the Boss.

However, I digress. M. was pretty livid about Pym getting the bum's rush, and decided to show Hopalong what she was made of. Signal transmitted to this crazy bugger with the scrambled egg all over his hat ic the Fleet, with instructions to get their arse into gear and storm ashore on South Georgia to raise the Jolly Roger. This mission was duly accomplished, whereupon the Boss went ape in front of the TV cameras and the other reptiles, and announced that we had won a famous victory as if it was Trafalgar, exhorting the proles to rejoice.

Personally I couldn't see the point of this. I don't know whether you remember 'Doc' Hoolahan, the Irish medico who used to hang about the Grapes in Burwash, but I met him in the Club the other day, and it transpires that he spent the War in Georgia, having been drummed out of the Merchant Navy. He told me it's a bit of rock a hundred miles long, wind whips through you like a knife, and the only solace to be found is the penguins. As for recapturing it, he said it was about as much use as invading Rockall. I thought of relaying this bit of information to the Supremo, but sensed that in her D-Day mood it might be out of place.

I think the whole grisly business is probably my fault for not speaking out at an earlier stage. I'm naive enough to think that someone in charge must have a glint of intelligence or some idea of what is going on, but they always end up bringing one down to earth with a ghastly bump sooner or later. Eg my mistaken admiration at one stage for Peter Carrington. What Pym and the F.O. Pinkos repeatedly fail to understand is the nature of Johnny Foreigner. You and I having got our knees brown in the 45 Show, would have spotted a mile off that the Argies weren't going to come to heel just because we waved the big stick. All those mixed races are very excitable, and the moment you start threatening them with GBH they rush out into the streets waving their arms about, setting fire to anything they can lay their hands on, signing on in droves at the recruiting office and giving whatever thug happens to be in power that week-end carte blanche to lead them all to Gory Death.

I'll tell you another funny thing, Bill. You remember when the Polish business blew up I was having a drink with Furniss at the Natwest? Well, I was in there, trying to sort out my possible investment in Maurice's Scandinavian Brick enterprise, and Furniss told me that it's exactly the same all over again. The Argentine is mortgaged up to the hilt, huge loans from the NatWest and most of the others, not the hope of a snowball in hell of getting it  back, and if things get any worse it could be Wall Street all over again. I said couldn't they lend their money to sensible people like the Japs who could be relied on to give it back, but he said the Japs had got money coming out of their ears, and at the time it seemed like a good idea because the Argies were 'buying' a lot of British weaponry, not to mention that aircraft carrier.

To crown it all, we have to put up with a flood of ex-Falklanders coming to the house and telling us to stop sodding about because they're perfectly happy living in Ruislip. I told the Boss that by the time the fighting was over the whole place would be even more uninhabitable than it was before, but she's got her hackles up, and is scanning the popularity polls with a very nasty look in her eye. Saatchis keep telling her that if she sticks at it she's got the next election in the bag, but between you and me, Bill, I think there might be considerable sighs of relief heaved on all sides were we to find ourselves back to square one at Flood Street.

Keep the home fires burning,
    Yours aye,

DENIS

10 Downing Street
Whitehall

21 May 1982

Dear Bill,
I do hope you didn't think I was too stand-offish not coming down to Frant for the Sponsor-a-Seawolf Bring and Buy. I'm afraid the Major rather jumped the gun putting my name on the poster. Don't imagine for a moment I'm not sympathetic to your line on biffing the Argie, it's just that when you're at the centre of things matters of this nature do take on rather a different complexion.

I've got rather friendly with old Pym during the last day or two, and I think he's probably quite sound. His point of view is that sooner or later, whatever they say in the talking shop, we've got to hand the sheepshaggers' stomping ground over to the Gauchos, and in the light of that it would seem rather pointless to spend millions of pounds on a full-scale D-Day scenario when it could be quietly earning interest on deposit in the NatWest.

Whether the Boss goes along with all this it's hard to say. I told Pym that from my knowledge of the beast she tends to go over the top, often without warning, on the ils ne-passeront-pas routine, e.g. Rhodesia, Mineworkers, etc, however if you sit back having made your point in a reasonable manner, retire behind the lines to the Mess for a quiet pipe and a snort or two, you often find she puts down smoke and sneaks back to a more defensible position when no one's looking.

The danger is, of course, as I outlined to Pym over a large sticky in the dining room while M. was doing one of her Panoramas, is that this Admiral Sandy Whatnot, who is clearly a very jumpy little bugger, may get browned off with steaming round in circles laden down to the gunwales with puking soldiery and decide the best cure for mal de mer is to unload them all into landing crafts and let them take their chance in hand to hand combat with the tin-helmeted gorillas. Pym said there was no chance of that, it was all under very tight control from the hut in Virginia Water, but having seen round said hut and not having been unduly impressed I wouldn't put it past little Sandy to take the law into his own hands.

By the by, have you seen that prize charlie from the MoD who reads out the score on TV? I said to Pym they might get a slightly cheerier cove like for example that friend of the Major's who used to be a Bingo caller. The present incumbent puts me very much in mind of your sky-pilot chum outside Tonbridge during the war who did time following complaints from assorted mothers in the neighbourhood about incidents during lantern slide lectures. Not that I am implying for a moment old Frankenstein is similarly inclined, he just has that same graveyard look and a lack of what Saatchis would call pazam.

But I am wandering off the point. At the time of writing, the UN man is banging heads together in New York, and Pym is preparing hearts and minds at this end for a swift twitch of the rug from under the few remaining loyalist sheepshaggers. This is called being flexible. You may have noticed the talk about their wishes being paramount has rather faded on the air and are probably bloody angry about it, but when you see the way these chaps run the show you'd probably be quite grateful to see them climbing down off their warhorses.

I hope this doesn't cost us our friendship Bill, but quite honestly I am sick to death of the whole ghastly business. I feel more and more like that very old man who's always on the gogglebox saying he can't wait to turn his toes up. You know the one I mean. Lives near Battle.

Yours in the Lord,

DENIS

10 Downing Street
Whitehall

4 June 1982

Dear Bill,

I'm afraid our Algarve jaunt is going to have to be shelved. As you know, I'd been banking on the war putting paid to Hopalong's State Visit, and I naturally presumed that Old Redsocks would similarly take a hint and stay firmly ensconced in the Vatican. Not but what the Boss isn't giving him a very cold shoulder, especially as he has been trying to stick his oar in on the Falklands. According to Boris this is because the Argies are RCs and I suppose he feels a duty to stick up for them, dirty little dagoes though you or I might consider them to be. Needless to say Runcie is smarming about the place showing his teeth as per usual and talking about a merger between the Left Footers and ourselves in the C of E. Not to mention a lot of canoodling and hanky panky for the cameras.

Meanwhile the Boss is still in a state of euphoria. Imagine how you or I, Bill, feel after a dozen or so really large ones; the fire in the veins, the light in the eye, the spring in the step, an all-pervading sense of confidence and achievement for no very good reason. She somehow manages to get it all without recourse to the screw cap. Amazing, isn't it? As you know, I've taken rather a back seat on this one, and Pym wasn't any too keen either. However from desultory visits to the Hut where the Brass Hats run the show with their Space Invader machines, I did get the impression that shovelling the boys ashore  was by no means a piece of cake and hats off to them. But the question that has been troubling me ever since the kick off, is what happens next? I managed to raise the matter with Brother Nott when he came round to be programmed by the Boss. Nott, en passant, is some kind of tax lawyer, completely out of his depth, and I'm told he was mixed up in the Rossminster business. I am constantly getting him mixed up with Frankenstein who reads out the scores on the TV for the MoD. Anyway, M. being upstairs taking a transfer charge call from her new fancy man, President Mitterand, I took the opportunity of probing our bespectacled friend on the long term scenario. Assuming the Argies run up the White Flag and the sheepshaggers are rehabilitated in their huts, Parish Council re-elected etc, what then? Of course, as usual, it turned out the politicos hadn't given a moment's consideration to such matters. Nott rolled his eyes, shuffled his feet, and burbled away a bit about 'opening the place up'. Biggish garrison, longer airstrip, all the usual guff. He even tried to spin me some yarn about enlisting Jap know-how to harvest the seaweed, which according to the boffins has magical rejuvenating properties. I said where would this leave the sheepshaggers? After all, they'd only gone there for a bit of peace and quiet in the first place, now they'd been bombarded from arsehole to breakfast-table, and here we were talking about erecting seaweed factories.

You know these lawyers, Bill. Nott looked at his watch, burbled away about options and getting round the green baize to thrash it all out, but not a word of sense to be gleaned from his discourse.

You ask what it's all going to cost. According to Boris, who has had a look at Howe's sums, the bill so far is pushing £3,000 million. All of which makes the talk about M3 and the Cuts look a bit bloody stupid. However, that sort of nonsense has been swept under the rug and Saatchis are talking about a khaki election. If you ask me, they've all got completely carried away and the sooner they sober up and face the music the better it will be for all concerned. Even Pym has taken to wearing red, white and blue underpants and raving on about how we've recovered our national pride. I'm beginning to think Peter Carrington probably got it right in the first place. The FO scheme was to smuggle the whole bang shoot over to the Argies under cover of darkness while everyone was watching Brideshead Revisited on the telly, and if the buffoon Galtieri hadn't jumped the gun with his scrap merchants everything would now be tickety-boo. However no one gives a damn what I think so I may as well save my breath to cool my Toddy.

Pax vobiscum,

DENIS

10 Downing Street
Whitehall

18 June 1982

Dear Bill,
A lull at long last in the mad rush of distinguished visitors. The Supreme Pontiff has toddled off to try and talk a bit of sense into the Argies, and Old Hopalong has been driven away in his charabanc full of gorillas for his Eight-Capitals of Europe in Four Days Tour. I must say, Bill, I was pretty glad to see the back of him, not to mention his better half. I couldn't make out why they wanted to come here in the first place: I suppose at their age they like to travel a bit and see the sights before they come to hand in the dinner pail, and if so they clearly got their money's worth with a personalised reception by H.M. the Queen and a Disneyland-style ride round the Park with H.R.H. doing his Christmas Card number dressed up as Mr Pickwick.

I was on parade for the big speech scene at Halitosis Hall, fortified I may say by a quart or so of Pimms very kindly laid on by Boris prior to our departure. The heat was stifling, six hundred sweating MPs, old Hailsham sitting there in his horsehair wig scratching himself, all those geriatric Labour peers

149

wheeled out of the Old Folks' Home adjusting their hearing aids. So you can imagine the pong. Then the most amazing thing, Bill. Hopalong finally lopes onto the stage in his corset and full make-up, and blow me, reels off a proper rip-snorter of a tirade lasting the best part of two hours. All very sound, Red Menace to be fought tooth and claw, ancient values, wit and wisdom of old Winston sprinkled in

for good measure. Your Rotary at Deal would have lapped it up, and the Boss was wriggling about in her seat fair purring with delight. But this is the amazing thing, Bill, the old stager did it all word-perfect without a note in sight. I was absolutely bowled over, and gave a nod of approval to Boris, who had managed to infiltrate the ranks of security men lurking among the floral decorations. He, to my surprise, only tapped his nose in a knowing way and gave me a broad wink. Later when we were shuffling out of the hall, he drew me aside and showed me how it had all been done with mirrors, the speech rolling off a treadle operated by one of Hopalong's handlers, and reflected on a sheet of glass where the old cove could read it with ease, all unbeknownst to his wondering audience, just like they do on the telly. The whole thing's frightfully ingenious and packs up the size of a suitcase. I asked if they could get me one from America for my Rugby dinners, as it would save an awful lot of time and angst if I could get Maurice's smutty jokes off pat rather than having to bugger them up and ask him for the real punch line, thus incurring the bread roll treatment from the Tunbridge Wells brigade.

Meanwhile our lot seem to be getting a good deal of stick behind the scenes over the South Atlantic Farrago. Even Boris is having some difficulty in cracking the telegrams flying to and fro from the Min. of Def. If you ask me M. is anxious to avoid too embarrassingly large a cull of Argies. Hence the dropping of free-offer leaflets, and the midnight phone calls to General Mendoza telling him to come out with his hands up and his trousers round his ankles, all of which as you or I could tell them is an absolute waste of time. The orders from Brer Galtieri are clearly to do or die for the Fatherland, the individual Argie on the spot doesn't know whether he's having a shit or combing his hair, and short of the SAS putting sennapods in their water supply it looks as though a pretty grisly ding dong is on the cards.

I can't see the sense of it myself, and I can't really believe that the sheepshaggers are exactly relishing the prospect of seeing their little wooden homesteads blown to smithereens. Why they wanted to go there in the first place I can't imagine. God knows there are enough uninhabitable islands dotted about our own inshore waters if that's the kind of thing they want. Take for example the Isle of Muck where you may remember I was forced to spend a brief holiday under the roof of the puce-faced old miser, Lord Margolis or whatever he was called, while Margaret bagged the grouse.

Hasta la Vista, amigo mio,

DENIS

10 Downing Street
Whitehall

2 July 1982

Dear Bill,

It seems as though I misjudged the temper of the Argies on the question of Menendez' Last Stand. As you probably saw on the gogglebox they ran up the white flag pretty smartish following the usual negotiations from a callbox, since when the Boss has been on Cloud Nine and shows no signs of coming down to earth, despite the fact that Brother Weighell and all the other Union Jackasses are playing sillybuggers again and the country has virtually ground to a halt.

Nonetheless the Old Girl's confidence seems well based. Having popped over for a brief champagne celebration with Hopalong, she is now back and planning a Victory Parade not to mention her own visit to the newly reconquered territories to receive the homage of the grateful sheepshaggers, all fifty-nine of them. I should say that I am being pressed to pose for a photocall at the Bar of the Upland Goose, but quite frankly going that distance for a drink when there's not even so much as a clock golf course and they're all half cuckoo and cross-eyed is not my idea of a lark.

Worzel misjudged the public mood yet again by trying to make mischief with the help of some Conservative activist woman from Gerrard's Cross. The reptiles dredged up a letter this old bag had addressed to Margaret on the eve of the Argie Invasion, to which M. had replied that as far as we were concerned fifteen marines armed with catapults and one Alsatian dog were quite sufficient to keep the gauchos off the guano, everything tickety-boo etc. Of course at the time this was perfectly true, and anyway like all these letters it wasn't actually written by Margaret in the first place, but cobbled up by one of Carrington's minor weirdoes at the FO. This didn't stop the smelly socks side, including the old salt Jim Callaghan, from trying to make capital out of it. Needless to say the moment things started to look ugly the Boss fired off one of her Exocet ripostes, pointing out that Worzel, if he'd been in charge would have done bugger all and left the sheepshaggers to their fate. No bad thing Bill, entre nous, but one can't really say that in public – and the Opposition front bench blew up as per usual and was sunk without trace in a matter of seconds.

I am sorry to hear about Maurice's troubles. The SDP was always a pretty dodgy line in my view, not that that is any reason for turning the gas on. Did he realise this North Sea stuff wasn't toxic? However the explosion can have done him no good and I'll do my best to go and see him at the Bin as soon as the weather gets better. I hope he's in a fit state to mark his card for the Men's Singles between Fatso and Dr Kildare. What a prize pair of twats! Apparently old Fatso's stock has gone straight through the floor. He seems really out of his element at Halitosis Hall and sat out the hostilities on the back benches arms crossed without a word escaping his lips, whereas the keen young Doctor was constantly on his feet, having learned off yards of the UN Charter by heart, precious little use though that was, so he could pip the old gastronome at the post. Not but what Owen isn't quite clearly a vicious greaser, the kind of interfering little houseman you often find in clinics who tells you to take a grip of yourself, cut out the booze and fags and live as miserable an existence as he quite obviously does. The only time he ever showed any signs of humanity was when he tried to strangle that Trot student who was throwing rotten tomatoes at him.

See you at Gatwick,

Yours in anticipation,

DENIS

10 Downing Street
Whitehall

30 July 1982

Dear Bill,
I presume you are now back in the country. I do apologise for my no show at Gatwick, but I was creeping out at the crack of dawn with the clubs and tropical kit when the Boss flung open the door of her operations room where she had been at work since half past four, confiscated my travellers' cheques and British Caledonian documents, and said there was no question of my going away

while our gallant lads were still trickling back from the South Atlantic. Presence was required in the quayside with Union Jack bowler, 'Welcome' balloons, poised to join in the Chorus of Land of Hope and Glory. I hope nonetheless that Florida was a success and that you managed to find someone to go round with.

As you may gather from the above, every effort is still being made by Saatchis to wring the last possible drop out of the Falklands. It is already being repeated as a major drama series by the BBC, Runcie has been roped in to give thanks in St. Paul's, and various showbiz johnnies have been persuaded to appear in gala performances of the Royal Tournament. As if this were not enough in the way of Good Cheer, Murray's Smelly Socks came to heel and clobbered little Buckton without Margaret so much as raising a finger, the first time I've seen any sense out of that lot since the General Strike. You can imagine that even I was less depressed than usual at the way things were looking. To crown it all, no invitation from the Isle of Muck, so prospects seemed bright for two weeks of relative p and q at the country flat down at Lamberhurst. However, in the words of Shakespeare, the best laid plans often run amuck.

As I may have said before Whitelaw is a perfectly decent old bean who likes the sauce as much as any of us, but he is totally out of his depth in the modern world. You've probably seen all the sniggering in the gutter press about this mad navvy who climbed into bed with the Queen. They'd scarcely got over that one when the top royal minder, one Commander Trestletable, was caught out by the reptiles with his pants down carrying on with some bumboy in his leisure hours. Crikey, Bill, all hell was let loose. Uproar at Halitosis Hall. Heads must roll. Poor old Oystereyes put in to bat by the Boss goes down under a hail of body-liners, and with a cry of 'Leggo, you rotters', retires to drown his grief in Members' Bar where he is seen sitting head in hands, his huge frame shaking with uncontrollable sobs. I must say if I were him, Bill, I'd have thrown in the sponge long ago and sodded off pdq to the little shooting lodge in the Lake District.

Personally I couldn't understand why on earth our chaps were getting their knickers in such a twist. Anybody who's ever put a foot in Buck House has seen the kind of thing that goes on. You probably remember the time the Major was taken short at that Garden Party and stumbled across a couple of guardsmen in the shrubbery. When I was last in the Superintendent's office looking for a little more soda the smell of cheap perfume was quite overpowering, and there were a couple of sailors being royally entertained who as far as I could see had come straight in off the street. I have indeed frequently raised the topic with the D of E, who lines up with you and me on the Gay Question having seen a thing or two in the Navy, but he says that even in George the Sixth's time the place was crawling with wooftahs of every size and shape, number one culprit being the old Queen Mother who makes a point of employing nothing but bumbandits and brownhatters in every possible post. Blunt, as the Duke says, was only the icing on the cake.

On a more serious topic, I see that Lillywhites have got a summer sale on. Do you want me to get you one of those electric barbeque trolleys that Daphne hankered after when we stayed with your friends near Lisbon? (Hadn't they come unstuck on intensive pig rearing?) I think there's something like £99.99 off, which in these days of hardship and recession is not to be sniffed at. I managed to drop in on Maurice last week, by the way, and he was sitting up in bed, though not making much sense. Apparently they've given him those happy pills, and he is trying to join BUPA retrospectively.

Hasta la vista, as the Argie said when he saw Johnny Gurkha coming for him with his cutlass.

Yours aye,

DENIS

10 Downing Street
Whitehall

13 August 1982

Dear Bill,

I can't remember whether I missed the post last time over the St Paul's Thanksgiving affair. Saatchis had planned the whole thing as a major boost for the Boss, full coverage on the telly, Royal Family filling the front pews, herald trumpeters, fanfares, Old Contemptibles wheeled out, Worzel in his donkey jacket shifting about uneasily in row Z. Somewhere along the way, however, the whole thing came unstuck. As I may have said before one of the Boss's biggest-ever mistakes was appointing that silly bugger

Runcie to the C of E hot seat. Over and over again at the time I stressed the merits of old Archie Wellbeloved, and over and over again I was told not to talk nonsense. Even in the state he is at present, plugged into all kinds of wires and apparatus, Archie would have laid on a better show than the grinning chimpanzee from Canterbury.

I had taken the precaution of ingesting a few pretty stiff ones across the road in the Barbican Arms, and my recollection of the opening moments is not all that clear, but I realised as soon as the Proprietor made her entrance, in total silence without so much as a breath of applause, let alone the massed trumpeters or Cup Final cheering we had expected, that someone had blundered. When Runcie finally minced up into the pulpit and adjusted his frock, instead of rendering thanks to the great Bartender in the Sky for the sinking of the Belgrano and all his other mercies viz unexploded bombs, crass bungling by Argies, massacre at Goose Green etc, we got a lecture, would you believe, on the evils of war with the strong suggestion the whole episode need not have happened. (Of course he may well be right, but that was not the time or the place to say so.) M. inevitably was fit to be tied, shredded her programme, looked at her watch several times during the homily, and when it came to shaking hands with the Primate at the West Door, gave him a radioactive look that left him smouldering.

If you ask me, Bill, the C of E is entirely up the spout. The latest news, as you may have seen in the *Telegraph*, is that they've re-written the National Anthem so as not to offend the Argies, another of friend Runcie's little wheezes. The next thing you know it'll be women priests. Didn't Daphne put herself down on the waiting list at one stage, or am I mixing her up with Maurice's old flame from AA? I know the Major got mixed up with some frightful harpy who went in for speaking with tongues after she'd had a few.

I am very glad to hear that Maurice is out and about. I passed on to little Geoffrey Howe the cri de coeur of a small businessman with a lifetime of experience in double-glazing and export contacts in the Middle East, and the message of cheer from the Treasury is that HP restrictions are being lifted; the logic behind this being that as people haven't got any money, they should be enouraged to get themselves as deeply into debt as possible by lashing out on three piece suites, a second refrigerator, and microwave ovens. Double-glazing is therefore due for a boom, ditto Maurice's brick contraption, though the last I heard of that, when he was coming to in the Home, writs were being issued for infringing the Swedish patent.

The latest for the Buckton treatment are the floorswabbers at the NHS. According to the Boss and that little creep Fowler they've been offered a very decent three per cent, which may not be a great deal on the amount they're earning at present, but you can't have everything in this life, at least they can't, and Margaret has obviously spotted another soft target for her salami treatment on the Unions. Personally I can't help feeling a twinge of sympathy for them. Maurice had two very nice little male nurses holding him down when I went to visit him in the Bin and knowing the old boy I doubt very much whether he left them any kind of gratuity when he finally discharged himself through the window.

We are now off to Switzerland to stay with one of Margaret's ole chums in a moated grange. It is slightly preferable to the Isle of Muck, but only just. The widow Glover is not one of life's merrier souls, and I have asked Boris to load one false bottom in my suitcase with the necessary supplies. In my experience all you ever get in the Alps is some ghastly sticky made out of rotting Edelweiss.

Ski heil, alte Freund, and yodel-ho he ho.

DENIS

27 August 1982

c/o Frau Glover
Schloss Bangelstein
Birchermuesli
Switzerland

Dear Bill,
I wonder whether you got my PC from the airport. Not much time to scribble more than a line as I was rather under the eagle eye and thought the joke about the mountain goat might be deemed in poorish taste.

As I foresaw, high life at the Schloss is uneventful, to say the very least. The whole idea was for the Boss to put her feet up and get the Falklands out of her system once and for all, but as usual it hasn't quite worked out like that on the ground. She gets up every morning well before dawn, buggering people in England about and running up an immense phone bill for the Widow, Boris the while being dispatched to the local W.H. Schmidt to bring back all the English papers, these being an average of two days late, though you couldn't tell that from looking at them, and costing £1.50 a go. Then more ringing up, endless heaps of official letters, autographed pictures and the like to be carried down to the Postamt by Boris.

There follows a frugal repast – apple juice, black bread and ten varieties of cheese, and if I'm lucky a thimbleful of some Alpine sticky out of a cut glass horror in a wicker basket that plays The Sound of Music at a deafening level of decibels if one so much as brushes one's hand against it, thus putting an effective stop to any nocturnal forays.

The afternoon is given over to motor excursions, when M. and I are allowed out sandwiched between several burly Swiss detectives in the back seat of the Glover Rolls, the Widow comfortably ensconced in front beside her very elderly chauffeur Hanfstaengel, drawing our attention to the various peaks on the horizon. Matterhorn, Schmatterhorn, when you've seen one you've seen them all.

On one occasion I made the mistake of suggesting we stop at a roadside hostelry of fretted wood with waitresses in embroidered pinafores. It took a bit of time to find seats for all the detectives, but when things settled down and the Boss was busy with her giant aerosol 'taking out' the wasps I managed to obtain the drinks list, four foot square and all in Bosche, from one of the frauleins. Inevitably I ended up with a glass filled a good six inches over the top with vivid green chunks of pineapple, chocolate, nuts and a paper parasol on top. Alcoholic content nil per cent. Hanfstaengel and the Heavies in the meantime lowering their bulbous noses into bottomless stone mugs with little metal lids.

As dusk falls, Herr Zwingli, the gloomier half of the Widow's live-in couple, appears with further trays laden with apple juice and dried fruit to draw the curtains and switch on a forty-eight inch colour TV, given over to the preliminary heats of the Eurovision Yodelling Knock-Out, interviews with incomprehensible goatherds and lengthy reports — keenly studied by the Widow G. — from the Zurich Stock Market on the movement of the Swiss Franc against the Yen. After this, an early bed in my carved cot under the low rafters, where I toss miserably to and fro wrestling with one of those ghastly giant eiderdowns filled with duck feathers, comes as a positive relief.

In contrast to my own somewhat disconsolate condition, the Boss remains on a level of intolerable euphoria, particularly at the recent polls showing Worzel and Fatso in the doghouse. She drones on to the Widow about her plans for the next fifteen years, how she's got the Health Workers in a hammerlock, interest rates tumbling, inflation bottoming out, everything in the garden lovely.

You notice that Pinko Prior waited until the cat was away before putting the boot in on unemployment. I used rather to admire his pluck in standing up to the Boss, but I imagine a year in exile among the mad Orangemen has taken its toll. If you ask me, poor old Whitelaw was never the same after his spell on the Bogside.

If you see Maurice, tell him I spent four hours in some dreadful Bierstube near Geneva Station, listening to relays of grinning zither players, waiting for his double-glazing contact Kornfield to turn up. A very elderly barmaid who had a smattering of English told me that someone of that name had been arrested the afternoon before and taken off in handcuffs, but it may not have been the same person.

Next stop Balmoral. Another milestone on the dreadful road.

Yours aye

DENIS

BALMORAL CASTLE
ABERDEENSHIRE TEL. BALLATER 3
SCOTLAND STATION: BALLATER

Dear Bill,

So here we are, doing our annual penance in the great gothic pile. Usual crowd, various Royal throwbacks, chinless sprigs of the aristocracy, and the stray coon basking in the conservatory. Good deal of gossip behind the green baize door to the effect that the Phillipses aren't getting on too well. I asked old Mrs Donaldson who very kindly came in to run a flat iron over my plus fours after we'd been rained out on the links if there was any truth in it, and she muttered somewhat cryptically in her thick highland brogue that folks like me 'didna ken the half of it' and that 'puir Captain Phillips couldna have been all there in the first place'.

You see poor old Nott has finally cracked and decided to quit. Personal reasons was what they said on the wireless, but if you ask me after the Falklands blew up and it transpired that if it had happened a few months later all we'd have had to send was a couple of vomit-stained Sealink ferries and the wreck of the Mary Rose, the Boss had made it pretty clear to him that he'd better hang on, as there had to be someone to carry the can if it all got cocked up but after that he was free to bugger off back to his daffodil farm. Apparently the little fellow had been hankering after Howe's job, though why anyone in their right mind should want that bed of nails being bounced up and down on by the Boss night and day beats me.

Personally, I never had much time for Brother Nott. He's some kind of city lawyer, who I am told was mixed up in the Rossminster business. Anyway he always looked pretty out of place shinning down a rope onto the heaving deck to welcome back the Boys in Blue. Altogether a very gloomy streak of piss and I shall not be sorry to see the back of him. I don't know who the hell they'll find to preside over our dwindling divisions, but I imagine Margaret has got some little creep up her sleeve.

What else is new? As I foresaw the latest poll suggests that the Falklands Factor is on the wane, so Saatchis are doing their damnedest to kick a bit of life back into it. The latest wheeze is for some kind of Victory Parade with captured Argies led in chains around the Barbican, contingents of grateful sheepshaggers, Johnny Gurkha riding on a special *Daily Telegraph* float, hooded SAS veterans parachuting out of the sky trailing smoke and a simulated Exocet attack on the GLC. The latter was my own suggestion, unfortunately vetoed by Nott on the grounds of expense. Another good reason for him to get the boot.

As usual, wetting one's whistle in this miserable mausoleum is proving an uphill task to say the very least. Fortunately the Queen Mother has a secret supply, and during the Charades last night she led me away to an old gun room where we quaffed some very acceptable Highland Fling Malt Whisky she keeps in an old croquet box. She told me a priceless story about Noel Coward and Lord Mountbatten on holiday in Tangiers which involved a visit to a Turkish Bath and the British Ambassador losing his trousers, but it was rather late and neither of us was too clear in our grasp of detail.

On re-reading the above, it all seems a bit pointless but it may serve to give you some insight into how we pass the time as the rain buckets down and the stags peer in at the windows.

Here's looking at ye.

DENIS

24 September 1982

INN OF THE SEVENTEENTH HAPPINESS
SOMEWHERE NEAR THE STATION
DOWNTOWN TOKYO
JAPAN

Dear Bill,

Forgive the fragrant rice paper, but it's all they provide you with.

I can't remember whether you've ever been to the Land of the Rising Sun, but it takes a bit of getting used to after Tunbridge Wells. To begin with there aren't any numbers on the houses, and even with a phrase book it's very hard to make oneself understood. As you may have gathered from the *Telegraph*, the name of the game on this trip is to try and persuade Mr Yamaha, the Head Nip, to stem the flood of Hondas, Datsuns and other miracles of modern technology into the British Isles, and in exchange to spend several billion yen on importing the Michael Edwardes Junk Collection. Another wheeze is for one of their big Video operations to set up shop in Toxteth or somewhere like that, thus solving unemployment at a stroke. As usual the Foreign Office has come up with an absolute stumblebum non-starter. The only things we make that the Japs want to import are various pansy products like Fairisle liberty bodices and Fortnum and Mason jam cosies, and can you imagine the workshy yobbos in the outer darkness responding to Changi-style discipline and the crack of the stock-whip? The Boss and I having just returned from a Space Invader factory on the outskirts, I can tell you Len Murray would have a fit. 05.45 clock in, 05.46 ritual obeisance to image of the Chairman, Mr Y.K. Bonzai, singing of National Anthem, five hundred press-ups, and off they waddle for a fourteen hour shift on a handful of dried seaweed and a tin mug of herbal tea, under the watchful eye of the TV cameras, and woe betide any slacker who fails to achieve his regulation output of 25 Space Invaders by the end of it.

159

The Boss was absolutely bowled over by the whole thing but I think even she realises that John Bull might be wriggling under the wire if they tried it at British Leyland. And who can blame him, say I.

I managed to miss the banquet at the Mitsubishi Bank last night, pleading hypertension and sore feet, and made contact with your old chum 'Harpic' Connolly, who I gather was already fairly far gone when he came out here. He's now a rep for some American Whisky firm, and certainly looks the part. He turned up in the hotel lobby wearing a suit and sandals with a presentation pack of samples for me to savour before we hit the town. He then conducted me to his gas guzzler and we drove out into the neon-lit nightmare. Our first port of call was one of these twenty-four hour fully automatic golf courses, all blazing with floodlights, clusters of Nips padding to and fro in shiny boots on the astroturf, barely room to swing a club, all with many an 'Ah-so' and an oriental oath, balls whizzing hither and yon like bullets. Give me Huntercombe on a wet afternoon any day. I drew the line at nine holes, especially as Harpic was seeing double by that stage and slicing the ball very badly meanwhile shouting abuse at the injured Nips and throwing their tartan hats into the air-conditioning.

We took refuge in the nineteenth, which was decorated roughly in the style of a Munich beercellar, and who should we run into but poor old Ginger Watkins? Leg in plaster after an accident in the revolving door of an umbrella factory in Kyoto, but glass eye agleam and raring to go to one of these Massage Parlours he'd read about on the plane. Harpic said he knew just the place, and after a few little cups of Japanese tea, a pretty lethal brew apparently made out of fermented bamboo shoots, we climbed into Harpic's convertible and traced an erratic course through the speeding traffic to the Forbidden City, though it all looked much the same to me, especially by night. Harpic assured us that he knew the way, but it became pretty obvious after a while that he hadn't the remotest clue and was badly lost.

By no means discouraged, he drew up outside a luridly lit establishment called the Golden Cock Geisha Palace and we all piled in, Harpic tossing the keys to an impassive attendant who drove off into the night. Smiling ladies plastered in make-up and wearing Madame Butterfly outfits then ushered us into a dimly-lit saloon where we were expected to squat on the floor and cram our legs under a sawn off table while the giggling Geishas

160

shuffled away carrying our jackets, spectacles and shoes, returning after about half an hour with three face flannels soaked in boiling water and two roses floating in a shaving bowl.

The words snort and snifter, it eventually dawned on us, meant little to these Oriental handmaidens, whose grasp of English only ran to telling us the show would be beginning in a few minutes. A good while later the lights went out altogether, and two women in pink kimonos came on with fans, swaying to the rhythm of a few old gongs and the usual chopstick music. By this time both Ginger and Harpic were beginning to get a bit restless, shouting a lot about Knocky Knocky, and throwing their flannels at the ladies. This did not turn out to be a good idea as we were immediately given the bum's rush by ten plainclothes Samurai warriors and unable to find the way in again.

Two more days of this insanity and we are off to rub shoulders with Hu Flung Dung who is proposing to do a Galtieri on us over Hong Kong. I'll keep you informed.

Sayonara Blitish Pig.

DENIS

PS I looked round the supermarket for one of those electric backscratchers for Daphne but they said they were out of them.

10 Downing Street
Whitehall

22 October 1982

Dear Bill,

Grim tidings about the interest rates coming down. Furniss broke the news to me when I dropped in to get a new cheque book on my way to the Club. Very apologetic, sherry to hand, and as usual no explanation of the wide gap between the ten percent to the borrowers and the six percent to the wise virgins i.e. you and me. I don't mind admitting I tore into him on the topic of Mexico, Poland and the Argies Dictatorship, but he laid his arm round my shoulders, gave me that shifty smile of his and began to talk about his chrysanthemums which apparently won some sort of prize at the Datchet Show. Howe keeps urging me to go into National Savings, but I'm buggered if I'm going to give him my money to squander on new by-passes for juggernauts just to boost the standing of that grizzly little streak of piss David Howell.

Did you see we had all the Top Brass round for a hot meal? The idea, according to Saatchis, was to keep the Falklands uppermost in the public mind pending the next election. As far as I could gather, most of them spent the whole show yomping to and fro from the bar at Virginia Water. I didn't know who half of them were, although I did recognise old Dracula face from the Min of Def who used to read out the scores on the box. He seemed to have smartened himself up for the occasion, and was obviously a bit miffed about not getting a gong. Apparently some people were also exercised about poor old Sam Salt not getting anything, but as I said to little Nott, if you start dishing out decorations to everybody whose ship sinks where would it end?

By the way, did you happen to see Nott's fracas with Sir Robin Day on the telly? I missed it, following a rather heavy evening's imbibing with Podmore and his friends from the Home at a little club in Hove, but apparently when Day called him a here today and gone tomorrow sort of chap he got very shirty, unplugged the mike and minced out in a huff. I've never had much time for Day myself, far too pleased with himself if you ask me, very opinionated, loud voice, wears those common-looking bow ties from Burtons, but I thought on this occasion it was perfectly fair comment and revealed what an unbalanced little pratt Nott really is.

A propos the Falklands gongs, the Boss was spitting tintacks as you probably saw because the reptiles jumped the gun and broke the embargo. According to the scenario worked out by Saatchis, the idea was to get maximum coverage of the Party Conference, final wind-up speech by the Boss followed by general last night of the Proms jubilation, Union Jack bog rolls being thrown about etc., monopolising the prints, and then as a 'grand climax' let loose the gongs on the Monday morning, flattening the SDP. As it turned out M. had a pretty grisly night with that gag-writer johnny with the long cigarette holder and padded dressing gown, dishing up one bum one-liner after another, then Hopalong's magic mirror prompting device started working sideways half way through and put up the racing results. So when to cap it all the VC's started dribbling onto the front pages the following day, no wonder she hit the ceiling.

Anyway morale was restored by the big march past in the City a few days later. This had all been laid on to make up for Runcie's flopperoo at St Paul's which sounded entirely the wrong note and was dreamed up by a lot of conchie sky-pilots of the type you always find lurking about having a cigarette in the vestry. The Boss was very carried away, burst into tears, VE Day all over again. Personally I thought it was all a bit pointless, but I suppose if Brother Scargill gets up to his pranks it's nice to know the Army can now be counted on to restore order. The only good laugh of the day was old Worzel on the saluting base in a suit. Shades of the Cenotaph, what?

By the way, I couldn't help feeling a surge of sympathy for poor old H.M. on the Prince Andrew front. Having had enough trouble with my own gangling great yob of a son and heir gallivanting around with various unspeakable bits of fluff, pursued by a horde of reptiles and bringing the family name into disrepute, I did think of giving her a bell when it came out that Randy Andy was shacked up in his aunt's tropical love nest with this ghastly stripper called Koo. Boris however advised against it on the grounds that relations with Buck House are strained as of late. Apparently H.M. doesn't like another woman getting in on the act and keeps the Boss standing to attention throughout their weekly pow-wows, never even offering her as much as a large Scotch.

Maurice is very euphoric about the Stock Market and is thinking of going public with Picbrick. I don't know whether you heard he set the chimney on fire at the Walmsleys' house-warming, so I wouldn't have thought it was the soundest of moves, but when he's on a high there's not much you can do to stop him. Did you see him at the SDP Conference not making very much sense about the Unions and getting the red light treatment from the woman with the messy hair? I thought it was a mistake to call him so soon after the lunch break, but I don't expect they've got the measure of him yet.

Tootleoo

DENIS

10 Downing Street
Whitehall

19 November 1982

Dear Bill,

I expect you heard the news about old Leonid B. turning his toes up at long last. Boris was very cut up about it and wanted me to put the flag at half mast but the Boss vetoed the suggestion.

Re the latest election plans, I don't know if I've ever told you about Margaret's South African Guru, a chap called Van der Pump who lives up a flag pole somewhere on the East Coast. He really is a most extraordinary little cove. He's spent most of his life, as far as I can piece together from what he has told me, roughing it with the pygmies. According to Van der P. they can fill their bums with water like camels' humps and walk across the desert for days on end. I don't believe a word of it myself, but that is one of the yarns he spins. The Boss is frightfully impressed, along with the Heir to the Throne, who has appointed Van der P. Godfather of the Royal brat.

This old S. African johnny, who was very thick with Mountbatten by the way (and take that as you like it), is a great believer in dreams, and if he's had pickled onions the night before you can bet your bottom dollar he'll be on the blower at dawn holding forth with a message for the nation. During the Falklands Show he was constantly hogging the hot line to Margaret. I remember on one occasion he'd had a dream about a bear eating his trousers while he was in the bath, and when he took a shotgun to it the bear gave them back neatly pressed and wrapped up in one of those plastic bags you get from the dry cleaners. This, according to Van der P., was obviously a signal to send off the Task Force and blow hell out of the bear, i.e. Johnny Argie. I said to Margaret at the time I thought this was pretty daft as the Task Force had left some weeks before, and asked her if she'd like to hear a dream I'd had about me and Maurice stuck up a tree at Worplesdon with Fatty Soames driving an ice-cream cart round and round the trunk. This only elicited a frosty look from M. and it was clear that Van Der P's effort was a clear winner in the dream stakes.

Anyway, M. being away getting to know Herr Schidt's successor, ludicrously enough called Herr Coal – though Germans always have pretty peculiar names in my experience, and good riddance en passant to that ghastly old snuff-taker in the sailor hat – when blow me, Van der P. comes through on the scrambler with the latest news from the world of the sub-conscious. Having retired to bed after a fairly fierce curry at the local Khyber Pass, the old boy had nodded off and found himself alone in a strange landscape thickly wooded with banana trees. Judge of his surprise when a huge owl fluttered down, bearing in its talons an alarm clock. I stopped listening at this point, being rather preoccupied with the *Daily Telegraph* crossword puzzle, but anyway the message I was to give the Proprietor on her return was to go for a snap Autumn election in 83. He repeated it several times, obviously thinking I was half cut, which I was, and wouldn't remember to put it on the Memo P, which I didn't.

Anyway the Suffolk Soothsayer has had his way and the Cabinet have been told to clear their desks in preparation for all-out war with Worzel in nine months time.

I find it hard to disentangle M's thinking on strategy, but according to Boris the scheme is to flog off the North Sea, British Rail and the BBC to the small punter in the interim. So tell that broker of yours — Meinerzhagen? Fellowes? anyway no matter — to get off his fat arse and beatle down to the Exchange before all the Japs get in on the act. Brother Howe has been told to pull a few rabbits out of his hat come budget day, and then they plan to stand back and watch while poor old Gummidge falls to bits, the Boss romping home on the You Know It Makes Sense ticket. A pretty grim prospect, what? Another four years in Colditz for Yours Truly could bring about his premature demise, what with the medicinal intake necessary to see one through the stresses and strains, lack of conviviality with old chummoes, constant exposure to frightful Euros, Wogs, Orientals etc.

A propos Maurice, the whole Picbrick thing has blown up in

his face as I predicted, taking with it a good deal of the Major's diligently accumulated pile. You may remember lunch at the RAC some months ago with the wordless Dane, when they all got carried away by the technicolour brochure. Of course it now turns out that Per Olaffsen, amusing drinking companion though he was, had failed to obtain the patent, and that his original scheme for compressing old copies of the *Daily Telegraph* into handy building blocks bore a striking resemblance to one being marketed in Reading by a subsidiary of General Motors. Writs showered down like autumn leaves on the wretched Maurice, Olaffsen having by this stage done a bunk to South Africa, and there is now talk of the bailiffs moving in and sequestering the stall at the Antique Hypermarket that I always thought belonged to his WVS lady with the smudged lipstick and the pekinese. All this bodes ill, I fear, for our friend's fragile sanity. The medics warned me when they let him out last time that there could be a yo-yo effect in terms of a rapid return to the bin unless any sort of stress was steered well clear of.

Dos vidanya!

DENIS

CHEQUERS

31 December 1982

Dear Bill,
By the time the idle yobbos at British Telecom or whatever they call postmen nowadays have got round to delivering this I imagine you will be back from five nights of invigorating North African sunshine and ready to look the New Year in the face. The nearest I got to a trip abroad was the Red Star Delivery to Northern Ireland and back as part of the Boss's pre-Christmas morale boosting whistlestop tour of the front line. I must say, Bill, the old peace-and-good-will-to-all-men sounded a bit thin when relayed over the Bogside to the accompaniment of exploding cars and the rattle of small-arms fire courtesy the Shamrock League of New York. Saatchis seemed very satisfied with the whole exercise, but personally I felt a bit of a mutt traipsing round the hospitals in the Royal wake with Margaret doing her

Florence Nightingale act for the TV cameras. Quite honestly, Bill, if you'd just been blown up by the IRA and were lying there listening to Radio One on the earphones, would the sight of the Proprietor attended by Yours Truly plus a bevy of brasshats and reptiles all bearing down on you with a lot of damnfool questions like 'How are you feeling now?' do much to promote a swift recovery?

I had a word with poor old Prior while we were being shunted up in the Laundry Lift for Security Reasons, and he said the whole thing was a nightmare. No sooner talk a bit of sense into one side than the other lot of mad bogtrotters start jumping up and down howling for the death of King James the First or some mediaeval Pope, and as for the talk of Margaret 'getting on top of the gunmen' when we've got several battalions of our own constantly inflaming the Left Footers with the Knock on the Door in the Night she might as well whistle for the wind. I always find the old Farmer a trifle hard to understand, but when he tried to outline his schemes for a new Talking Shop I found the glazing over processes began to operate instantly, and I had to pop behind a trolley of soiled laundry for First Aid from the hipflask.

Meanwhile here at Chequers a mood of solemn despair reigns in all quarters. Clearly scenting a free beano, Mark turned up on Christmas Eve, as usual unannounced, and offering as pretext madcap scheme to take over De Lorean Cars with funds made available by Robert Maxwell and some perfume manufacturer in Hong Kong — this inevitably going down like a cup of cold sick with the Boss. As we were trying to get ourselves into the mood for the obligatory attendance at the Midnight Service in Great Missenden I did my best to discourage him from bringing his latest belle along, a rather portly South African number who does PR work for one of those shady Save the Animals organisations the poor D of E falls for from time to time. My advice unheeded we set off four in the back seat, Mr. Wu reluctantly at the wheel. Miss Joleen bubbling noisily into a handkerchief throughout the carols and the pious words, drawing many a black glance from the Heroine of the Falklands.

What put the tin hat on it as far as I was concerned, just as I had folded the specs on the bedside table at 0.15 hrs approx and composed myself for sleep, was the urgent jangling of the telephone at my ear. For a moment it crossed my befuddled mind that the Argies might be storming up the beaches at Folkestone as some kind of tit for tat, but it turned out to be the old crackpot Van der Pump, against whom Margaret will hear not a word, with his Almanack for 1983, as compiled from a recent dream. After half an hour of him crackling away into Margaret's ear about great white sheep roaming the mountains devouring everything in their path I took two pillows and slumped off to sleep on the sofa under the Christmas Tree and woke in agony from pine needle acupuncture.

Better to draw a veil over the more intimate miseries of

Christmas Day. With the distant gleam of an election on the horizon, Margaret had thought up the wheeze of inviting all and sundry in for a fork lunch on Boxing Day, casting by Saatchi and Saatchi. As usual the absolute scrapings of the barrel, rather like some glorified Parky Entertainment: out of work actors, dilapidated peers of the realm, assorted odds and sods crowding round Margaret and roaring their silly heads off at her damnfool jokes, specially composed by the old fool in the dressing gown who is always wheeled in to help out on such occasions.

Meanwhile the telephone has never stopped ringing, the word having got about that the Boss is poised to reshuffle, following the departure of that prize ass Nott, who as I have mentioned before, appears to have burned his fingers quite badly in the Rossminster business. Poor old Willie Whitelaw who had clearly been hitting it fairly hard, came through, his voice choked with sobs, convinced that he was for the chop, all he wanted to do was to retire quietly to the gun room with his Labrador and do the decent thing. I assured him the Proprietor would never hear of it. Ever since Reggie Maudling's liver came out with its hands up the Boss has looked to Willy as the last surviving relic of the Grand Old Days. This also incidentally explains why she insists on keeping on Hailsham, long after human charity would have dictated he be put out to grass at the funny farm. It makes no sense to me, Bill. M. keeps reading the Riot Act when she discovers from the *Telegraph* that another rapist has been let off with a caution, and who does she have in charge of law and order but two old buffers who couldn't keep the peace as night nurses in a geriatric ward.

May the great bird of the New Year let fall its blessings upon your head.

Yours aye,

DENIS

CHATEAU
ST. DENIS

1983
BOTTLED

14 January 1983

Dear Bill,

First things first I wouldn't bother if I were you to go up to town for the Lillywhites sale. I had a quick whizz round en route for the Ritz Bar, and quite frankly, apart from the evil-smelling horde of Arabs hurling athletic supports from hand to hand in the jogging department there didn't seem much of interest to you. I made do with a set of thermal Japanese golf hats in pastel shades, knocked down to practically nothing. Maurice's friend with the funny leg swears by them, and I thought they might enliven the scene at Worplesdon.

You'll forgive me for not giving you prior notice of this present little excursion, but we were all sworn to keep absolutely mum, lest the Argies bomb the airstrip prior to our arrival.

When it was first mooted, in company with assorted brasshats and other Whitehall buffers all drawing her attention to the various hazards attached, I wrung my hands imploring M. to think again. Pym however seemed singularly sanguine urging her to press on and fulfil her destiny. (I wonder why?)

Needless to say the Boss had her way, but agreed to throw sand in the eyes of the reptiles with talk of a cancellation, and limit the operation to an Ulster-style 'inner and outer'. I thought it only right and proper to motor the old girl out to Brize Norton and flutter my hanky from the waving base, telling her as she studied her red boxes in the passenger seat of my deep regrets that I couldn't come along and enjoy all the fun. After she said 'But you *are* coming, Denis' for the third time the penny finally dropped and I began to feel very queasy indeed. Not only was I unsuitably accoutred for the Antarctic, but I had several dates lined up on the old While the Cat's away the Mice will Play syndrome, and therefore had to ring round from the only available telephone in the Nissen Hut at the drome. All slightly embarrassing.

Next thing I know it's up a little ladder into the boneshaker, chocks away, and eyes down for seven hours hardarse non-stop to Ascension. The worst thing about it, Bill, was that not being forewarned I was deprived even of the solace of my little flask which I always pack for these occasions. I tried to light a gasper, but it was immediately knocked out of my hand by some Air Commodore, roaring above the din of the engines that I must be mad, didn't I realise I was sitting on forty thousand gallons of high octane fuel? You can imagine my mental state when we tottered out at Ascension, a godforsaken spot if ever I saw one (or so I thought until we reached the Falklands). My hopes of a quick dash to the Duty Free were immediately put paid to as we were frog-marched up another ladder into an even older biplane, and off for another thirteen hours of unmitigated hell, teeth chattering with the vibration, as we nose-dived towards the sea to take on fuel from a stalling nuclear bomber, Margaret unruffled by it all still deep in her boxes and writing her Christmas thank-you letters.

Finally I was awakened from a nightmarish doze and hustled out into the blizzard to be met by that awful little slug Hunt, who used to be the Governor, and a small crowd of blue-nosed Sheepshaggers, the surrounding view bringing back unhappy memories of our grisly holidays with Lord Pucefeatures on the Isle of Muck. M. strides in, a dreadful gleam in her eye, and begins to press the flesh, a half-witted photographer from the local roneoed news-sheet The Shaggers' Weekly falling about in the background popping off his flashbulbs.

I think we had shaken hands with the entire population of the benighted settlement before the wretched Hunt's better half brightly announced that she had put the kettle on. We were then, if you are still with me, invited to climb into a ridiculous London taxi, and driven off through the minefield to Mon Repos, locally known as Dunshaggin where we are greeted by a smouldering peat fire, tea and rock buns arranged on tasteful doylies. Hunt, catching the light of insanity in my eye, mutters that if I like to accompany him upstairs, he has something that might interest me. This proved to be a captured pair of underpants once belonging to General Menendez, now mounted by his good lady in a pokerwork frame.

Controlling my emotions, I suggested a stroll to stretch the legs after our long ordeal. Resisting the fool Hunt's suggestion of a trek up Mount Tumbledown, I reached the Goose six minutes later, only to find the bar crammed with inebriate reptiles, brasshats, airline stewards and one or two cross-eyed Sheepshaggers of idiotic mien sitting in a corner reminiscing gloomily about the good old days under the Argies when at least they could get a drink.

As I write our time of departure is still very much under wraps, Margaret having toddled off to a small thanksgiving service at the local tin tabernacle and showing every desire to stay on indefinitely. At least, thanks to Mine Host, Bill Voletrouser, I am not well prepared for the return trip, a miniature in every pocket and a fire extinguisher full of the amber fluid for discreet in-flight refuelling.

Yours in transit

DENIS

10 Downing Street
Whitehall

28 January 1983

Dear Bill,

I'm sorry I had to miss Podmore's seventieth birthday celebrations but I was still pretty flaked out with Shag Lag. I had in fact to be brought back from Brize Norton on a stretcher, rigor having set in somewhere over Ascension, and Dr O'Gooley who was summoned round by the Boss diagnosed severe stress complicated by dehydration. I then swallowed a handful of brown bombers, washed down with your generous two-litre bottle of Bells with the handle on the side and was unconsious for seventy two hours.

I woke up fresh as a daisy to find that Wonderwoman had meanwhile zapped the Bank of England, bollocked the Usurers, and propped up the pound with one hand while blaming it all on that seedy little man with the pot belly and the quiff, Peter Shore, who had taken advantage of her absence to spread panic and despondency.

Our lot are tremendously cock a hoop about the Report on the Falklands. I don't know if I've mentioned him, but Margaret has this dogsbody called Gow, a bald, chubby, brown-tongued little fellow from somewhere on the South Coast, what the Yanks call a gopher, i.e. gopher this, gopher that, usually M's handbag. Anyway this prancing pixie was duly dispatched to the newsagents to bring back an armful on the morning after Franks hit the stands: surprise surprise Maggie Not To Blame, P. Carrington perfectly nice little man and only doing his best, poor old Nott much maligned – you may see that Lazards have taken him on board at forty grand a year, so much for the back to the daffodil farm routine, what? – F.O. going through all the necessary motions to the best of their ability.

Implausible as all this might seem it came as no surprise to me. Franks, you may not know, is One of Them, having done time as Our Man in Washington before bumbling off to spend his twilight years being Professor Branestawm among the dreaming

172

spires. It was hardly to be expected therefore that this old boffin would name the Guilty Men, i.e. the F.O., a nest of every conceivable variety of pinko, queer, Trot and deviant known to medical science, each one of them ready at the drop of a nicker to sell us down the river to any foreign swine that hoves into view, be it Galtieri, Andropov or Chu Chin Chow.

Whatever reservations I may have had however were as naught to the consternation at Smellysocks House. Worzel and his cohorts, who have been going through a baddish patch these last few years, had been pinning their hopes on Comrade Franks doling out a goodly quota of mud to fling at the Boss. As dawn broke on publication day they were therefore to be seen eagerly queuing outside the Stationery Office, clutching in their sweaty palms the seventeen pounds fifty necessary to secure a copy. Holborn then crowded with malodorous men in dirty raincoats hastily thumbing their way to page 506 where His Lordship finally concludes 'I therefore lay the blame entirely on the Argies.' Clatter of dentures on the pavement, collapse of elderly parties. How now to spin out four-day emergency debate demanded by Worzel in first flush of excitement?

Talking of derelicts, who should I see weaving his way along Whitehall the other morning at a very unsocial hour but M. Picarda, en route for a Mass Rally of the Faithful at Temperance Hall to relaunch the Alliance, which as you may not have noticed has been aground for some months. As I told him they could hardly have chosen a worse moment with the Boss rapidly climbing back into the charts following her ENSA tour of the Minefields. How hiring the Temperance Hall and wheeling out Ol' Foureyes is going to help their cause I have no idea. Maurice himself seems to have a shrewder grasp of how to woo Johnny Public. He tells me he has booked an upstairs room at a pub in Sevenoaks to revive his own local prospects, and has already engaged the services of two strippers. His son by his first marriage has formed a pop group and threatens to participate. I agree it sounds absolutely grisly but I did promise to show my face, weather permitting, and throw a bread roll or two. Any chance of your being let off the leash?

Yours in anticipation,

DENIS

10 Downing Street
Whitehall

25 February 1983

Dear Bill,

By the time this reaches you the fartarsing-about down in Bermondsey will be over, and in any case the result will in no way dent the rising line of Margaret's graph, which seems set fair to go off the top of the board with an all-Tory House of Commons as soon as she blows the necessary whistle. Boris says it'll be June according to the Kremlin, but they don't always know. The thinking, according to him is that the inflation will be down to four per cent by the summer, and before it roars off into double figures again in the autumn they can go to the hustings with a lot of flashy talk on the lines of look what we've done. In fact, as you and I know perfectly well, it's sod all to do with M's mob and is fixed by a lot of greasy little money-lenders over in Wall Street, but obviously nobody can say that in public.

Not surprisingly, spirits over at Smellysocks House have hit an all-time low, and the horny-handed sons of toil are beginning, albeit slow-wittedly, to move towards the idea of an Ides of March scenario for Worzelius Tribune of the Plebs. Picture the scene, Bill, as the poor old buffer shuffles down to the Senate, his ill-fitting toga flapping in the breeze. Enter R. and L. assorted malodorous conspirators, Wedgius Lunaticus in the van, Healius of the interwoven eyebrows, Tatchellus Arsebandicus in minitoga bringing up the rear. Then, as the white-haired loon paused to expectorate across the Forum the H of C cutlery flashes in the air, and the poor old bibliophile slips with scarce a groan to the garbage-littered pavement. This, I should say, is the one thing our lot dread like poison, for fear of what may follow after, though quite frankly, Bill, the idea of that pot-bellied scruff Shore, let alone Old Swiveleyes Benn marshalling a force to be reckoned with seems to me fairly remote.

Will you tell Daphne I can't give away the prizes at her Disabled Jockeys Ball, as I promised Squiffy's Sawbones friend in the North I'd slip into the bib and tucker and offer myself for target practice to the Hibernian bread roll hurlers at Carnoustie, who have very generously volunteered to make me an Honorary Member of their club, free set of Jap irons and a couple of crates of Glen Kamikaze thrown in.

Yours in haste,

DENIS

10 Downing Street
Whitehall

11 March 1983

Dear Bill,

Thank you for ringing me up to tell me I was on the telly the other evening. By the time I got to the screen, inevitably, it was all over, but Boris seemed very amused and toasted my driving ability in his mother's 1982 plum vodka. Trust the reptiles to try and make me look a BF, and succeed by all accounts.

Ever since the Metro launch in Birmingham a couple of years back, the Boss has had a soft spot for the shower up at British Leyland, and despite my continued harping on what happened to poor Maurice Picarda when the steering wheel of his Metro came away in his hands as he was going the wrong way down the M4 after that Masonic shindig at Chippenham, she continues to lend her name to promoting their ramshackle assemblages of cheap scrap-iron. The latest British-built number, indistinguishable as far as I could tell from any of the little Jap runabouts the Major's friend sells down at Tunbridge Wells at half the price, was brought to the door by their PR man, an oily little greaser by the name of Smythe-Pemberton, who claimed to be a friend of Squiffy's. All over the Proprietor with his sales talk, reclining ashtrays, digital rear wipers, swivelling sidelights etc., immediate delivery six months to a year. Boss then stage-managed out onto the doorstep, all aglow with wonder at latest triumph of British knowhow – I'm told the engine, by the by, is eighty-five per cent built in Taiwan – reptiles seven deep on the pavement, obediently recording the event with popping flashbulbs, whirr of cameras, etc. M. jumps in, poses with arm upraised in royal wave, and purrs effortlessly away from kerb for one minute thirty-second test drive. Wonderful, marvellous, now it's your turn Denis.

As it was by now half-past ten in the morning, I had taken a couple of large ones on board, and strode forward to play my part in the Birth of the Boom. Slammed door, turned key in ignition, foot down, and off we shot. As the reptiles scattered, a woman apparently sitting in the back seat told me to fasten my seatbelt. I turned round, Bill, and would you believe it? Not a soul in sight. Gave me a pretty nasty turn, I don't mind telling you. Brakes on, beads of sweat forming on the forehead, is this a return of the old trouble, pink spiders up the wall etc? Bring vehicle to shaky stop alongside the kerb, narrowly missing Smythe-Pemberton's Lamborghini, very badly parked incidentally, whatever they may have said, and eject from vehicle to cries of 'Good old Denis!' and guffaws of laughter from the various flag-waving yobbos who hang about in Downing Street with nothing better to do.

Smythe-Pemberton explained later that all these kamikaze jobs are fitted with an I-speak-your-Weight device that reminds you to empty the ashtrays and so forth as a sales gimmick. I said it seemed a damn fool idea to me and could cause a lot of accidents.

What of Worzelius, you may ask? Ides of March scenario, like everything else organised by Smelly-socks House, an absolute cock-up. Worzelius alert-ed to the raised daggers by the reptiles, leaving the conspirators to resheathe the knives and forks and explain on TV how loyal they were to the old party, heaven forfend that any of his white hairs should be harmed etc. The day of reckoning in other words now postponed till after Darlington, much to the relief, I should say, of our side, who had been dreading the spectre of an Opposition with Koalaface in charge.

I gather Maurice P. is on something of a high following the bum's rush administered to young Tatchell by the good burghers of Bermondsey. The Sevenoaks SDP immediately doubled their membership to eight, and Picarda finished up in the cells after overdoing the victory celebrations and writing off the garage. Did the Major ring you about Venice? Seemed a damn stupid idea to me. Squiffy was very scornful. Apparently they had a reps' conference there in November, and those who didn't go down with Montezuma's revenge walked out of the hotel after dinner and fell in the lake.

Do give us a bell if you have any better ideas. This time ideally not after one a.m.

Hasta la vista.

DENIS

10 Downing Street
Whitehall

25 March 1983

Dear Bill,
I couldn't agree with you more about friend Howe's abysmal performance with the tattered red box. The reptiles did their best

176

to make it look as though all of us on over fifty thou were going to clean up, but I've done my sums and what with the 25p on my morning bottle of the hard stuff, fags up yet again, and 4p extra on juice for the Roller, I should say we were roughly speaking back where we started from, i.e. despite little Howe's giddy trigonometry, $x = 0$.

This, from where I sit, is not the stuff to give the troops on the eve of the great battle with Worzelius, whensoever M. in her infinite wisdom decides to fire the first cannonade. In any case the idea of that crepe-soled little creep, Brer Howe, the so-called Mogadon Man, giving us the Gentlemen of England Now In Bed speech from Henry the Fifth, would seem to smack of brainstorms in the casting department.

Head above the clouds, however, the Boss remains unperturbed. With that mule-like obstinacy I have come to know in private life for over a quarter of a century now, her new wheeze is to promote the hoary old Mastermind MacGregor to take over the pits, give little Scargill's balls a tweak, block up all the coalmines, and then get to work on dismantling British Rail. Margaret has always preferred a gas fire and has never been on a train in her life unless forced to do so. As for that little greaser Parker, she can't wait to have him broken up for scrap. This is what she calls long term strategy, though if you ask me they'll get poor little Howe pissed in the summer and wheel him out with the bribes prior to going for gold in October.

Sorry to miss you at the Worshipful Company of Spoonbenders. I would have given a lot to see the Major being given the bum's rush by the Security Wallahs. Full marks to him for pulling the Lord Mayor's head through his hat before they got to him.

Yours aye,

DENIS

10 Downing Street
Whitehall

22 April 1983

Dear Bill,

Re your coloured brochure of the Algarve 15 days half-board at the Mountbatten Motel for £143.75 including VAT for the first half of June. It all looks very enticing, I agree, and I am told by Whitelaw that the Course is a sheer delight to play on, very obliging caddies, and a nice little Englishwoman, Mrs Flack, a merry red-headed widow from Morecambe, who runs the bar.

However, as you may have gathered from the DT, there has been quite a lot of talk about M. going to the Polls at that juncture, and I thought it prudent to check with Head Office before putting down the deposit. The Boss had her paperknife out, dealing with her fan-mail, and seemed in an agreeable enough mood, so I broached the vital Q. Sorry to interrupt and so forth, but any chance of a 36-hour pass come raging June? No reply. Realise it's still some time off, but in my line of business one has to plan ahead. Crippling look, ugly stabbing movement with paperknife. Feel I am now commanding her full attention, press on. Chap needs to get away from time to time, recharge the batteries, change of air, been rather on top of each other in recent months etc. M.'s eyes assume gimlet-like intensity.

I was about to come to the point and produce my Dataday, when blow me, with scarce a tap at the door, in blows little Pym. Ever since he slipped into the hastily abandoned boots of Peter C., our bespectacled friend has had the crushed and doleful mien one would expect of an ageing pugdog kept on a v. tight leash and never allowed out of its kennel except for walkies once a week. Besides which, spending time with the poofs and closet weirdos down at the Foreign Office have never done wonders for any normal cove's morale, witness the sad decline of his predecessor the noble peer, now, I am told, working as office boy for a firm of usurers in the City.

It transpires that Puggy P. has come hotfoot from Amman, where he has been closeted with the little bald bloke who went to Harrow some time before Mark and now runs Jordan. Old Hopalong, when not threatening to bombard the Russkies with Death Rays from Outer Space, had cooked up some scheme to bring peace to the troubled West Bank, which had predictably fallen through, as Begin is busily occupied with building skyscrapers and Kosher Meatball Stands on every vacant lot remaining, offering cut-price mortgages to the Chosen Few through their equivalent of the Nationwide, and is about as likely to hand it back to the Arabs as Hopalong is to hand Manhattan back to the Indians. Nonetheless at his mistress's whistle, Bonzo Pym scampered off, convinced in his doggy mind that where Hopalong had failed he would succeed. Hence his gloomy expression as he now stood, hands behind his back, under the chilling gaze.

Having delivered his tidings and taken his medicine, Pym shuffled out, closing the door, leaving me to gather up the threads of my enquiry. What about it? A blank stare. Would Margaret care for a drink? Was I aware of the time? Very well, would she mind if I had one? A predictable pattern of response: she had ceased to mind years ago, if that was the way I wished to destroy what was left of my brain then I was at liberty to do so. You probably know the form; we all do. Emboldened, I returned to the fray. What price a June holiday? Could she acquaint me with her electoral intentions one way or the other as I was a busy man?

At this the floodgates opened, and I was borne from the room on a tide of invective, still no wiser as I sit mournfully stabbing the Olivetti here in my little den.

As far as I can gather from Boris it all now hangs on Van der Pump, the South African seer. Her own inclination is to soldier on until the Spring, thus showing that she means business and is not one to heed the siren voices of Mori and Nop. However, should the old sage, on looking into the seaweed and consulting his stockbroker, come to the conclusion that a Bandit Raid on the electorate in June is the will of the Gods, then Bandit Raid it will be. I realise that none of this helps you much with old Mr Vidler at the travel agent's, but I'm afraid it's the best I can do.

Should the balloon go up, the main worry on our side is that Worzelius will raise the tasteless topic of unemployment. Everyone has therefore been told to dream up ideas, under the baton of little Bertie Mount, the one-man Think Tank, and very entertaining some of them have been. The only one that has got off the ground so far is a damnfool scheme from Tarzan to recruit a kind of Heseltine Youth, equipping a select number of school leavers with old 303's, paying them half a crown a week, and marching them up and down for twelve months, with the option they can bugger off whenever they feel like it. I said why not bring back National Service and what a difference it would have made to young Mark but I got my head bitten off again, and retired hurt.

Pip pip,

DENIS

10 Downing Street
Whitehall

6 May 1983

Dear Bill,
You really must forgive me for blowing my top on the phone last night, but if I haven't found out about my availability for the Algarve trip it isn't for want of trying. On sober reflection I think your best plan is to book the other ticket in the name of Smith, and then if the worst comes to the worst I'm sure Maurice P will take my place. You may not fancy two weeks sharing a Portuguese chalet, albeit with patio, with the poor old soak, but it would do him good to get away from this new home computer nonsense. I don't know if you've been down there recently, but he has somehow or other raised a loan to buy a warehouse full of obsolete word processors in Milton Keynes, and is currently working with

an unemployed Jap waiter trying to decipher the assembly instructions.

It's not often, as you know, Bill, that I lose my rag with the old lady, having learned the consequences of such folly at an early stage in our ongoing matrimonial experience. Last evening, though, some moments before your reverse charge call to Downing Street, I took the opportunity to broach once again in the most tactful and diplomatic terms the question of the electoral timetable. M. was doing her red boxes over supper, including Whitelaw's latest cock-eyed scheme for channelling 57 Varieties of colour TV into every chicken coop in the land – Memo: possibly an opening here for Maurice when Picatel bites the dust – and after a few preparatory coughs and a refill of the nosebag, I produced my diary, and let fly on the following lines: 'Ahem, ahem, Margaret. Excuse me for distracting you from weightier matters, but I wonder if we could have a word?' The Boss, tearing up Whitelaw's proposals: 'What is it now?' Self: 'Forward planning. It is not solely the question of my Portuguese arrangements, as you appear to think: a whole range of important engagements are hanging fire as a result of the uncertainty. Look at this. "Mr Terry Wogan on behalf of the Royal Order of Sewage Rats requests me to take the chair at a fund-raising It's A Knockout Evening in aid of mentally-handicapped Rugger Referees, on June 23rd 1983." And here's another. "The Grand Barker of the Worshipful Company of Water Buffaloes requests the company of Mr D. Thatcher to propose the Loyal Toast at the Essoldo Ealing on June 15th. RSVP." "Mr Danny La Rue and Friends request the pleasure of Mr Denis Thatcher at a Celebrity Golf Tournament at Troon on July 1st. All proceeds to The Queen Mother's Fund for Indigent Acrobats" . . .'

Three strong cards, I think you must agree, and quite enough I would have said to force the old girl to show her hand. I laid them on the table in front of her and sat back, explaining in a firm tone that it was quite impossible to live one's life without being able to give a firm answer to these very important people. Somewhat to my chagrin, I saw that Margaret was now forking M & S lasagne into her mouth while simultaneously wielding the blue pencil on other proposals from Cabinet.

At this point, for the first time in seventeen years, my reserve gave way, and I rose to my feet, overturning a chair, and struck the table a painful blow with my fist. Was it too much to ask that my feelings should be taken into consideration? At some time in the next year, no doubt to be determined by that pompous fathead Van der Pump and a couple of oily wops from Denmark Street, I would be expected to sacrifice three weeks to traipse round the country by fast car and helicopter, crammed in with the evil-smelling little Gow and smartyboots Bertie Mount, thrown out to press the flesh of thousands of malodorous proles, a permanent grin making my face ache, an object of uproarious derision to the reptiles of Fleet Street all waiting for me to put my foot in it, listening to the same fatuous platitudes night after night, clapping like a demented monkey at the ghastly jokes of Sir Custardface, snorts snatched from my hand, digestion ruined, blistered mitts, sore feet, and all I would have to look forward to at the end of it another four years of purgatory, locked in this hell-hole, when we could be living in quite retirement at Lamberhurst like everyone else.

I was still in full flood when I became aware that Margaret was telephoning Dr O'Gooley on the scrambler, informing him in injured tones that I was having one of my turns, after which she left the room, locking the door behind her. The medic, I must say, could not have been more understanding (when he turned up two hours later) and told me in confidence that he often had the same sort of trouble with Mrs O'G. Boris, who is also very supportive on these occasions, produced a magnum of some unspeakably vile Cuban whisky, and we spent a pleasant enough evening watching a smutty video confiscated by Whitelaw in one of his lightning swoops on Huddersfield.

Arrivederci antiquo amigo mio,

Yours aye,

DENIS

10 Downing Street
Whitehall

20 May 1983

Dear Bill,

Well, the whistle has finally blown, as you may have gathered from the newspapers. So much for Portugal, and I hope you will enjoy your fortnight in the sun with Maurice. Do make sure he takes his Antabuse. I know from experience the only way to do it is to actually see him swallowing them, and don't let them substitute Aspro like poor Squiffy's mother-in-law used to do towards the end. The only thing he's not allowed to have is cheese or asparagus.

They finally got the old girl over the sticks by cornering her at Chequers. M. until that point, as you know, had been hopping round like a parrot telling everyone she would not be pushed about, and the nerves of the Cabinet were as much in tatters as mine. Whitelaw in particular seemed in danger of apoplexy, and poor old Hailsham who doesn't know where he is half the time anyway was obviously heading for the funny farm.

Enter at this juncture the strong men, to wit Alberto and Luigi from the advertising agency, armed with all manner of computer printouts, little graphs, market research bulletins and assorted sales guff. According to the Corsican Brothers (absolute baloney as it turned out) Worzel was on the up and up, a discernible trend with A, B and C consumers, liable to peak into Margaret's share of the market by late August. This could produce a downturn in sales figures for the month of October in image-related selling profile, spelling doom for an Autumn scenario. You remember the way those buggers at Burmah Oil used to carry on at the sales conference. What were they called – Carfax and Malpractice? I never believed a word of it, and I think they are now working for Breakfast Television. Anyway you could apparently see, according to Boris – I was upstairs at the time unpacking my weekend iron rations from Hedges and Butler – that M's eyes were clouding over with self-doubt. Here she was, her whole act as far as the plebs is concerned based on unflappability, determination to see the job through, no time for siren voices etc, how was it going to look if she was seen to be behaving like a human being, snatching at the first straw?

The meeting before lunch broke up in a mood of quiet desperation, Howe and Pym gnawing their nails down to the knuckle, both taking refuge in my little hideaway under the roof and polishing off a goodly proportion of my emergency supplies before being summoned with shrill tones to go down for their packed lunch supplied by THF in the Conference Room. Imagine their surprise, after three quarters of an hour trying to unpick the clingfoil and extract the khaki-coloured chicken leg, when the Proprietor swept in, all smiles and announced that after long and careful consideration she had decided to go on the TV and explain to the nation how imperative it was to bring an end to all this uncertainty. Pretty rich, I think you will agree, Bill, after she's spent the last two months refusing to give a straight answer to any question on the topic.

What had happened in the interim, you may ask? I will tell you. At five past one I took a call from an obviously excited Van der Pump, the South African explorer wallah who guides the nation's destinies from behind the throne. Could he speak to Mrs Thatcher at once as he had urgent information to impart. Knowing that M. has such a soft spot for this oddball, I took the liberty of listening in on the extension as she came to the phone.

The old boy was plainly on a terrific high, enunciating his words with a frenzied precision. He had been up in his observatory all night, gazing into the heavens, all the wonders of the starry sky spread out before him. Margaret at this point told him to get on with it, much to my relief, as I had left my snort in the other room. He would come to the point at once, he said. A magnificent comet trailing a great banner of light across the firmament was approaching the earth at a speed of three million miles an hour and would be clearly visible with the naked eye in a night or two's time, weather conditions permitting. 'What does it portend, Prime Minister, you may ask.' 'I do ask,' came the somewhat impatient rejoinder. 'Victory,' breathed the sage in a voice fraught with strange significance. 'For those born under the sign of Libra this is an important week with regard to a vital business decision. Colleagues' advice should be heeded. With new heavenly movements affecting your cusp, now is the time to end uncertainties and tell your nearest and dearest of your decision. Your love-partner will be relieved, as he or she will be able to make plans at last in the realm of leisure activities.' 'You can say that again,' I unwisely expostulated, only bringing down on myself a torrent of abuse from M. for eavesdropping and a command to hang up at once.

What worries me, Bill, at least the way things look at the moment, is that my worst fears about another four years of misery cooped up in purdah in a back room at Downing Street seem all too justified. With a two hundred seat majority, can you imagine what she'll be like? You don't think you could have a word with your Grand Master to pass the word round among the brethren that a vote for Labour might be in order, just to balance things out a bit? Otherwise I can see myself following old Hailsham into the Priory.

Pip, pip,

DENIS

10 Downing Street
Whitehall

3 June 1983

Dear Bill,
Only another week to go before polling day, thank God. My hand is already calloused and misshapen from pressing the proletarian flesh and Dr O'Gooley had to pop in the other day to give me an anti-lockjaw inejction after three weeks of solid grinning. Then last night I woke up shouting 'Hear Hear' in response to Margaret's snores, which will give you some idea of how far things have gone. I wish I could be more sanguine about the future, but it does now look as if I must face the prospect of another four to give years incarcerated in Colditz SW1. Picturing you and Maurice hot-footing it over the sprinklered sward of the Algarve en route to Mrs Flack's beachside Smugglers' Bar only serves to twist the knife in the wound.

Personally, I blame Worzel for all this. The poor old fool's always been hopelessly out of his depth in that tank of piranha fish and you can tell from the expression on his face that they've got to him. Immediately the charge was sounded half of his Red Lancers turned on one another, pigsticking away as if there was no tomorrow, while Uncle Jim Callaghan sounded his own private tally-ho shortly afterwards to distract the remaining ditherers from the battle. All that remains now is for that old twister Wilson to crawl out from under his stone and inject his lethal venom into Worzel's unprotected hinder parts, and they'll have to blow up for a walk-over. When you've seen our lot at close quarters, particularly that fat ass Howe, little Bertie Mount beavering away with his Roget's Thesaurus trying to think of something new for M. to say, Sir Custardface on call with his dressing gown and gag book, and Gow fartarsing about the place, you'd think anyone with a grain of intelligence could blow them off the map.

As it is the projected majority gets bigger every day with all the grave implications that entails for the Boss's mental equilibrium. It was plainly this thought that occurred to Brother Pym when he blurted out on TV that the last thing he wanted was a landslide. Of course he was immediately summoned round to explain himself to the Supreme Commander. It is quite pathetic to see these men, Bill, crumbling before one's eyes under the impact of the deadly gamma rays. Afterwards little Pym got very tight with some reptile and told him he wasn't budging from the FO whatever happened, but I think if truth be told he's already reconciled to the heave-ho come the July purge and has been seen scanning the Occupations Vacant column in the *Farmers' Weekly*.

Old Oystereyes is in much the same boat, and has, alas, been looking pretty deep into the glass in a forlorn attempt to muffle the pain. Fatty Prior, poor old sod, remains in exile in the Bogs, and if he is waiting for a recall I fear he may wait in vain. The Monk is keeping very quiet with the help of a big bottle of green pills which he stores in his briefcase and shovels into his mouth every ten minutes in generous quantities.

The only good thing to come out of the whole farrago so far is that the fat cat Jenkins has quite clearly thrown in the towel as far as a career in politics is concerned. I always told Maurice they made a great mistake when they put him in charge, and I bet little Steel is absolutely livid: being seen about with the old fool must have cost him ninety-nine per cent of any seats he hoped to win. Apropos, I'd be very interested to know if the voters of Sevenoaks have realised that their Social Democratic candidate, Maurice Picarda Esq, has hopped it to Portugal, taking with him, I gather, a large proportion of the campaign funds. How much will he give me, I wonder, for not ringing up the Sevenoaks Chronicle and spilling the beans? I gather quite a lot of the SDP folk have deemed it prudent to go abroad till the whole thing blows over.

I hope you can read this, despite the odd typing error, but I am writing in the back of the Saatchimobile haring up the M1 to some derelict marginal in the North West. The Corsican Brothers are sucking spaghetti through their moustaches at the other end of the table, and friend Gow is on his back with a screwdriver trying to mend Margaret's Hopalong Teleprompter which went on the blink at the last whistlestop and caused a good deal of Proprietorial gnashing of teeth. Little Cecil Parkinson, unruffled as ever, is chatting up the Boss with a look of doglike devotion in his eyes, and giving me a frosty glare every time I have recourse to my flask, as much as to say how could a man married to this paragon possibly be in need of any other solace or stimulant. Little does he know.

Roll on death,

DENIS

10 Downing Street
Whitehall

17 June 1983

Dear Bill,

Well, that's it! What a ballcrushing disaster! In all my wildest nightmares I never visualised it being quite as bad as this. Another five years of guaranteed hard labour as a tailor's dummy being wheeled on to grin to order every time the Boss plays host to the likes of Hopalong, Big Chief Coon or Ahmed ben Wog. The trouble is I've seen them already, and if the novelty was ever in danger of wearing on, it's certainly worn off now.

One of the reptiles the other day, while we were being shuttled from A to Z, told me en passant that Jackie Kennedy negotiated a pretty fat retainer for staying on in the supporting role. I did think of approaching Top Management with a strike ultimatum, proposing a minimum three months in six off the leash, all expenses paid and a company flat in sunny parts, but the Boss is still in overdrive after Friday morning's results and shows no sign of shifting into a lower gear.

Boris, to whom I confided my post-election thoughts of self-destruction, said I should look at it more positively. It was tempting to sit on the sidelines, large tincture in hand and carp at the passing show, encouraging a mood of Scandinavian despondency. Far better to plunge in while I was still active, and play a more decisive role in the affairs of state.

It may have been his silver tongue or possibly the effects of a second crate of his widowed mother's plum vodka, but the prospect began to seem a great deal rosier. I mean quite honestly, Bill, with all the power in the country concentrated in the hands of wets and waverers like Norman Tebbit, what hope of any real upturn? Now, surely – this is what Boris said – we have the chance to crack down on troublemakers, pack up the railways and other drains on the motorist's pocket, remove tax from heavy spirits, hand over the NHS to BUPA, introduce imprisonment without trial for all shop stewards, bring back the black cap and other long overdue middle-of-the-road reforms. Rather late at night admittedly, I noted down a few of these ideas on a paper doily and stuffed them under the door of little Bertie Mount, Margaret's one-man think-tank. And as you will see from the reshuffled Cabinet, some of my notions are beginning to trickle through, and I have reason to hope that as time goes on I shall be able to get my hand more firmly on the tiller.

I still maintain we could have been out from under it altogether and sipping the pina colada chez Mother Flack beneath the thatched parasols of the Algarve, had it not been for that frightful old stumblebum Worzel Gummidge and his entourage of hopeless clowns and kamikaze wallahs. By the end of it even Koalafeatures lost his marbles altogether, and was throwing away votes like confetti. I've no idea who they'll find now to preside over the salvage operations on the Red Titanic, but I understand the leading contenders are that red-haired Welsh windbag called Pillock and some wheezing fat cat from Birmingham who contributes would-be humorous pieces to Punch. I can't understand why they don't just pack their bags and bugger off back to Moscow.

There were one or two happier moments on Thursday night I must confess, eg Benn walking the plank, ditto Benn junior. Margaret only really showed her teeth when the woman with the messy hair came unstuck at Crosby. I was also personally very gratified to see a frightful little greaser called Sprat or Sproat bite the dust: he's tried to oil up to me at the Club once or twice affecting an interest in golf, but it was perfectly clear he didn't know a mashie from a swizzle stick. Maurice, I see, managed to scrape in just ahead of the National Front despite his absence on foreign soil, and incidentally thank you very much for your postcard: I couldn't decipher the old boy's remarks but I liked the photograph of the lady holding her hat on and the bloke lurking in the shadows with a snorkel.

The musical chairs in the Cabinet began on Friday morning. Poor little Pym trotted round to the Headmistress's study soon after breakfast and was told it was to be six of the best and immediate expulsion for dumb insolence. Old Oystereyes blubbed a lot, put an arm round the boy's shoulders and pleaded for his chum in a very pathetic way. The Boss however remained unmoved, giving them both the gamma ray treatment. Pym got five minutes to pack his tuck box before being driven to the station. Oystereyes himself has been kicked upstairs and given an

Hereditary Peerage. I said to Margaret what was the point of this as his only male relative is a bus driver living in Scunthorpe but she only gave me a frosty smile. I suppose she must be allowed her little joke. Talking of jokes old Hailsham will not after all be heading for the funny farm, but is to be kept on for the sake of the tourists. Lawson and Brittan, those two frightful little creeps who Margaret has taken such a shine to, have both been promoted for services to the brown-tongue industry. But more of them later.

So there we are. I don't know whether you've ever made a will, but for some reason or other the thought had never occurred to me until last Friday morning. Furniss has a printed form you can fill in, costing 30p, and I said I didn't mind what he put as long as Mark didn't get his grubby little hands on any of it and there was some provision for scattering my ashes in the bunker opposite the Club House at Worplesdon. Furniss said there wasn't a space on the form for that kind of thing. Could I leave it to you to make the arrangements when the Reaper comes to call? On a more serious note, M. owes me a favour if nothing more after my loyal laughter and rigid lips-sealed policy vis-a-vis the reptiles. What price three weeks in Gib before the FO wooftahs hand it back on a plate to King Coca Cola?

Adios,

DENIS

10 Downing Street
Whitehall

15 July 1983

Dear Bill,

As you see, I'm back from my little hol, not too much the worse for wear and already wishing I wasn't. Whoever it was, though, who told you that there was some lovely golf to be had in Malta is talking through his arse. Either that or he meant somewhere else. The place is a rock-strewn dump inhabited by swarthy degenerates, Spanish waiters and sex fiends on the run from Interpol. I tried to look up Purvis, who as you remember retired there with his pile of chips in the early sixties, but according to the woman living in the house, he was driven out some years ago by this little commie Dom Molotoff, who now runs the place. You probably remember his daughter threw a sack of donkey droppings into the House of Commons some while ago; probably the only decent thing any member of that family has ever done.

I got back to find Margaret in no way improved, and chuckling over the news that poor little Steel can't stand the pace and is sodding off back to bonnie Scotland to collapse in a deep armchair for the summer. The Boss was very amused when one of her brown-tongued brigade on the back benches pointed out that since June 9th Worzel and Woy had both jacked it in, Kinnock had lost the power of speech, and now little Steel has had a nervous breakdown.

One unhappy consequence of the recent musical chairs is that old Howe alias Mr Mogadon, but a very quiet neighbour given to padding cautiously about in his brothel creepers accompanied by a mildly talkative wife droning away in the background, has now been replaced next door at Number Eleven by Mr Nicely Nicely Lawson. According to Frognall, who lost a packet on John Bloom with the washing machines, Lawson used to be some kind of share spiv for the *Sunday Telegraph*, offering the punters likely tips on the City Page. I gather his wife ran off with some randy egg-head from Oxford, for which I must say I can't entirely blame her. He is now encumbered with a librarian woman and presides, if that is the word for it, over an unruly family, definitely the non-nuclear variety, hence the thump of pop records mingled with the squalling of babies hourly audible through the wall.

I can't quite fathom what the Boss sees in him myself. We had them both round for a snort a couple of evenings ago, a social occasion that could, I must say, have gone more smoothly. Mrs L rather a nervous little body, sat primly to attention, listening to Margaret banging on about the future of the Falklands, nodding tentatively every ten minutes as if afraid she was going to bite her, and Lawson himself got very man to man with Yours Truly, shovelling salted peanuts into his mouth and saying 'I think Denis, that you and I have at least one recreation in common, and it isn't golf, eh?' I couldn't see what he was driving at. Then he winked, nodded at the bottle, and held out his glass, which I refilled, still very mystified. It was only after he'd gone, that Boris suggested he was probably suggesting I was a piss-artist. Cheeky little bugger.

Anyway, he seems to have got off to a good start, announcing without so much as turning a hair that we weren't on the road to recovery after all, but that on the contrary we were up the familiar creek fabled in song and story in a barbed wire canoe sans paddle, and that the axe must therefore fall on all the various sacred cows paraded out at the election. I gather Ginger Jesus, which is what old Hailsham calls Heseltine, is absolutely livid as only the day before he'd announced the biggest-ever shopping spree for the Brasshats, including a new Tumbledown International Airport for the Falklands, devised by some bright spark as an inducement to the Sheepshaggers to pack their bags and whiz away to healthier climes. Personally I don't think they're clever enough for that, and when they're all pulling down a million and a half per man, woman and sheep from the British taxpayer one can't really wonder at their staying.

The Boss's other bright-eyed boy, called Brittan, is a smarmy lawyer from somewhere in Transylvania, who has taken over from poor old Whitelaw; Oystereyes having finally been wheeled away to the red-leather Geriatrics' Ward just across from the H of C. I thought he'd made a promising debut, with plans to bring back the rope, something in my view they should have done years ago. All the wets like Whitelaw and Runcie go on about it being barbaric and so forth, but certainly in the Club people are queueing up to pull the lever, and from a humanitarian point of view I'm told that most killers would prefer to take the short sharp shock any time rather than wither away in jug being visited by that awful old RC chap in the dirty raincoat.

They've now got round to a vote on it, but when it comes to the crunch and Dracula Brittan gets up and shows his fangs you can bet your bottom dollar it'll be the usual woolly *Guardian* rubbish that will win the day. I can't help suspecting that the old girl's heart isn't really in it. Whatever she says it hasn't got mass consumer appeal like the Falklands.

Yours incoherently,

DENIS

10 Downing Street
Whitehall

29 July 1983

Dear Bill,

How are you coping with the heat down in Kent? Up here it's quite intolerable, yobbos loafing about in their underpants, every kind of tourist riff-raff loitering outside the door with Instamatics waiting for something to happen. When I turned the sprinkler on the other afternoon little Bertie Mount came scurrying out with a message from the Boss to turn it off immediately or Red Ken would be over the wall before you could say knife. I can't understand where all the water goes to, can you? Two months ago it was bucketing down like Niagara Falls and it can't have just disappeared.

I've spent most of the heat wave in a pair of Lillywhites shorts sprawled in a canvas chair in front of the TV watching Birkdale, my silver locks ruffled by a fan borrowed from the Cabinet office.

Boris doesn't like the heat at all, and has come out in a rash on the soles of his feet which makes him very grumpy. By the by, your Golfer's Portable Oasis from that mail order shop in Texas has come in jolly handy during the drought. I put the Pimm's in first thing in the morning, fill the ice compartment as per instructions, and it's still delightfully chilled when I drain the last snort before toddling down to the Club for a quick one at noon.

You saw they cocked up the hanging business as I confidently predicted? Personally I blame little Dracula Teeth Brittan for the fiasco. Here were the new boys, no idea of the form, all perfectly prepared in their rather numskulled way to kill for Margaret on command, and where was the clarion voice to tell them where their duty lay? Instead, up pops the Hammer film hero, poised as one might think to outline the advantages of slow strangulation, all the colourful nostalgia of the black cap, the last hearty breakfast, the walk to the scaffold, the creak of the lever, the light in the executioner's eye as the trap falls open and a ragged cheer goes up from the chaplain and bystanders. Not so. The oily Transylvanian hums and hahs, vaguely trying to catch Margaret's eye to see what it is she really wants, and eventually sits down leaving the new recruits under the impression that what would really bring a smile to the Proprietor's lips is a vote against the rope. Which may in fact have been the case, if you ask me, but I have long since stopped expecting any kind of logic from the Boss.

Next on the agenda at Halitosis Hall is the question of how much the useless prats thought they ought to award themselves in the way of a pay hike. They were already taking home what you or I would call a bloody good screw for unskilled middle management, not to mention 'expenses', ie secretaries, chauffeurs, cut price snorts in the basement, and on top of that as you know most of them are moonlighting to the tune of several thou a year sitting on boards, running fish and chip shops and so forth in their spare time. The Boss made a very generous offer of four per cent, upon which a howl of outrage went up from the assembled deadbeats and idlers, all of whom had got their sights set on the prospect of thirty rising to sixty over the next three years. As it is they're all about to bugger off for two months' fully paid holiday. The latest proposal put forward by that smarmy greaser Edward du Cann acting as ACAS is that they should be kept in line with civil servants with index-linked perks and a full pension after six months on the job. I understand now why Maurice was so keen to do his bit for the community.

Did you read about little Pillock's amazing prang on the M4? It said on the news he was stone cold sober, and I suppose one should rule out foul play with the monkey wrench by the Hattersley Dirty Tricks Brigade, which makes it all very mysterious. It crossed Boris's mind that the whole thing was a shrewd publicity stunt, which would explain why the Newbury News photographer was standing by on the hard shoulder when he landed. Can this be right? No matter. The feeling in this neck of the woods is that Pillock has got the job in the bag and a damn good thing too as he is just another version of Worzel only Welsh and younger and not so intelligent.

Still no news from the oracle about the hols. From the various runic inscriptions in Margaret's Dataday it could be Balmoral, or, horror of horrors, the Isle of Muck. Maurice Picarda has been ringing very persistently. He and some of his Sevenoaks rotarians have formed a consortium to buy the Southern Railway, or at least the profitable bits, when it comes on the market. I said I didn't think there were any profitable bits, but I would ask Lawson the next time we have our usual disagreement about parking spaces. I think it's beginning to dawn on the Boss that she's made a bit of a boo-boo letting poor old Howe off the leash and bringing in this new wide boy with his long eyelashes and lah-di-dah ways. Apparently he used to tip shares on the *Sunday Telegraph*. Did I tell you that before? I find I am constantly repeating myself these days. I find that I am constantly repeating myself these days. I shall be forgetting my own name next.

Yours through the haze,

BORIS

SCHLOSS BANGELSTEIN   12 August 1983
BIRCHERMUESLI
SWITZERLAND

Dear Bill,
As you see from the above, the Widow Glover won on points over Lord Pucefeatures and the Reagan Ranch House, and thus it is that I find myself typing this on the deceased's electric Remington to the sound of cuckoo clocks and distant alpenhorns. The routine chez Mere Glover is if anything more grisly than last year. I put this down largely to the bulky presence of the Widow's Swiss friend, Herr Doktor Bosendorfer, an elderly bearded shrink and close friend of Van der Pump. In addition to his other quirks, ie deafness, inability to speak comprehensible English, unsteadiness on the pins etc, the Doctor is a teetotaller, who tells me he regards my own way of life as pathologically unstable.

In order to escape the presence of this heavy-footed weirdo on whose company circumstances here inevitably thrust me for a good deal of the time, I have been forced to invent a business contact in Bern called Herr Zwingli, with whom I arrange regular assignments, working lunches, and even occasionally small dinner parties. At whatever hour of the day or night I return Dr Bosendorfer is always there waiting to interrogate me about our business, other guests, the menu and so forth, nodding at my answers and saying 'Ya, ya, ya. Please go on,' like some mad gestapo chief questioning a recently recaptured squadron leader from Colditz.

You must have read about M's eye operation. She's knocking off fifty thank you letters every morning before breakfast, so I've no doubt she'll get round to you eventually thanking you and Daphne for the white stick, and you'll receive your signed photograph to put on top of the piano with all the other ones.

The trouble with the Boss of course is that she hates to admit to any form of weakness, and has been known to hit Cabinet ministers who stand up and offer her a seat. I spotted that there was something agley even before the Election, when she started going cross-eyed trying to read the Hopalong Teleprompter Screen, and advised her to have a word with Dr O'Gooley. I was told not to be ridiculous, he was a hopeless drunk who couldn't read a thermometer even if someone held his hand to stop it trembling, and anyway he was National Health and wouldn't be able to see her for months.

When things worsened and tempers became frayed as I inevitably knew they would, some very sharp little number was summoned round from Harley Street who I think must have been a friend of Lawson's. To begin with they tried to keep the whole thing secret and Dr Kildare, or whatever his name was, offered it as his opinion that it could all be sorted out in a couple of shakes after closing hours with a blast of his death ray machine. We were all accordingly swept round under cover of darkness to some sort of Star Wars set-up at fifty guineas a minute. Of course it turned out that Margaret fused the machine and the whole thing was a complete bloody waste of time, at which point I suggested trying O'Gooley again. I might as well have been talking to the wall, and probably was by that time. Second Doctor wheeled in, a very smooth little BUPA chap called Pankhurst or some such name, his line being a simple little op, he does fifty of them a week, nice quiet clinic in the backstreets of Windsor, very tasty food, same butcher as the Castle, far from prying eyes of Fleet Street, he'd have her in and out in a couple of days and no one would be the wiser.

You probably saw our arrival on television, police having to hold back photographers. Someone below stairs had let the cat out of the bag and from then on it was sheer hell, yours truly being picked on by the powers that be to give the nightly bulletins before the cameras and respond to the barrage of idiot questions from the foul-breathed yobbos. 'Is she working under the anaesthetic?' 'What's the hospitality like then, Denis?' and similar impertinences. Even so I think I managed to keep my end up and scored a moderate hit with the little man at Saatchis who does the TV advertising.

What had her really hopping mad, even under the anaesthetic, was the allegation that no proper chain of command had been established to deal with any emergency in her absence. It transpired that in the event of war breaking out while she was in the operating theatre, the man in charge was poor old Willie Whitelaw, or Lord Lakedistrict as he is now. I said the chances were he'd be out on the links anyway, if he wasn't half cut, or both, and even then I very much doubted if he'd be able to find the button with both hands. Apropos, I may have said this before, but it seems a damn silly idea giving hereditary honours to two old buffers with no male heir. What's the point? If that's the qualification, why not give one to our seafaring friend Ted Heath, or Stevarse for that matter? I made the mistake of suggesting this in a rash moment the other night when Margaret and the Widow Glover were watching the stockmarket prices live from Zurich, and it went down like a lead balloon, especially when Dr Bosendorfer woke up and asked to have it explained.

Tomorrow we climb the Matterhorn in the funicular for a picnic with an aunt and former patient of the Doctor who lives in a chalet and has a collection of English glass paperweights. I fear Herr Zwingli may have to send one of his telegrams summoning me to crisis talks in the Etoile Keller. Auf Wiedersehen, mein alter freund.

Bergmanns Heil!

DENIS

SCHLOSS BANGELSTEIN   26 August 1983
BIRCHERMUESLI
SWITZERLAND

Dear Bill,

Many many thanks for your aerogramme, which was brought up from the village yesterday by Herr Bosendorfer who had been down to have his beard trimmed. Any little contact with the outside world here is like a puff of smoke on the horizon to a man marooned on a desert island, and I was very moved. The *Telegraph* arrives at the station kiosk three days late, which makes pretty good nonsense of the weather forecast and rather takes the thrill out of the crossword.

I suppose you're still basking in the heat wave in easy strolling distance of the Merry Leper, with Daphne safely packed off to her American friends in Portugal. You lucky bugger. You ask, apropos, whether there is a news blackout on our activities. The fact is that it is so boring here that even the Telegraph stringer, a little man in leather shorts called Ackroyd, went away in despair after two fruitless days lurking in the shrubbery with his telephoto lens. What the hell did he expect? At half past nine old

Bosendorfer toddles down to the summerhouse with a leather bag full of case histories to mull over, the Boss meanwhile, having been at her papers since six, sits in the tower dialling away on the telephone to bring this minister or that sloshing out of swimming pools from Tenerife to Dover to give an account of their daily doings. Your old friend, having discreetly avoided the Widow, lying face down on the massage couch being slapped by elderly karate expert Rose Klebb, now sets off on his constitutional via the back gate and down to the village to the Kaffeehaus Wandervogel. There, having purchased the aforementioned out-of-date copy of the *Daily Telegraph* from Herr Blasius the newsagent, he spends the next two hours wrestling with the crossword with a litre bottle of some colourless but potent sticky at his elbow to stimulate the grey tissues.

I thought, thanks to an alpine hat and dark glasses, that I had managed to remain incognito, until the other day the Coffee House keeper, Herr Davis, brought his own foaming stein of beer, and placing his considerable bulk directly opposite me asked whether I would settle a bet he was having with his dentist. Was I not Herr Thatcher, staying up the mountain with the Widow? I thought for a moment of doing by halfwit act – never too difficult at that time of the morning – but in the end I owned up. There followed a riveting half hour listening to an encomium of the Boss's achievements, her superb skills as a war commander, gallant defence of firm currency, admirably truculent attitude to the Russian Bear. Since then I have had to lend an ear every morning to similar confidences, and today the dentist friend, one Herr Weidenfeld, a small excitable man with protuberant eyes, was presented, and put a number of questions about Margaret's new teeth and how much each had cost, which I was quite unable to answer. Tomorrow Frau Dr Dentist Weidenfeld and their eight children are to join us at our table for coffee and Black Forest gateau with cream.

Lunch at the Schloss is taken in silence, punctuated only by the occasional sharp explosion of the Widow's crispbread slimmers' biscuits and the soft tread of white-coated menials replenishing Herr Bosendorfer's glass with mineral water. At five to two I fold my napkin and am allowed to retire to my room to finish the crossword and try to think up excuses for cutting the afternoon excursion in Herr Hanfstaengel's limo. The fictitious Herr Zwingli of Bern, a mysterious business contact who constantly requires my eagle eye to sort out some little item of double-entry book keeping at the Etoile Keller, has been of invaluable assistance, and I have managed so far to miss the Matterhorn, an exhibition of Gruyere cheese making, a glockenspiel concert, a visit to Calvin's birthplace, and hot chocolate with a retired Canadian stockbroker who once had control of the Widow's considerable investments.

Maurice P however having entrusted me with a triangular brown-paper parcel to deposit in Lichtenstein, I agreed to join the official party for a trip to Vaduz, capital city of the pocket-handkerchief-sized principality, the only country on earth where the Royal Family outnumbers the rest of the population by two to one. The Prince, who walked down to the border to meet us, seemed a nice enough cove in plus fours and a fairisle pullover, and said he'd heard all about me from his close friend the D of E, a fellow preserver of World Wildlife, and would I like to stay for a boar shoot the following day? If not perhaps I might prefer to see his collection of postage stamps? Foreseeing another morass of tedium, and noting that Margaret and the Widow were scheduled for a conducted tour of the conservatory with the Archduchess Brunhilde, I asked His Serene Highness if it was all the same to him if I popped down to the town to buy a pair of shoes. Imagine my horror, as I slipped past the sentries at the gate, to see Herr Bosendorfer, who had been eyeing me strangely and no doubt suspects me of every kind of secret vice, tottering along in my wake. I gave him the slip easily enough by taking a short cut through the cathedral, and had no trouble in finding the International Head Office of the Pan-African Bank, located with fifty other undertakings in the front room of a small terraced house. As I rounded the corner however the sight of two burly agents of the law lurking on the threshold fingering their riot sticks, and a third sitting in a car opposite talking to base on his walkie talkie made me think twice about entering. Sure enough at that very instant a man carrying an identical parcel to mine arrived at the door, was snatched roughly off his feet, and thrown into the boot of the car.

Back at the Palace for tea with various old fossils in coronets and eight rows of pearls who had been wheeled out for our inspection, all totally gaga, I heard Bosendorfer, mopping his brow and with his suit clinging to him from his exertions, observing to the Boss that he had no idea I was so deeply religious – 'A whole hour in the cathedral! Tell me about his mother.' The Boss gave us both a pretty beady look and was fortunately swept away to see His Highness's showjumping trophies.

Roll on Balmoral!

Yours in extremis,

DENIS

BALMORAL CASTLE　　　　　**TEL: BALLATER 3**
ABERDEENSHIRE　　　　　**STATION: BALLATER**
SCOTLAND

9 September 1983

Dear Bill,

What news from Castle o'Doom? Well, not since the Isle of Muck have I undergone such humiliations. At least at Schloss Bangelstein one was left in peace and treated as a private patient. This lot here subscribe to the Gordonstoun Bugger Them About school of thought. Half past five yesterday morning, thump thump thump on the bedroom door – M. already knee deep in international dispatches – and a mountainous Scot with a thick red beard and a kilt strides into the room, depositing a plate of concrete-like porridge on the bedside table, tearing the clothes off the bed, announcing that he has run me a cold bath and that the shooting party will be leaving in three minutes. Then there ensues a twenty-five mile drive in an ancient landrover, most of it over trackless rocks and heather, the porridge refusing to lie low despite its immense weight, three princelings of the Blood Royal singing lavatory songs at the tops of their voices and the Duke with a foot hard down on the accelerator shouting abuse at the sheep which scatter before our bouncing wheels.

Finally we ground to a halt at the head of a dark glen where a knot of purple-faced piss-artists in plus fours and green wellingtons bowed and scraped and dutifully laughed at the D of E's early morning obscenities. A bottle of whisky was passed from hand to hand but when it came to my turn the Duke snatched it from my grasp and said No no, he'd promised Margaret there would be nothing for me before lunch and then it'd be a can of shandy if I was damn lucky. (Ha, ha, ha, from the puce-featured contingent.)

After a good three hours' slog across the moor by which time my Lillywhites so-called waterproof golfing shoes were asquelch with brown water and my trousers sodden to the knees, we arrived at the butts. Amid more laughter and a further rotation of the hard stuff the Duke said that we should now draw straws for Butt Number Thirteen and Mr MacLevin. I drew last and needless to say got the short straw. More guffaws and MacLevin was brought up, also apparently in on the joke. I can never tell those two Princes apart, but the one who was in the Falklands show and mucks about with the American tarterino offered to point the way to my position, a distant speck of rock on the shoulder of a great hill where a little red flag could be discerned through binoculars fluttering on the skyline.

Come noon we were in situ. MacLevin, a former sergeant major in one of the Highland Regiments, was not a man clearly I could look to for any sympathy. He loaded my gun, thrust it into my hands, and told me I'd be lucky if I saw much game as it had been a hot summer and the heather was as dry as tinder. There was, he said, 'nae monny a groose tae tak a pottie at.' The occasional rare bang from down in the valley confirmed this view. After about an hour of further misery I at last, like that chap in the poem when the creepy things come on board and they've all got the DTs, descried a welcome shape flapping towards us at zero feet, and was raising my firing piece to prang it, when a swarthy hand grasped me by the back of the neck and hurled me to the ground. 'Dinna shoot, ye mad fule,' Mr MacLevin cried, 'can ye no tell a seagull when ye see one? His Royal Highness would hae yer breeks for garters for gunning doon the wild life.' Thinking it pointless to enter into a debate as to why the grouse should bite the dust and the seabird escape unharmed, I lit a cigarette and decided to wait for lunch.

Moments later we were engulfed in smoke, and despite MacLevin removing his kilt and attempting to beat out the burning heather the fire spread very rapidly over a sizeable area of Aberdeenshire and a pall of black smoke still hangs on the horizon as I write. Yours truly inevitably blamed for the whole episode, non grata with HM the Queen, Boss furious, officially placed on jankers by D of E, told to report to his room five times a day in different kit for an earful about the threat to vole and grasshopper, invitation from Royal and Ancient to toddle round with their pro and Lord Lakedistrict (Oystereyes as was) cancelled 'owing to lack of transport'.

Any chance of an extended lunch at the RAC on the 20th?

Greetings frae bonnie Deeside,

DENIS

10 Downing Street
Whitehall

23 September 1983

Dear Bill,
You ask me in yours of the 11th inst about this little prat with the glasses who has taken over Parkinson's job, J. Selwyn Bummer as he is known round the office. I can tell you very little about him, except that no one can understand why he has been singled out for the distinction. Boris tells me he's a Bible thumper who prints tracts of an improving nature for distribution at bus stops, and that he's got it in for the likes of you and me as limbs of Beelzebub with our miscellaneous weaknesses of the flesh. I have occasionally seen him having a giggle with Runcie at his ghastly sherry parties and he's certainly a prime candidate for the OBT (Order of the Brown Tongue), particularly where Margaret is concerned. Beyond that I'm afraid I can enlighten you no further. We shall have to wait for the Rocky Horror Show at Blackpool, where Mr Bummer will be called upon to wield the gavel and try to keep the NF contingent in order before marking his card.

Strictly entre nous, Bummer's promotion, coming in the wake of such arch creamers as Lawson and Brittan, has been interpreted by one or two sage heads here as a sign that the old girl is finally cracking up. Would that she were and we could hot foot it away to Dunleadin, Lamberhurst, Kent! Unfortunately the Opposition refuses to play along with this scenario, and until the emergence of any serious contender from Smellysocks House, the SDP mob or the Libs, she's clearly going to cling on, whatever her state of health. The reptiles did their best last week to boost the smarmy-haired little houseman Owen but as I may have said before the only decent thing he ever did was to try and break the neck of that Trot who threw a tomato at him. And as far as new SDP ideas are concerned they've obviously all been copied out of the manifesto Bertie Mount did for our people. As for Steel, the chap is clearly ripe for Picarda's open-plan funny farm. I blame *her* quite frankly. She looks like the kind of woman who stands behind the door with a rolling pin waiting for the poor little sod to totter in from an all-night sitting to crack him one over the nut. If *he* jacks it in God knows who they'll dredge up. It's early days yet for ginger Pillock, but as hammer of the Trots I wouldn't give him the chances of a snowball in hell.

Searching for allies or even civilised drinking companions in the Proprietor's new Cabinet is a pretty hopeless task, especially now poor old Oystereyes has been moved to the bed nearest the door. It may admittedly be lack of any reasonable alternative, but I could eventually come round to Heseltine. My reason for saying this is that listening to Boris's tapes of last week's Cabinet I was delighted to hear Tarzan laying into Fatty Lawson and his cheap cuts in no uncertain terms and also being very sound on the need for dumping the Sheepshaggers once and for all. Lawson came on very pompous and started on a lot of guff about M3 and the Snake, an old gambit that Howe always used to resort to when I got him in a corner and asked him about my deposit account. But I formed the impression that Tarzan's got him marked down for his hate book. Say what you like about Heseltine, at least he was working hard and making his own way in the world like you and me when Lawson was gobbling down the canapes and pocketing the cigars as a reptile pushing dubious shares in the *Sunday Telegraph*. Including I may say those of the rascal Bloom, that funny little geezer with the beard and the washing machines. You remember the Major's first wife was in deep shock for three weeks after hers exploded and the Major himself came a very nasty cropper with the equities.

Now, if you please, Lawson is toddling round slamming our fingers in the till on off-shore funds and tax concessions to the big oil boys. By all means nail the pen pushers of Whitehall down to 0.003 recurring on pay increases over the next twenty-five years, but Furniss at the NatWest was saying to me only this morning over a few scoops of cooking sherry, it used to be the rule with our mob that you had people like Lawson on the inside pissing out, not the other way about.

Any chance of a day out at Wentworth, which I see is looming up yet again? If you get the limo I'll do the booze at Attwoods.

Yrs in haste,

DENIS

10 Downing Street
Whitehall

7 October 1983

Dear Bill,

Did you ever read about the man who was buried in a coffin for six months with only a tube connecting him to the outside world for some damnfool scientific experiment in France or somewhere? Well, after my five-continents-in-four-days tour with Margaret I know exactly what he felt like when they brought him up.

I can't remember whether you've ever been to Canada. I know at Burmah it was always regarded as the equivalent of the salt mines, and you probably recall poor old Wally Forbes who was sent out to look after Montreal that time they caught him in flagrante with the Chairman's secretary during the staff outing to Ostend. Quite frankly I can't think how the Canadians stand each other. If I was left alone with that many million bores for half an hour I'd go berserk with a meat axe.

Their leader, a fluffy little antique dealer called Trousseau, whose wife very understandably took to hard drugs and ran off with a pop-singer, is absolutely wringing wet vis-a-vis the Bear, and had M. frothing at the mouth from the moment he came prancing down the steps of their equivalent of Number Ten. This distaste was very clearly reciprocated, and Trousseau insisted on the Proprietor holding forth in Froggish, sniggering the while behind her back as it became clear that neither man nor beast could understand a word she was saying. Then to cap it all he paid some hooligan to give her a nasty fright when she was going walkabout. To get her own back, M. had a much-publicised reception for the Leader of the Opposition, a real crasher even by Canadian standards, who could only talk about the cent by cent rise and fall in the price of paper over the last forty years. He invited us to pop up to his cabin in the Rockies for three months any time we felt like a spot of orienteering. Would you believe it?

Naturally enough I got blind drunk on touching down and stayed that way for the duration of our visit, with the result that I was very seriously ticked off for snoring during reptiles' question time!

When I tell you that it was a relief to arrive in Washington and be greeted by old Hopalong, needless to say holding hands with his tiny and emaciated spouse, you will get some idea of my feelings about the Land of the Maple Leaf.

I hadn't seen the old cowboy since his House of Lords spectacular when he came to launch his new autocue screen, and it was quite a shock. The more hair dye he puts on the weirder he looks and he can only hear if you shout into his breast pocket very loudly indeed. He put me in mind of

that former Chairman of Cobbs the haberdashers in Tunbridge Wells who stayed on till he was ninety and kept being mistaken for a dummy. They used to say he had an Indian man who came round on Thursday mornings to inject powdered monkeys' balls into his bum. (You probably remember one of the window-dressers got the push for trying to get his trousers down.) I can't say for sure that Hopalong is on the same kick, but he certainly has that waxy look about the wrinkles and finds it hard to turn his head from side to side.

Things in general have not been helped by the Boss's strange new Churchillian Iron Curtain mood. It all began when Van der Pump, our South African seer and backstage Rasputin, came down to Chequers one weekend and showed us his slides of the Kalahari. This was pretty ballsaching as you can imagine and I slipped away under cover of darkness to wet the whistle down at the Waggonload of Monkeys in Great Missenden. When I got back they were still sitting there, with the projector turned off and the lights on while the old sage fixed her with his hypnotic eye and spun her a yarn about some tribe of little bushmen who bore holes in rock by looking at it. Not that this was the point of what he was saying: his burden was that these bare-arsed Johnnies are convinced that when their Big Chief turns his toes up his spirit hovers about moaning in a kind of limbo until it finds a worthy successor, at which point it moves in and everything's tickety boo. 'It's as if,' he added, his eyes glowing with a mysterious fire, 'the spirit of Winston Churchill had been waiting all this time, and now at last had found its home.' I gave a nervous guffaw at this point and asked the Boss if she'd like a glass of brandy, but the other two made it clear that they found my remarks in poor taste, and it was cold tongue pie for supper that night as far as yours truly was concerned.

Anyway, the long and the short of all this is that the Boss spends hours every night in the old War Room down in the bowels of Westminster reading the Collected Speeches , and has regurgitated them all over North America whenever she has been called upon to speak. I don't know what it does to Andropov, but by God it terrifies me.

Take it easy now. Have a real nice day buddy boy and may the Good Lord take a liking to you.

DENIS

10 Downing Street
Whitehall

21 October 1983

Dear Bill,
What a shambles! If I ever needed convincing of the virtues of alcoholism in preference to a little bit of fluff on the side, this whole sad tale of Cecil Parkinson and his love child has hammered it home good and proper. Quite honestly, Bill, I never took much of a shine to him. Altogether too much of an arse creeper as far as the Boss was concerned, and he really got my goat during the election campaign by bagging the seat next to the driver on the Bus and forcing me to sit at the back with the reptiles, all singing Roll Me Over In The Clover and tossing beer-cans out of the window at the unemployed. You or I could tell he was an HMG with his eye on the main chance, but the Boss is always far too busy to notice things like that. All she saw was the flashing smile, the Brylcreemed charm, clean-cut appearance and sober demeanour.

Of course, I knew aeons ago that our Mr P. and his typist friend were up to a bit of malarkey, though I thought it imprudent to tell you at the time. It was the Major's chum, Four-Eyes Entwhistle, who spotted them canoodling in a wine bar in Chester and inevitably put two and two together. Major on the blower next morning, wasn't it my duty to tell the Boss? I said absolutely not. Whatever I thought of our Cecil, we chaps must stick together etc. If one person starts blowing the whistle on that kind of caper where will any of us be? And in any case I deemed it probable that a messenger bearing such tidings to the Boss would have a life expectancy measurable in seconds.

Come election night on June 9th, champagne corks popping, M, self and Cecil pull in from the window after our eighth curtain call from the cheering winos in the street below, CP clears throat, 'Prime Minister, I have something to tell you. Could I perhaps speak to you privately?' Margaret, still in euphoric mood, bids him proceed, all friends here. Out comes a lot of romantic novelette drivel about how he is deeply in love with a very wonderful woman, she has taught him the true meaning of the word for the first time, would like Margaret to be the first to know that she is expecting his child, will she be the godmother? Crikey, Bill, did she hit the roof! Talk about cruelty to animals! Had he ever considered his duty to his employer, the little woman waiting up night after night at Downing Street to hear his report on morale in the constituencies? And all the time his thoughts had been elsewhere! Parkinson stammered something about Lawson having got away with it – you probably remember Bill, his wife skedaddled with a randy egghead from Oxford and he sought solace in the arms of a lady librarian at Halitosis Hall, all pretty squalid I agree but that's the way things go. The Boss however refused to be diverted. Had he forgotten that the election had been won with the help of young Bertie Mount on the platform of The Family? Unless he pulled his trousers up pronto and got himself taken back into the bosom of Mrs P and PDQ it was curtains as far as his political career was concerned. What the hell could have got into him etc, all over again, you know the form, and I was finally moved to lay aside my personal feelings, crack a bottle of rotgut and force it between his chattering teeth.

Time goes by, all apparently tickety boo, the whole thing swept under the carpet; this however reckoning without the reptiles or indeed Miss Keays. Hell hath no fury etc, as Picarda discovered that time he ditched the big woman from Harrods' Food Halls who subsequently came at him with the broken bottle. Come September, reptiles on the line to HQ every morning asking for a statement. Boss belatedly realising that solids are about to hit air-conditioning, gives CP heave-ho as party chairman and moves in little Bummer, who, whatever his other shortcomings could not conceivably be accused of being a part-time swords-man. I could tell that her patience was beginning to wear a trifle thin however when it all blew up again on the eve of the Blackpool Circus. Once again CP was hauled in, given the gestapo cellars treatment and ordered to come clean, tell all, and Saatchis would push the loyalty line, the Party's readiness to move with the times etc.

A sticky wicket, I think you'll agree. We arrive at Blackpool – hordes of reptiles loving every minute of it. Parky goes in to bat, all the delegates instructed to applaud. Boss already not in best of moods, the Conference as a whole being pretty grisly, Brittan, Lawson et al getting the bread roll treatment and a lot of murky little blackshirts and gay-boys crawling out of the woodwork to make it all look very seamy. This, mark you, supposed to be the Party's celebration for the greatest victory in recent history! M, however, always sanguine, is convinced she can dispel any unhappy memories with a great Churchillian speech on the Friday, annihilating the critics, blasting the wets, knocking cocky little Pillock off his perch, and above all burying the whole Parky episode as a nine-day wonder a thousand feet underground.

Picture the scene in the early hours of Friday morning. After a sleepless night in our hotel bedroom with Bertie Mount and Sir Custardface the gag writer complete with silk dressing gown and cigarette holder having beavered through the hours of darkness to get the great oration ready for the Hopalong prompting screen, the telephone jangles to inform us that Miss Keays has blown the gaff and is plastered all over the front page of the new look gutter *Times*. I don't think Parky will forget the moments that followed as he ruminates about what might have been on the verandah of his sheep farm in Australia.

On the whole just as well you didn't come. I think apropos my own retirement plans at Dunleadin, Lamberhurst, that I begin to espy a light at the end of the tunnel. Thank God there is a real feeling of defeat in the air at last. It has come to something when Norman Tebbit is looked upon as our Great White Hope.

Yours,

DENIS

10 Downing Street
Whitehall

4 November 1983

Dear Bill,

Forgive me for breaking off rather abruptly in the middle of our jaw about Grenada the other night, but Margaret's temper has been getting very frayed of late. You were, I think, asking why the hell the old girl had come out strongly against Hopalong, when surely we were all a hundred per cent in favour of exterminating the Red menace wherever it shows its ugly head.

The answer, which I could hardly give to you with the Boss hovering at the back of my neck, was that she was extremely miffed at being left out of the act. Personally I couldn't quite see what all the hoo-ha was about. As you probably know it's about half the size of the Isle of Sheppey, and largely given over to the manufacture of postage stamps. Scatty Longmuir once spent a holiday there by mistake, under the impression he'd booked into the other place in Spain – a perfectly understandable error if you go to your travel agent straight after lunch. He said the only difference was that it took much longer to get there, and the local restaurant didn't serve paella. Otherwise it was just a lot of chaps sitting about in shorts drinking rum.

Be that as it may, the first wind M. got of it was when the landing craft were churning up the beach. It then transpired of course that the FO wooftahs had masterminded yet another utter ballsup. God knows, Bill, after the Falklands business, you'd think they'd have cleared out some of the human refuse clogging the Office in question, but no. Telexes rerouted to some Swedish mail-order firm in Soho, everyone convinced that lynching the Prime Minister and massacring the Cabinet are all part of the tourist drive, and in charge of this shower old Howe shuffling about in brothel creepers with his specs steamed up not understanding a blind word of what was going on.

I always said it was a mistake moving him from the Exchequer, where he was in his element, sorting through the tax returns and occasionally going on the television to assure us all that there was light at the end of the tunnel, and meanwhile would we like to invest our remaining savings in some of his new bonds at a very generous five and a half per cent before tax? Probably if you'd had a few you might even have believed him and no doubt many did. But put him on the gunboat platform on the other hand or prop him up in the House to wave the flag for Queen and Country and he cuts a pretty sorry figure. No wonder Johnny Foreigner lays in supplies of the stale bread rolls whenever he appears over the horizon.

Had little Howe or any of his pansy advisers been on the ball, M. would of course have been fully briefed well in advance, and yomped in there with the Boys from Belize, scorching the arse off every Cuban in sight within a matter of minutes. Nothing she would have liked more than a bit of Cuban arse-scorching hand in hand with old Hopalong. Ever since the Falklands show in fact she's been longing to have another crack at a bit of war-war, to quote her favourite character in fiction, and it would have done wonders for the ratings.

Another blow to her carefully laid plans was little Cocky Kinnock's first day at school. According to her scenario it was to be full turnout of Smellysocks and reptiles, Cocky K on his feet ranting away about the evils of the NHS Cuts – if you can be said to rant with permanent laryngitis – Boss sits there smiling, letting out the line and then wham, reels him in and clocks him over the head with a mallet. (Cue for Smellysocks to wonder if they've made the right decision. Would they have done better with Fattersley?) As things turned out the Grenada storm blew up engulfing Howe and leaving the Boss shouting away about her deep respect for Hopalong, how only the dearest of friends can hurl abuse at one another etc. Roars of laughter, catcalls and general derision from Smellysocks, M. ashen-faced and eyeing Howe's jugular in a very nasty way.

Yours at the ringside,

DENIS

10 Downing Street
Whitehall

18 November 1983

Dear Bill,

I've just come back from the annual Remembrance Day Parade in Whitehall, where I was lucky enough to bump into Peg-leg Hartridge, who was marching past with his British Legion  contingent from Staines. I managed to wink at him as he stumped by the saluting base, and we met up afterwards in the Guardsman's Arms, for a couple of large ones and a few guffaws about old times. He was tickled pink at the way the Boss had stopped any nonsense about that shifty little greaser Dr O getting in on the cenotaph act and having his photograph in the papers looking statesmanlike. As Peg-leg said, the most the little Doctor had done in the service of King and Country was letting off a few blanks on Salisbury Plain during his days in the school OTC. Of course you could say exactly the same of Steel and Cocky Kinnock, but as I pointed out to Peg-leg, you can't have too many conchies cluttering up the plinth, and he absolutely agreed. Allow the Doctor on in his funeral gear and where would it end? Next thing you know there'd be Scargill on parade with a CND banner, not to mention hosts of frightful wooftahs representing the fallen gays in two world wars. You may chuckle, Bill, but that's the kind of thing we're up against nowadays.

Talking of which, I thought the Lord Chief Justice was very sound when he said they ought to bring back the rope for buggers. An unfashionable view, Bill, but it is high time somebody spoke up for the silent millions of people like you and me whose whole way of life is under attack.

Poor old Howe is still getting stick, I see. You remember last year he lost his trousers on the train. We all had a good laugh at that. The latest tale relates how he poured a pot of hot coffee into his crutch in the Executive Class en route for Athens and another shouting match with our loyal comrades in Europe. I gather he had to borrow a pair from Lofty Smallhouse of the FO to avoid the spectre of walking naked into the conference chamber. Gales of merriment nevertheless from the evil-smelling foreigners as he shuffled in.

It all points again to the fact that the Boss made a major boo-boo in ever moving him from the Treasury and replacing

205

him with our friend at Number Eleven, Mr Nicely Nicely. God, Bill, what a prat! I know that the Good Book instructs us to love our next door neighbours, but that man would try the patience of a saint. Here we are, pledged to reduce inflation to zero, rising prices the number one evil, sworn to give British industry the shot in the arm it needs to get it off the slab, and up comes Nicely Nicely authorising huge increases in the retail cost of gas and electricity. As you know from Smallbone, these sods are making massive profits as it is. All they ever do is sit around in white coats in huge humming laboratories reading the *Guardian* and occasionally looking at a dial or twiddling a little knob. Makes no sense to me.

I taxed Nicely Nicely with it the other morning when he was watering his hair in the downstairs gents prior to popping in to see the Proprietor. I was given the usual snooty brush off, and made to feel that until I got an A plus in O-level economics I shouldn't bother him with my views and might as well save my observations for my fellow winos down at the Club. Fair enough no doubt in today's abrasive society, but I was brought up to treat my seniors with more respect.

How are you finding your new clubs? I'm told the Korean ones are twice as good at half the price, but Lillywhites were out of stock so I won't know till Christmas. God, to think that's all looming up again! Still, when you get to our age I suppose you can't complain. All I notice is that the drinks seem to get weaker. Has that been your experience?

Yours as the shades lengthen,

DENIS

C H E Q U E R S

30 December 1983

Dear Bill,

I must apologise for the black-edged communication informing you of my demise due to over-indulgence: this was one of Mark's little Yuletide jokes that as usual misfired as I may say did the Major's Singing Gorillagram on the 23rd who was summarily arrested at the gate and bundled off to choky, security having been beefed up considerably since the IRA's pre-Christmas goodwill mission at Harrods Stores. Apropos, you probably spotted me on the Nine O'Clock News doing my business-as-usual bit. At the time I was fairly browned off, having left the house en route for Lillywhites and a last minute foray into the Golf Department to collect my Japanese ball-washers for miscellaneous chummos, including yourself I may say, when up goes a window and the Boss calls me back: Saatchis have a limo waiting at the corner to ferry me down to Harrods, buy whatever I like on M's account as long as it doesn't cost more than fifteen quid, and back in time for the photo-call at half six.

I don't know when you were last in Harrods, Bill, but I still have happy memories of going there for a bit of fun in the zoo and a tickle of the ivories in the piano department before they opened at the Bunch of Grapes. Always a very nice class of person in there, and you usually ran into someone you knew in the banking hall. My God! What would poor old Potty Fergusson say if he could see the swarms of great fat begums in beaks and Allah-catchers busily shoplifting everything they can lay their dusky hands on, followed by their pathetic little sheikhs, none of them housetrained and all smelling like polecats!

I tracked down the sports department somewhere on the upper deck and asked for a dozen of the Jap ball-washers. Very sorry Sir, not much demand, temporarily out of stock, expecting consignment early in the New Year; had I thought of trying Lillywhites? I eventually left the store with a collection of assorted miniatures to hang on the tree and an Old Millhillian cricket square for Mr Wu who has always admired mine. Back at the barracks reptiles all assembled, contents of bag emptied out with much tut-tutting and headshaking by the creep from Saatchis, shunted off in the direction of the camera lights and told to say something Churchillian on the need to keep the tills rattling at Christmas tide come what may. In the event I rather lost my temper, but the Major told me it came over very well on the bulletin. Needless to say by the time I got down to Lillywhites they were shut.

By the by, do you see that furry-headed little cookie-pusher Brittan is having the fountains in Trafalgar Square drained for New Year's Eve? You might warn your friends not to make the trip this year. As I told him, revellers could easily hurt themselves very badly, jumping off the statuary in the expectation of a jolly good splash and landing flat on their backs on the concrete. As for his crack down on drink and driving, I've never heard anything so monstrous. No wonder the IRA get away scot-free when every copper in creation is lurking in the hedgerow with pencil licked eager to book the public-spirited boozer for doing everything in his power to prevent unemployment in the Highlands.

I am sorry to say I missed most of the festivities, having passed out after unwisely opening Mark's present on Christmas Eve, a bottle acquired at the duty free shop in Macau and called I think Number One Tiger Breath Whisky. The son and heir did his usual act of descending unannounced, on this occasion in the company of Mr Monty Glew, a swarthy little chancer from Finchley who he introduced as his accountant. Having plied me rather too obviously with my own very expensive gin within moments of their arrival, they broached the little matter of an interest-free non-returnable loan to help tide them over until they receive a promised order for seven gull-winged convertibles, to be sold to an influential client in Dubai. I could tell from the cut of his jib that little Mr Glew was up to every trick in the book, his eyes flickering over the furniture and fittings, no doubt with a view to how much they would fetch in the Portobello Road, and my cheque book remained firmly tucked away in the breast pocket. Mark later tried a bit of the Lawson-type flannel on M. about confidence returning, leading out of the recession etc, but she also kept her handbag securely shut and later rang through to the Waggonload of Monkeys to book a single room for Mr Glew overnight.

It was after lunch that I toddled up to the den, feeling the need for a stiffener, and made the mistake of starting in on the Chinese poison in front of the Channel Four Golf Highlights of the Year. When I came to it was Boxing Day and the chirping of a lone sparrow on the windowsill went through my head like the rattle of a Bofors gun. The only mercy, as Wu explained to me on the drive down to Hoddinott's surgery for a pick-me-up and emergency Kaolin, was that I'd missed the Howes who had come over on Christmas night, also Hopalong's personal video message not to mention Van der Pump's midnight phone call with his predictions for the coming year. Wu said it was the usual guff about some dream he'd had featuring Margaret as King Kong sitting on top of the Albert Memorial shying coconuts at David Owen.

I'm still feeling pretty fragile and taking it very gently with the intake of alcohol, rationing myself to no more than four large ones before meals.

A happy 1984, and remember Big Mother is Watching You.
Regards,

DENIS

10 Downing Street
Whitehall

13 January 1984

Dear Bill,

Do thank Daphne for the bed on New Year's Eve. My memory of events after about two am is necessarily blurred. Did Maurice Picarda suddenly come into the Spread Eagle with a monkey on his shoulder? And was the Major breathalysed on the way back from Maidstone or did I dream that? I presume we all got home because I woke up in your granny annexe with Mrs Plimsoll pressing a welcome cup of Instant into my shaking hand with the news that you'd left on the morning cheapo from Gatwick. I suppose one is getting a bit long in the tooth for making whoopee on these occasions, but that's no reason to stop doing it.

Saatchis felt it necessary for the Boss to dispel any sense of doom at the coming of the New Year. I couldn't see that it was any more necessary than usual, but apparently some old Etonian dropout called Orwell made a lot of money just after the last show with a book called 1984, foreseeing a bleak scenario of Britain under a pretty tough law and order regime – some ugly mug running the show with the help of a Databank and sniffer dogs. Contrast this, say the Saatchis, with the bright new world under the Boss, a radiantly beautiful if mature woman, with everyone free to do whatever they like so long as they can afford it, plenty of colour TV sets for all, inflation growling in its cage, altogether a boom boom boom situation.

By the by, I don't know if you saw but I thought it was a bit rich of the Saatchi Bros to launch out as television critics, and issue an in-depth bollocking to ITV for failing to come up to scratch. Obviously the Boss's patronage has gone to their heads and the next thing you know they'll be criticising the Test Team or telling the Archbish to pull his socks up. Not a bad idea incidentally, but hardly the sort of thing one wishes to hear from a couple of jumped-up Eyetie icecream pedlars.

My own contribution to getting the country back on its feet again was to drop in on Furniss at the NatWest on the first working day after Christmas to see how my deposits were looking in the wake of the Xmas battering. He too was doing his best to dispel the Orwellian despair with a glossily produced pornographic calendar which he offered to me discreetly wrapped with the compliments of the management. Would I care for a beaker of his new Cyprus sherry? Our bald friend proceeded to sound a note of steady optimism waving the inside pages of the FT at me in a grandiose manner and producing graphs showing growth on its way through the ceiling. I had the usual feeling of deja vu, asked for my printouts and another slug of the Cypriot filth, and rather stopped him in his tracks with what seemed to me a logical query: if everything in garden so delightful, why he jack up mortgage rates?

Thoughtful pause, fingertips together, brow creased in cogitation, then rapidly turns conversation to holiday plans, the wife and kiddies v excited about a brochure called Tunisun etc.

What else is new? Poor little Howe has been given his jabs, ten pairs of spare trousers and sent trundling off round the Middle East, and the Monk who we'd all assumed to be languishing in the funny farm suddenly resurfaced with a three-hour speech on the need for more 'O' level passes. Everybody seemed very impressed by this, but I think that was probably only because they thought he was in the funny farm in the first place.

You saw that Mark is taking out some rock-laden heiress in Texas. Fingers crossed we might even get shot of the little sod once and for all and see a return on our money. Who knows, I may follow in the footsteps of President Ford and get a walk-on part on Dallas: 'Here honey, meet my paw in law, the Limey Wino.'

May the Lord bless you real good.

DENIS

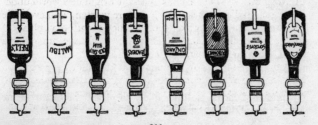

10 Downing Street
Whitehall

27 January 1984

Dear Bill,

What a very enjoyable trip to the Land of Apartheid and Sun. Every time I go there I can't understand why everyone makes such a fuss about their local rules and regulations. Looking at the smiling faces in the street you could tell that a pretty good time was being had by one and all, and as Mrs Van der Keffersbesher said at the farewell wine and cheese, we whites have got to stick together against the reds, blacks, pinkos and everybody else. All common sense stuff, but if the Boss was to stand up and say as much on the TV the roof would fall in. Don't ask me why, it's just the mad kind of world we live in.

You probably saw on our return that the reptiles, having failed to trace us in the Transvaal, are trying to make trouble for the Proprietor over the boy Mark. I don't need to tell you the difficulties we've been through with the little bugger in the past, first of all with advertising rubber goods on the side of racing cars, then all the hoo-ha when he got himself lost with a French bint in the Sahara and had to be rescued by the combined forces of the North African Treaty Organisation, not to mention his latest exploits flogging Japanese plonk and Hong Kong scent on behalf of some fly-by-night outfit at present being scrutinised by the Revenue.

Now the Smellysocks are trying to make trouble about him getting mixed up in cement in the Middle East. I don't know if you recall a particularly grisly tour the Boss and I undertook to Sidi Barrani and points East three years ago. I didn't tell you at the time because it seemed of no conceivable interest, but during a scheduled stopover in Oman, who should come breezing into the VIP lounge in dark glasses and a girly mag under his arm, but the son and heir. What a coincidence etc, temporarily strapped for dibs, could I bung him a few travellers' cheques, and while we were about it, could he tag along for the cocktail sausages at the Sultan's Palace as he hadn't had anything to eat since Gatwick at breakfast time?

I was pretty livid having finally cornered the Grand Vizier Abdul Abulbul and tried to do my sales pitch on behalf of poor Maurice's double-glazing caper, then, as you may recall, poised on the brink of bankruptcy, when Mark charges up, would you believe it, brushes me aside, lays an arm round the sheikhly shoulders, and draws him off into a corner making great play of family solidarity, nothing likely to please the Great White Mother more than three hundred million or so towards another close relative called Cementation Limited knocking them up a little polytechnic on a suitable site overlooking the harbour. Interested nods from friend Snaggleteeth, new gleam in the eye, and thumbs down from a menial on Maurice's double-glazing.

Be that as it may I thought nothing more until it all floated to the surface again last week, questions asked in the House, Margaret being 'got at' through Mark, as if either of us were in any way responsible for the little twerp at his age. I told her to get up at Halitosis Hall and say as much, but Saatchis advised a no comment approach, Margaret's bloke i/c reptiles to complain to lobby about unfairness etc, which means that it will fester away for months with yours truly getting regular bollockings from the Boss into the bargain, and all murky business contacts, to wit you, Maurice and the Major constantly under surveillance.

What with one thing and another M. has had a pretty trying time. She was all set to get a new war going on the Red Barons at County Hall, who as you probably know are always shovelling public money into the handbags of every conceivable variety of queer and weirdo – a long overdue campaign that had the full backing of Saatchis and was scheduled to rocket her back into the charts like greased lightning. Instead of which the wets decide to protest against what they term interference with local democracy, the resulting uproar awakens Captain Ted in his hammock a-sleeping there below, and he comes rumbling out to put the boot in to roars of helpless mirth from the Smellysocks. What the blue-rinsed hero always fails to realise is that his little interventions nearly always succeed in letting the Boss off the hook.

Not to be outdone, old Brer Enoch, weary of sniping at the Boss, decides to go one higher and take a pot shot at the Monarch, accusing her of pandering to the darkies in her Christmas TV show. Admittedly I was pretty far gone on Christmas afternoon, but it did strike me at the time as a bit odd that instead of sitting at her desk, surrounded by signed photographs of the Russian Royal Family in silver frames and a few nice chrysanths, she chose to address us from a camp stool on the lawn at Gandhi Towers. I assumed it was all to do with everything on the telly being about India nowadays, but what Enoch doesn't understand, bless his little cotton socks, poor barmy bugger, is that HM eats, dreams and sleeps all that Commonwealth nonsense, and her idea of bliss is being smothered in garlands and carried through the bush shoulder high by half-naked coons while a lot of little missionary-trained pygmy Johnnies throw their spears in the air and sing God Save the Queen. You don't get the same feeling riding down the Mall in a taxi on a wet Friday afternoon.

Yours restored,

DENIS

24 February 1984

Dear Bill,

Forgive me if I was a little short on the phone last weekend but life has been a regular whirlwind of social engagements, all of which have taken their toll of my fast-dwindling reserves.

Do you remember the old boy who used to have M's job and went to Moscow in a fur hat? The story goes that his medic gave him two weeks in 1963, so he threw in the sponge, retired to the country, summoned his family for the deathbed number, only to discover shortly afterwards that he was a hundred per cent fit and well, no more than the old gents' traditional waterworks trouble playing him up. Since then he's been sitting in the pavilion making sour remarks about his successors. Anyway, having turned down the various shoddy offers put his way by Heath, Wilson etcetera to keep him quiet, he apparently read in the *Telegraph* that M. had brought back Hereditaries for Whitelaw, whereupon he rang up and said now he'd reached the age of ninety could he have one too. Sod all that Margaret could do, I think you will agree, but put a brave face on it and cough up.

I presumed that the Proprietor could send it him through the post, but no. Saatchis in their wisdom decided that the occasion was to be marked by a champagne reception at the old buffer's country retreat down in Sussex on the way to Tunbridge Wells. So off we flocked. The old bird has always had a rather warped sense of humour and it came as no surprise as we were enjoying

our pre-lunch thimblefuls of Cyprus sherry, when a powder-blue Rolls drew up and Ted Heath got out, carrying a huge bouquet of chrysanthemums and a box of cigars. The geriatric jokesmith who had clearly planned the whole thing in order to create the maximum embarrassment, then introduced Heath to M. with a gracious wave of the hand murmuring, 'I don't know if you two know each other. I'm sure you have a lot in common.' Our seafaring friend coloured up to the roots at this, eliciting a snigger from the other guest of honour, the frail but sprightly Sir Alec Douglas-Home, looking very fetching in an old but carefully darned kilt.

A disgusting lunch was then served by an elderly domestic, all present preserving a frigid silence when the newly ennobled Earl rambled on about the Boss as though she wasn't there, referring to her as 'this woman with the ghastly voice who's put everyone out of work', and how in the Thirties it wouldn't have been allowed. The only good word he had to say for her was that she wasn't as bad as 'that awful organist fellow she took over from.' I could see old Deathshead Home smirking into his watercress salad at all this, and was delighted when the Ancient of Days suddenly transfixed him with a watery eye and asked whether anyone had ever told him that he bore a remarkable resemblance to that absolute ninny Alec Douglas-Home who in his opinion had started all the rot, adding that the worst thing he had ever done in his life was to hand over the reins to such a prize idiot.

Lunch broke up fairly early, and on the way back in the car M. said, charitably I thought, what a terrible thing senility was, especially when exacerbated by over-indulgence. I could have told her that in my view the old walrus was as clear as a bell and was even now shaking at his fireside in helpless mirth.

As if this was not enough there has been the grisly saga of the boy Mark. Having been told to keep his mouth shut about the Oman shindig on pain of death, the little prat was then splashed all over the front pages as having given a press conference in America, offering his version of events and pledging allegiance to Margaret, the Almighty and himself. (No mention of yours truly, needless to say.) Anyway, next thing I know I am summoned into the Proprietorial presence, expecting pretty severe flak on my involvement in Maurice P's double-glazing or the sauna units and barbecues business. You could have knocked me down with a feather when she announced that the reptiles were to be summoned to meet the son and heir at Chequers the following weekend, plus bint, in the shape of Miss Amy-Lou Fortnox, hospitality care of yours truly, church parade attendance obligatory, smiles all round and no drinking in public.

I smelt a rat at once, and was still recovering from the shock over a treble plum vodka in the pantry when Boris spelt out the plan. Saatchis have got the wind up and very understandably vis-a-vis Master Mark. After burning a good deal of midnight oil devising various schemes to neutralise him as a political threat, they hit on the weekend party as the first step towards a Not The Royal Wedding scenario, the announcement of an engagement to be made within the week, full dress ceremony at St Margaret's Westminster, where else, our hero, his Oman exploits long since forgotten, disappears shortly afterwards into the sunset equipped with a gold meal ticket for life.

All very well on paper, of course, but reckoning without the bone-headed stupidity and almost supernatural ability to foul up even the simplest of tasks that has been characteristic of the boy Mark since infancy. For further news, watch this space.

So long,

Your old granpappy,

DENIS

10 Downing Street
Whitehall

9 March 1984

Dear Bill,

Dunleadin here we come! As you will have seen, it does now look as if things are going badly for our lot. For the first time since he came in the ginger bloke with the bandy legs i/c Smellysocks has gone ahead in the polls and our poor little wimp at Chesterfield got his arse well and truly scorched by the electors, limping in only just ahead of the Raving Monster Down With Motorways candidate.

Chaps here at HQ did a bit of whistling in the dark after the result was announced, suggesting that Benn's return to Halitosis Hall spells trouble for little Pillock. I'm afraid there may be something in this: as well as being TT I understand our friend with the revolving eyes is now a fully paid-up member of the nut-cutlet brigade and eschews all meat. You remember what happened to Maurice during his brief period on the waggon when he took up with the lady from the health food shop in Deal. His behaviour was described by the magistrate when they found him jogging up Middle Street totally starkers as 'better suited to the monkeyhouse than a quiet residential area of a leading south coast resort.' According to Dr O'Gooley the body needs a regular intake of mutton chops to stabilise its natural rhythms, and total abstention from the amber fluid combined with a sudden intake of nuts does funny things to the brain. So Pillock had better stand by for explosions.

Talking of explosions, I have had my fair share up here at the sharp end during the last few days. After the poll came out I happened to mooch into the blue drawing-room in search of a packet of Senior Service and found M. deep in Monday's copy of the *Daily Telegraph*. A jocular reference to our retirement plans possibly being moved forward brought the barrier of newspring. down with a sharp rustle. 'I expect treachery from Edward Du Cann, not from you!'

Mystified by this reference to the slippery little Somerset card-sharper aforesaid, I made the mistake of lingering. 'What you fail to grasp, you and your pin-striped friends up and down Whitehall, is that there has been no error of judgement over GCHQ. I have singlehandedly taken on the combined power of the unions and the civil service and emerged triumphant. Don't interrupt, and if you must smoke do it out of the window. The workers at Cheltenham have rallied to the standard that I have raised. They have seen the light. Where is the defeat in that? Answer me!'

Knowing the form on these occasions I realised that it was pointless to argue the toss. 'Quite so,' I said, 'Quite so. I had not looked at it that way before. I am sure you are right.' 'Of course I'm right. And what is all this nonsense about me being autocratic and not listening to other people's views? When have you, Denis, found me intractable or unwilling to listen? Answer me this minute! When?' Stifling the thought that had I been so minded I could have cited instances galore of times when the spirit of give and take had been noticeably absent, I cleared my throat and inclined my head in deference to her views. 'And don't cough! Another consequence of your disgusting habit. And while we are on the subject was it you who mutilated yesterday's copy of the *Sunday Times*?'

I had hoped that at this point Act One Scene Two was about to be brought to an end by my rapid exit stage right, however the reference to the gaping hole on the front of the Sunday paper prolonged the agony. You probably saw it, Bill, or some friendly soul will have drawn it to your attention: further smears attempting to implicate me in the boy Mark's 'business dealings.' I myself found the whole story entirely baffling. All it amounted to, as far as I could discern, was that some snivelling reptile had rung up the boy's bank, talked to a clerk just after he got back from lunch, and elicited the fact that the boy's account was (a) overdrawn, and (b) guaranteed by yours truly. If this is the case I certainly have no memory of it. I do remember Mark turning up at Christmas time in the company of a small-time spiv called Mr Monty Glew. I am not denying that we had a few, and it may well be, Your Honour, that carried away by the Season of Goodwill, I allowed my hand to be guided across the page to affix some approximation of my signature.

Anyway, when this was all plastered across the front page of the rag in question, I deemed it prudent to cut it out, on the pretext that I was interested in a golfing report on the other side, rather than endure another helping of cold tongue pie at the breakfast table. I now got it however with knobs on and eventually retired hurt to Boris's pantry for an emergency transfusion of damson vodka. Boris in gleeful mood told me that the Kremlin were cock a hoop about the Cheltenham affair, as with everyone now predisposed to give Margaret two fingers their job of recruitment would be a great deal easier. I considered whether it was my patriotic duty to report this, but decided not.

I'll try to corner little Lawson some time this week to get you the gen on the Budget. My tip at this moment would be to turn off the electricity and stock up on the vital necessities of life. Talking of which, could you see if your friend at the Cash and Carry would deliver as far afield as Lamberhurst as measures at this end have been tightened up following the recent excitements.

Toodleoo,

DENIS

10 Downing Street
Whitehall

23 March 1984

Dear Bill,

The longer I live, the more mysterious I find this whole business. Take the case of Fatty Lawson, our pomaded friend next door. We were all agreed until a day or so ago that whatever abilities he might have shown as a share tipster and mortgage-wangler in days of yore, as Chancellor of Her Majesty's Exchequer the fellow was a total non-starter even in comparison with his predecessor, the sleepwalker in hush-puppies, whose budget speeches reduced the back benchers to a snoring heap on both sides of the House.

Then suddenly, last Tuesday or whenever it was, Fatty throws off his crumpled three-piece gents' natty suiting and Shazam we are confronted with Supernigel, master of the whirling figures, saviour of the universe, number one in line to step into the Boss's shoes should the Number Eleven bus snip through the web of destiny. Damn me if I can see why.

As is my wont on these occasions, I poled down to the NatWest on the morning after to assess the damage, and found Furniss poring over his *Telegraph*, calculator in hand and sherry at the elbow. After a good deal of scribbling in the margin of the financial page he announced that a man in my position,  ie retired executive, working wife, one wastrel son, one other female dependent, could expect to be 33p a month better off, but added with a disrespectful smirk that he didn't expect that in my own case, any small gains on such swings would compensate for losses on certain other roundabouts.

All of which makes the metamorphosis of Mr Nicely Nicely even more difficult to comprehend. I bumped into him the other evening, while I was putting the car away and it was pretty clear to me that the ecstatic notices he had received from the financial reptiles had gone to his head, already swollen in my view as it was. 'Ah Denis!' he cried with a boyish grin, flicking caviar off his waistcoat, 'Been filling up, have we? I would have thought that you and Mark could have got a tanker sent up from one of your chums in the Gulf! Ha ha ha etc.' I thought it best to still him with a chilling look, rather than retaliate by referring to the Major's experience when he invested in John Bloom's washing machine shares as a result of matey's own spiv-like recommendations in the *Telegraph* some years ago.

Incidentally, as far as this Oman business is concerned, I am rather pinning our hopes on Sailor Ted coming to the rescue as so often in the past. Just as things were beginning to look a whit dodgy with all the Smellysocks queuing up to sign a chain letter deploring the existence of the boy Mark, up jumps the Broadstairs maestro, jowls awobble, to say it was high time Margaret came clean, rinsed through her smalls in public, and let him have his job back. Margaret's lobby-fodder immediately rally to the flag, put down several motions to the effect that nothing can be more admirable than a mother defending her brood however misshapen and demanding the chick in question may be.

What with the approach of Spring and the bird man of Number Eleven, spirits here have taken a depressing turn for the better, and all the talk of banana skins is now behind us. To add to the euphoria Comrade Scargill is deemed to be playing into our hands by ordering his yobbos into the fight, grinding the faces of the honest miners while old MacGregor sits on his pile of coal chuckling away and plotting his next move in the big run-down. For my part I can't wait till he's slammed down the lid on the last of the black holes, then the old boy can get to grips with ripping up the railway lines and other equally outmoded vestiges of the past.

Auf wiedersehen, Pat, as the German said when he pushed the Irishman over the cliff.

DENIS

6 April 1984

Dear Bill,

Do you remember that story about Fruity Podmore's uncle Sidney, the so-called black sheep of the family? As I recall he was commissioned in the Royal Somerset Dragoons, lost a packet gambling, got caught red-handed with the wife of a brother officer, fiddled the Mess accounts, collapsed after taking drink at the Queen's Birthday Parade, and his father old Lord Whatsisname gave him a one-way ticket to New South Wales. As far as I know he was never heard of again.

I could not help but be reminded of this chain of events when out of the blue I got the summons to Headquarters ten or eleven days ago just after returning from a longish lunch at the RAC with Maurice and his car-dealer friend Charlie Whackett. The Boss seemed unusually fraught, and was poring over a consumer research portfolio from Saatchis marked For Your Eyes Only. 'This is all your fault Denis,' was her opening salvo, 'you and your fly-by-night business friends.' For one terrible moment I thought the press must have got on to our greenhouse scheme and the little dispute with the VAT office and was steadying myself for the blow when she came at me from an entirely different direction. 'Poor Mark! If ever a promising young life was ruined by his father's total failure to give him a decent start!'

Perhaps if it hadn't been for the generous quantities of stickies ladled out by friend Whackett at the Club I might have held my peace; however on the topic of the Boy Mark I have a pretty short fuse even when sober. I therefore waded in. Had I not paid thousands in hard-earned cash to put the little sod through Harrow when Mill Hill had been good enough for me? Had I not paid for his junior membership of one of the best golf clubs in North London, indeed the one that wouldn't have Maurice? Had I not bought the little bugger the best set of children's clubs available in Lillywhites sale, only to see him make a bonfire of them?

Self-justification, as at all times, proved unwise. 'Like father, like son' she kept on repeating, and the moment she saw my Dutch courage begin to falter, inserted her blade and began the familiar twisting process. 'Listen to me, Denis. I have done my best to cover up for the pair of you, at risk to my own survival, but now I have had enough. It is clear that the forces of disorder are not going to allow the Oman matter to drop. You got us into this mess, you can get us out of it. See the boy on neutral territory and tell him that I have arranged for him to give this interview to the

Mail on Sunday. In it, as you will see, he admits amid sobs that he has brought disgrace on himself and his family, and is determined to live out his days in a far-off land in an effort to make amends.'

To say that a great weight fell from my shoulders at this moment and that I was inwardly moved to skip with glee would be no exaggeration. 'It will be hard for you,' she continued, 'to break the news to our poor boy, but I am sure you have ways and means of fortifying yourself for such a daunting ordeal.' I did my best to look concerned and worried at the severity of her sentence. 'According to MI5 you have just been having lunch with a man called Whackett who has connections in the motor trade in America. As a loyal citizen it is his duty to fix the boy up with some kind of sinecure. And now get out!'

I couldn't wait, and immediately gave the boy the news over the blower from the front hall, recalling the episode of the burnt golfclubs and many other milestones on the downward path, arranging for a motorbike messenger to take the interview to him for signature, and assuring him that I would put the contents of his room in Downing Street in the hands of the local refuse collectors.

All this has left the Boss ravenous for blood vis-a-vis the reptiles. Orders have gone out to Havers, the rather beaky old lawyer bird you and I ran into in the strip club during the train strike, to prosecute with the utmost rigour of the law any newspaper thought to have been in receipt of a leak, stolen memo etc, and especially the *Observer* who started the whole Oman snowball rolling. Rather childish in my view. Whatever your private thoughts about these ghastly vermin I always believe, with the D of E, that it's prudent to put on a cheery smile and say 'Good morning, gentlemen' when one actually meets them. Once their backs are turned of course it's another matter. Margaret however will have none of this, and was cock a hoop when one of Heseltine's typists got carried off to choky for talking to the *Guardian.*

I've got some very tempting literature from the bucket shop about Easter. What do you want to do? Return to the bosom of Mother Flack on the Algarve or try pastures new? I've no idea where Lanzarote is: it looks pretty bleak from the brochure but there's rather a nice photograph of the bar. Give me a bell next time Daphne's out to lunch. Did you forget Mother's Day like I did?

Yours in disgrace,

DENIS

10 Downing Street
Whitehall

20 April 1984

Dear Bill,

As you may have seen in the *Daily Telegraph*, the Boss has zoomed off to Portugal on one of her Common Market freebies. I had been hoping to get in on the act and snatch a few days tapping the little ball across the green before relaxing beside the pool at Mother Flack's thatched oasis, but the advisers have become very sensitive about the presence on the Algarve of my alleged former business associates who might emerge from the bunkers and be photographed by lurking reptiles eager to promote another Oman shindig. I pointed out that such a scenario was highly improbable to say the least, and that any resemblance between the Sheikh of Oman and Maurice's old accountant Les Whipple, now struggling to earn an honest living packing Japanese cigars for the Canadian market was pretty remote. Anyway no joy.

Talking of wogs, I got a pretty stony look when I offered the Sheikh of Bahrain some shares in the Major's new video company. I thought I might at least try and extract something of value from two hours of dry torture at the Dorchester, but it was not to be. Incidentally, the Queen Mother gave me a very good tip about how to get through on these Mohammedan junkets last time we were staying at Balmoral. Apparently she has little miniatures concealed in specially made pockets inside her ball-gown and nips into the ladies every quarter of an hour or so for a quick slug. You and I would obviously be at a disadvantage not wearing ball-gowns but perhaps that ingenious little Mr Rothschild of yours over in Deal could run us up something in the way of evening wear with spare room under the centre vent.

Meanwhile we're all shaping up for a showdown with Scargill, the main aim being to get our own back after the defeat of '74 and to show Heath, who has been up to his usual monkeytricks at Halitosis Hall, how it should

be done. I personally hae me doots as to whether Margaret's American geriatric has got the necessary will to win: he strikes me as being altogether too reasonable by half, and at his age I can't believe he packs the killer punch in the back of the neck necessary to flatten the Barnsley Bruiser. The kind of person we need in my view is someone like Prosser-Cluff in his heyday. I think when you knew him he had rather gone to seed and taken to flicking butter at the ceiling during boardroom lunches, but in his youth he was a terror. When he was in charge of our Singapore operation he single-handedly quelled a coolies' strike by locking up the ringleaders, bulldozing the native quarters, and cutting wages by fifty per cent. The funny thing was they loved him for it.

Mind you, I think the Boss has got something of a P-C about her, which is more than you can say for that pathetic squirt Tebbit or Leon the furry-headed cookie pusher who totally bungled the Bring Back Hanging Campaign. Given several months' supply of coal which no-one can afford to buy anyway, her idea is to keep a lowish profile, busy herself with trips to Portugal etc, and starve the buggers into submission, Scargill then to be led in chains through the City of London. A noble aim, I think you will agree.

Did you see the old girl doing battle on Panorama? I thought she won hands down, didn't you? The wretched Day was on the ropes from the moment the bell went and by the end so groggy he could barely stand up. I don't want to blow my own trumpet, but I like to think I played some small part in managing the contest. As usual they arrived at Number Ten some time before the show was due to start, and while Margaret was having her nose powdered and the various gorillas were rigging up the lights, I took Brother Day upstairs to show him my golfing trophies in which he unwisely expressed an interest. Once ensconced in the leather armchair and embarked on a non-stop stream of reminiscence – how he pushed Jeremy Thorpe in the river at Oxford, how he outwitted Harold Wilson, how he could be Prime Minister by now if he could have afforded the cut in salary and so forth – he was so busy crowing away that he failed to notice that the tumbler in his right hand which I constantly refilled, laughing and nodding the while, contained a pretty powerful mixture of neat gin and Boris's Moscow Knockout Drops. When the floor manager chappie came up to collect him it took him all of three minutes to find the door, so no wonder Daphne thought he looked a bit sleepy and seemed to find it quite hard to read his own notes.

A propos Daphne's ban on our Lanzarote plans, what are you doing on Easter Monday? The Battle of Britain contingent at Huntercombe are having a Celebrity March to raise funds to pay for our Rugby Tour of South Africa, so if I come it'll have to be the dark glasses and the beard as my recent trip to the Land of the Rand went down like a lead balloon with the Great White Chief.

Happy Easter,
Yours aye,

DENIS

PS Do you agree with Maurice Picarda that if you hear Scargill's voice on the wireless in the next room he sounds exactly like Adolf Hitler?

10 Downing Street
Whitehall

4 May 1984

Dear Bill,

I don't think we've spoken since the ghastly business in St James's Square. As you know the Boss had toddled off to patronise the Portuguese on one of her EEC freebies, so I took the opportunity of fitting in a long delayed lunch with Thumper Binsley, last seen doing his stuff on the Panorama programme about the Nazi resurgence on the Right of the party, which little Gummer got so upset over. As I said at the time I couldn't see what the fuss was about. Thumper made a number of very sound points which were in no way invalidated in my view by his insistence on wearing a swastika armband. But a lot of people apparently didn't see the joke.

Thumper's suggestion was that we should meet for a jar or twain at the East India and Sports in St James's Square, where he is a country member, and then proceed in a leisurely manner to the RAC. Accordingly I arranged a fitting at Gieves and Hawkes for my new golfing blazer with the special Queen Mother-style hipflask gusset for Arab functions, and emerged into Piccadilly as Fortnum's clock was striking twelve. Cross into Jermyn Street, and blow me, the whole place is cordoned off, sheets of blue plastic hung on everything, hordes of Old Bill swarming all over the place with shooters, reptiles thick on the ground and scant respect being shown for Joe Public going about his lawful occasions.

I had asked to speak to Sir Kenneth Newman, pointing out who I was and emphasising that I had important business in the Square, when I caught sight of Thumper, as usual pretty red in the face, umbrella raised in anger and clearly about to be taken away by the guardians of the law. I succeeded in intervening, and drew him still speechless with indignation into the snug bar of the Red Lion, where the effects of two large sharpeners soon restored a semblance of equilibrium. When he finally stammered out his tale of a crazed gang of trigger-happy wogs firing machine guns through the window at all and sundry in broad daylight, I must say I could quite see why his first instinct had been to get in there and sort them out, if necessary with the end of his umbrella. After all he did spend some very colourful years in the Trucial States, and has had considerable experience with the various Mad

Mullahs and bhang-befuddled bedouins who frequent those parts. As Thumper said, the only language they understand is the big stick wielded repeatedly and without mercy by the white Sahib.

Discussing these and related topics we sauntered down to the RAC where we took on board a few steadying schooners of one thing and another, toyed with the cold game pie, as usual fairly revolting, and returned to Downing Street by cab, bent on taking matters into our own hands. Thumper's scheme which seemed to me wholly sound, was to get on to his friend Hooper-Strangeways of the SAS, line up a re-run of the Prince's Gate show, and then, as soon as they were poised to blow their way in, ring up the Boss for her official go-ahead. Judge of our despair to find, squatting on the floor of the Cabinet Room talking on the telephone to Portugal with one finger in his ear, who but the smarmy little cookie-pusher Master Britoil, hush-hushing us and giving Margaret, who was obviously on our side, a lot of flannel about diplomatic protocol and the danger of retaliation in Tripoli.

I used to think Old Oystereyes was fairly pathetic, but at least he'd been in the army and knew one end of a gun from the other, whereas this fellow has spent his entire life sitting in a padded chair in the Temple counting money and musing on ways and means of screwing the next unfortunate litigant out of his precious savings. The result, as you probably saw, was humiliation. After a week of police snipers lying about on the rooftops sunbathing they decided that the whole thing was a waste of time and let the murderous little darkies trickle off home on a scheduled flight with their guns safely tucked up in the Diplomatic Bag.

I can't help feeling it would have been different four or five years ago, and I am beginning to agree with Thumper that the old girl may be losing something of her touch. Though to be fair to her, as the Major said on the phone the other night, some of our people have got an awful lot of money tied up out there. You remember that friend of Maurice's with the one arm called Macsomethingorother who's building a chain of motels in the desert. I suppose a lot of his shareholders would feel rather let down if the whole deal fell through. This chum of Maurice's, Captain Hook as they call him in the mess, is apparently a close friend of Gaddaffy, and says he's a very good sort once you get to know him. He's done a lot for the wog in the street, building hospitals and so forth with the help of our people, and holds very reasonable views on law and order at home. As I said to little Britoil after it was all over, Margaret could well take a leaf out of his book. So perhaps we did the right thing after all.

Talking of madmen, it looks as if old Scargill is beginning to sweat a bit. They're so thick these buggers they didn't realise the sun was going to come out and nobody would want their coal even if they gave it away. And I wouldn't advise Scargill to book a table at the Ritz on the strength of a whip-round by Benn. Not that I wouldn't put it past MacGregor to run up the white flag at the last minute.

Cheeribye,

Yrs,

DENIS

Dear Bill,

As you may have seen in the gutter press Operation Markscram has now entered its crucial midway stage. Charlie Whackett has done his stuff and fixed the boy up with some kind of Used Car Consultancy on the fifty-third floor of a very tall greenhouse in Los Angeles, the other wing of the pincer movement being the impending wedlock with Miss Fortknox. In furtherance of the second objective, a twenty-four hour Unwanted Aliens' Visa was issued to the son and heir over the weekend and he was ferried in to Chequers along with Miss F. and an entire Texan family consisting of twin brother Ben, a six-foot bruiser in a crew cut, mother Mrs Kay Fortknox with a knee-length handbag and engaging smile, accompanied by a retinue of smiling black servants, gloomy Mexican maids and an English butler called Mr Sammy Gielgud.

Saatchis had laid on a five-line whip for the reptile corps, the thinking being, quite rightly, that if everything is made public at all stages along the grisly path, the little rascal will find it extremely difficult to wriggle out of it. Accordingly we all put our smiles on and stood out on the lawn before lunch while the greasy winos of Fleet Street stumbled against one another with their cameras, shouting impertinent remarks – most of them levelled at yours truly who was expected as usual to provide some comic relief.

My own instructions from the Boss were fairly cut and dried, i.e. to refrain from hard liquor, speak only when spoken to and avoid disparaging remarks about the son and heir, Hopalong etc. A tough assignment, I think you will agree, and my immediate thought was that I would need a couple of very stiff ones if I was to carry it out. With these under the belt I advanced on Mother F. who was admiring a portrait of Mr Gladstone at his writing table. 'Why,' she cooed, laying a hand on my arm, 'I just adore your family portraits. He looks such a jolly old boy. And he has something of Mark about the eyes.' The poor woman was plainly under the delusion that the whole bang shoot belonged to us. I was all in favour of enlightening the old bird, but I could see Margaret was in no haste to disillusion her, part of the plan being, I should say, to impress on our Texan visitors that money was the last thing in Mark's mind in offering himself as their future son-in-law. However when Mother F. caught sight of Sailor Ted in pride of place on the first landing and exclaimed 'Now, Margaret, *that* must be your brother! What a handsome man, and what a delightful smile,' the subterfuge inevitably gave way. A hard light appeared in the Proprietor's eye and she gave our guest a brief history lesson to include an account of Chequers and the many inadequacies of its last Conservative occupant.

It was clear that the WAAF officiating with the booze had been tipped off to keep us in short supply, so after an hour and a half next to Mother F. at lunch I was pretty dazed and, unwisely as it transpired, slipped into the Butler's Pantry to solicit Boris for an Emergency Transfusion. Boris and Mr Gielgud had clearly hit it off remarkably well and the flood of anecdote and reminiscence was a good deal more entertaining than was the case next door. When I toddled back in, looking perhaps more cheerful than I should have done, the conversation had turned to the topic of Hopalong's possible re-election. You know my views on this, and I immediately trotted them out, saying that I could never understand how an old cowboy actor could be put in charge of running a country and that people over here would think it jolly odd if we had Donald Sinden as top cat. It was clear to me they had no idea who I was talking about and, though Margaret was fixing me with the gimlet eye from the other end of the table, I proceeded to my second theory, namely that he hadn't the hope of a snowball in hell if he persisted in stripping off and going for a swim looking like some halfwit from Butlin's Eventide Homes, certainly not if he combined it with holding hands with his wife. 'Look what happened to the fellow before, the peanut man who was always falling over. They soon got rid of him.' For some reason I found all this hugely amusing and it was a few moments before I realised that the company did not. 'I take it you are referring to our dear friend Jimmy Carter,' crooned Mother F. in a frostyish tone. 'Jimmy is godfather to our Ben here.' Ben nodded gravely at this and it was clear to me that I had plunged the pedal extremity into the ordure. The gamma quotient was stepped up from the head of the table and D.T. was once again reduced to a small smouldering heap of ash on the dining room chair.

However on other fronts my efforts in bringing about world peace have been more signally successful. I didn't mention it at the time, Mum being very much the word, but during my stopover in Jo'burg some months back where I was doing my best to interest the natives in Maurice's Picvid Film and Video venture, I presented myself at a reception given by Mrs Van der Kefferbesher and ran into their Supremo Mr Pik Botha. He seemed to me a nice chap, quite a decent handicap, and very sound on the Red Menace. After we'd had a few I suggested he come up for the weekend some time to smack the prune round Huntercombe. He seemed unusually excited by this idea and accepted with alacrity. He arrives next week. Needless to say the great unwashed will be out en masse with their placards and the usual Rentamob. I have asked Brittan to round up the ringleaders as a matter of courtesy but I shouldn't think he'll do anything, knowing the cut of his jib. However I thought it was the least I could do as a host.

Do you fancy getting legless at Littlestone to celebrate my sixty-ninth? Give me a blow.

Yours in the Lord,

DENIS

10 Downing Street
Whitehall

15 June 1984

Dear Bill,
'The tumult and the shouting fades, ti-tum, ti-tum, ti-tum, ti-tum,' as the old song has it. I am seriously thinking of going on the wagon. The last fortnight I seem to have been in bib and tucker from dawn till dusk, listening intently, or pretending to listen intently, to some barmy foreigner droning on about interest rates or the Gulf war, having to drink almost as much in public as I

normally do in private and never getting to bed much before four in the morning. All, as far as I could see, in aid of the scheme to rejuvenate poor old Hopalong sufficiently to wheel him in to the White House for another four years.

To this end the Irish Tourist Board agreed to a million

dollar ramp based on some fairly fraudulent 'research' by the Let Us Find You An Ancestor Service which is all the rage with the Yanks. Anyway they managed to dig up some half-pissed late Victorian turf-cutter whose signature in the parish register if held upside down might possibly be interpreted as Ryan. This was good enough for the White House, and the PR Circus, complete with ground to air guided missiles, descended on the un-suspecting inhabitants of Ballypoteen (pop. 29), a malodorous hamlet fifty miles from nowhere. The wretched Hopalong was then guided through a charade of lifting Guinness glasses, being given the freedom of the parish, reading out a lot of Bear-baiting rubbish to the alcoholics in the Dail, while Nancy, togged out as Miss Aer Lingus 1931, was wound up to perform a brief walkabout for the reptiles beside the green waters of the Liffey.

By the time we took delivery of them, O'Darby and O'Joan were therefore in a very dazed state, not certain what country they were in and pretty short on the small talk. I knew it was going to be hell the moment I saw them tottering down the aircraft steps hand in hand. The Boss very gallantly went into a clinch with the old gun-slinger for the benefit of the reptiles, and even I had to accept a bird-like peck from the emaciated spousette who clearly thought I was the Duke of Edinburgh. (I may say that after being mauled by the Dallas Giants during Mark's recent courting rituals I am used to this sort of thing.) I had even boned up on the kind of drinks they like and Boris and I concocted a knockout cocktail containing Bourbon and Drinking Chocolate with a cherry in it, which I felt sure would shut them up for the rest of the evening. Alas I had reckoned without the four regiments of heavily armed security men who came along for the ride, one of whom sniffed at my offering and ordered it all to be poured down the sink.

I had been hoping, as you know, to join the Major and his Royal Corps of Winos for the Normandy Anniversary outing, and I am told I missed a bender never to be forgotten. Apparently the old boy was so plastered by the time the march past came that he called the Eyes Right when the Queen was on the other side. But the Duke had had a few himself and it all passed off in gales of laughter. M., however, suspecting that she might be knocked into the B Team by Heads of State like Grand Duke Charlie of Luxemburg, had cried off, so I was forbidden to go on the charabanc.

Before you could say knife however Hoppo was back, this time for the damnfool Economic Summit, which involved cordoning off the whole of London, dragging the Serpentine, and the general buggering up of life as we know it. You might wonder what conceivable point there could be in laying on this Madame Tussaud's jamboree with all these famous faces crammed round a table having their photographs taken, reading out scripts they couldn't understand and listening to same for hours on end, little Howe shuffling about in the background trying to look pur-poseful. The answer is that, once again, it's all going to look good in *Newsweek* – the Court of Good King Ron with attendant Lickspittles, Vassals and Serfs Paying Homage. In fact, as you may have gathered, they gave the old boy a pretty rough ride on interest rates, the Boss's voice waxing particularly shrill on this topic and Trousseau wearing a CND badge jumping up and down like a demented fairy. All to no effect, needless to say, as Hopalong by this time had sunk into a coma, still muttering 'Glad to have you know me' and 'Have a nice day'.

Yours pro tem,

DENIS

10 Downing Street
Whitehall

29 June 1984

Dear Bill,
The great battle against King Arthur and his Squareheads rages unabated with no sign of a let-up at this end. You should have been with me at the RAC when they showed Scargill on the news 'falling over' during the Battle of Orgreave. Cheers? There wasn't a piece of furniture left intact. Windows broken, toupees thrown in the air – that old retired Brigadier in the wheelchair who hadn't spoken since the Coronation actually rose to his feet, threw his crutches away, had a heart attack and died. A good way to go was what we all said afterwards.

Back at HQ however they were less jubilant. MacGregor's latest wheeze was to send out a billet doux at phenomenal expense in postal charges to every miner in the country, telling him that his intentions have been honourable throughout, and that things have been hideously twisted by Brother S. for his own political ends, the hope being that the sooty-faced sons of toil will blub their eyes out on reading it and 'drift back to work'. Fat lot of good this will achieve if they are stopped in mid-drift by hordes of bottle-throwing yobbos bussed in by Wedgwood Benn.

The only solution in my view, as I told MacGregor the last time I caught him shuffling in through the tradesmen's entrance for his daily conflab with the Boss, is to bring in the army and give them a whiff of grapeshot. Some hope however of any such robust solution with M. and her cringeing band of paedophiles at the helm, trying to keep their spirits up with reading aloud manifestly forged letters from starving miners' wives pledging their support. They haven't even the guts to implement the new laws brought in by Tebbit although how the Boys in Blue are supposed to arrest the entire staff of British Rail and seize their Art Collection I agree is not altogether clear at this moment in time.

Did you hear my friend Princess Margaret on the wireless being in The Archers? I thought she did jolly well. Her voice sounded completely clear and the way she said 'Good Evening' moved both Boris and me to tears. Our own efforts for the NSPCC were a good deal more lugubrious, involving as they did a Mafia-style gathering at Number Ten attended by various padded-shouldered international hoodlums and share sharks who had paid up to five hundred grand a plate in their search for respectability. M's lot got the idea from Barbara Cartland and her moneygrubbing daughter who lure the Yankee Tourists into their crumbling pile on roughly the same basis. The 'guest of honour' was a retired Kamikaze pilot called Mr Phuwatascorcha, well over ninety and without a word of English. Apparently he subsequently asked for some of his money back on the grounds that I went to sleep while he was telling me via his interpreter of the advances made by the Japanese in disposable softwear. (You will remember in Maurice's case it turned out to be not so disposable as he hoped.) Obviously I wasn't asleep, and had merely closed my eyes in order to concentrate better on what the little Johnny was saying. But the reptiles got hold of it and I was back on the mat yet again at sparrowfart the next morning, threatened with compulsory drying out at that place Maurice goes to near Dorking.

I am still trying to get out of another Swiss Misery Tour at Chateau Despair. I gather the widow Glover is feeling fairly pissed off with M. descending year after year and treating the place like a hotel, but I don't imagine that will deter Margaret.

Yrs in extremis,

DENIS

10 Downing Street
Whitehall

13 July 1984

Dear Bill,

I'm afraid our little outing to Sandwich ended in disaster. Maurice has never been good in hot weather and with the temperature pushing ninety quite healthy people were keeling over like ninepins. That was in the bar. God knows what was happening outside on the fairway. According to one of the Battle of Britain boys, Maurice took one of the heavier trophies into the gents under his coat and by the time they'd brought him under control he'd done an estimated five thousand pounds' worth of damage to the vitreous enamel. They were going to call in the police but I pulled rank on the blower from Number Ten late that night and they've agreed to waive charges on condition that the sum is found by the end of the month and that we never bring him there again. A pity, as the old boy lives just down the road. I suppose there's always Littlestone and with so many weirdos down there, Maurice will seem like a pillar of respectability.

When I got back there was a message to call Furniss, asking me whether I would look in on the way to the Club next morning. It seems, as I predicted at the time of that barmy economic summit in aid of Hopalong's re-election campaign, that Wall Street has failed to respond to the massed European pleas for a dip in interest rates, with the result that the pound is rapidly going through the floor and the NatWest is jacking up its base rates with immediate effect. With this in mind, Furniss was hoping that I would see the advantages of their Golden Wonder Added Interest Deposit Account with the Three Day Withdrawal Facility. I took half a bottle of his disgusting sherry off him and said I would mull it over but between you and me I think the only hope is to shift the caboodles over to the US pdq. The Boy Mark is in situ and miserable little viper though he may be, I think he can be trusted to cross the road to the Chase Manhattan and fill in a couple of pink forms.

This cold wind from America seems to have concentrated M's mind on the Scargill Scenario and by the time I got back after lunch MacGregor had been whistled in. I bumped into him shortly after six coming in through the back door for an emergency pow-wow with the Boss and Walker, and it being Boris's day off I was drafted in to do my Old Heathers act with the

amber fluid. Margaret kicked off by saying yet again that the Miners' Strike was no business of hers, Walker sitting there nodding, and that she had no wish at all to interfere. This seemed pretty damn silly to me and MacGregor obviously thought the same, but the old boy knows when to keep his trap shut. The Boss then embarked on a long lecture about the economics of energy and how she couldn't understand what all the trouble was about. At this the old codger stirred feebly in his chair, wheezed heavily, and seemed to go a little wild about the eyes. 'But surely, but surely, I understood . . .' he began, 'I understood that it was your intention to squeeze Scargill until his eyes popped out. Wasn't that what you said?'

I could have told him from my long years under the Iron Heel that the presentation of hostile evidence never goes down very well and Margaret's eyes took on a steelier glint. 'Memory can play strange tricks, Mr MacGregor,' she snapped, 'particularly if people let themselves go . . .' Here a glance at Old Heathers tactfully replenishing his own tumbler set the socks a-smouldering. 'You know quite well that I have scrupulously avoided becoming involved in your undignified blood feud with the National Union of Mineworkers. Peter and I have always urged you to seek a compromise that was satisfactory to both sides . . .' The one-time City Nabob here made a cautious gesture with one hand: 'I think the Prime Minister means that we would have so urged, ahem, had we ever, at any time, been in touch with you, which of course we were not.'

I could see poor Mr MacG. twitching a bit at this, so I lunged forward with the silver tray to top up his trembling beaker. Shortly after that I was told to hop it, but the old boy was in there for a good solid hour before he tottered out looking white and shaken and was helped into his Roller. I was not surprised when Boris told me the next morning that secret talks between MacG. and Scargill were going on in a guest house in Moscow Road, Bayswater.

Did you see that Nigerian Airways are running a new one-way 'Chief Dikkoo' cheapo? Free dope before take-off, own tasteful stripped pine stateroom with personal air-conditioning and no charge whatsoever. Sounds to me as though they ought to introduce it on the Falklands Run.

The Widow Glover has been persuaded to let down her drawbridge yet again so your Mexican Tequila Package will have to wait. In the interim, I look forward to our little outing to the Algarve. See you at Gatwick 9.30 sharp in time for a pre-flight stiffener.

Yrs awash,

DENIS

10 Downing Street
Whitehall

10 August 1984

Dear Bill,
Goodness me, what a beano! The bill for breakages arrived from the Portuguese Embassy the morning after I got back, but I am pleading diplomatic immunity. I formed the impression that we may have been forgiven by Mother Flack herself, as she was fully insured and the thatched beach hut was never very solidly built, as you will remember from the time when Maurice did his gorilla from the crossbeam and had to be taken to the local Out-patients. Those ex-pats have always been too full of beans in my view and

fooling about with fireworks last thing at night is always asking for trouble. The locals' equivalent to the National Trust claimed five miles of coastal woodland destroyed but I'm sure they were exaggerating.

The Boss hasn't come down since her big end-of-term jamboree at Halitosis Hall. Kinnock and his chums decided that they would go out with a bang, Vote of No Confidence, all the big guns wheeled in, Boss to be brought to her knees and have her nose rubbed in it, forced to confess country ruined, she herself hopelessly incompetent, Cabinet a crew of bungling eighth-raters. You'd think under the circs they could have made some of it stick, but it is beginning to dawn on these thick-headed proles that Brother Kinnock, amiable enough over half a pint of shandy in the Varsity Bar, is just not of the stature to go ten rounds with Meaty Margaret the Iron Mauler.

The poor little bugger is in any case a martyr to chronic laryngitis, brought on, as with many of his compatriots, by verbal diarrhoea. (You remember Taffy Patterson in the REME who used to empty the mess at Catterick with his reminiscences of life in the Valleys. He always had a packet of Meggezones to hand to lubricate his wheezing chords.) Anyway poor little Pillock got to his feet to administer the coup de grace – French, as the Major's Mother always used to say, for lawnmower – croaked a few defiant scraps of Welsh rhetoric barely audible above the usual undertow of flatulence and Trotskyite heckling, whereupon the Mauler rose, twisted his neck in a reef-knot and began whirling him round and round her head much to the delight of her young cohorts. Lawson unfortunately then managed to put his foot in it when he said that the Coal Strike was good news for the City, then said he hadn't said it, and Tebbit had to get up and say he had said it and it was a jolly good thing too. The Boss was spitting tintacks at this as it was meant to be her Big Night and she didn't want Nicely Nicely and Mr Munster giving the gallery anything to get their teeth into.

Not that it makes much difference as the Old Girl is now so carried away with her Thousand Year Reich that she has declared a Polish-style amnesty for all the old wrecks on the scrap-heap and is even talking of bringing back smarmy-boots Parkinson, the evil lothario of yesteryear. A great mistake in my view. Once a chap has been caught with his trousers down behind the pav the chances are it'll happen again, Ethiop can't change his spots etc. As I said to Picarda in the Executive Jet on the way back from the Algarve, how do we know he hasn't got love-children everywhere like Prosser-Cluff, who had them in Singapore every colour of the rainbow. Of course out there it didn't matter.

Mind you the Cabinet is getting a bit like the England Cricket Team and the way things are going she may have to take any old tramp off the Embankment. Fatty P., as you probably saw, is taking voluntary redundancy after five hard years in Siberia, the Monk looks to me pretty near the edge most of the time, little

Jenkin (P.) is unanimously deemed to be ripe for the knacker's yard, and poor old Hailsham will have to give himself up to the men in white coats one of these days before they come in and get him. I can't for the life of me remember what the other ones' names are.

Howe, admittedly, seems to be gathering laurels from every side, though why I haven't got a blind idea. They all trooped off to the Land of the Yellow Peril and got a piece of paper from Mr Dung on the Hong Kong question saying he would allow the old China Hands, Opium Pedlars and other rickshaw fodder to live on in the manner to which they have become accustomed for another five hundred years after the lease runs out. But why anyone should believe a word those slit-eyed little fiends have to say I can't imagine. You and I have had dealings with Johnny Chink and know that all he understands is the big stick wielded by White Sahib with gusto and without pity. Howe, who has spent all his life pushing peas round his plate in the lawcourts canteen, doesn't begin to grasp these subtleties. Give him a beaker of fermented beanshoots Number Fifty Three and he's anybody's, to say nothing of his Foreign Office advisers. Nuff said.

You may have seen in the Court Circular that the Widow Glover, bless her elasticated stockings, has once again deigned to play host to the Old Codgers for a limited season. I've been trying to find out if that ghastly shrink who was there last year is going to be in attendance but the Widow plays her cards very close to her chest and all she vouchsafed over the phone to M. was that she was very taken with spiritualism and the F-Plan Diet and had either of us ever attended a seance? Margaret persists in the economic argument, i.e. five-star luxury, no reptiles, no bill. But every time I think of it my heart contracts with terror. No postcards from Ibiza please, I couldn't bear it.

Yours in a trance,

DENIS

SCHLOSS BANGELSTEIN
BIRCHERMUESLI
SWITZERLAND   24 August 1984

Dear Bill,
If I told you that I spent seven hours last night sitting in a padded box costing £4,500 for the evening listening to assorted members of the Master Race warbling away ad nauseam in incomprehensible Italian in a theatre crammed to the ceiling with overweight music lovers all of whom looked like Maurice Picarda's grandmother, you will understand why the Queen

Mother's hipflask gusset has been doing sterling service since our arrival here.

You may remember from last year that the Widow G., proprietor of this Alpine morgue and inheritor of a vast collection of daubs all authenticated by the late Sir Anthony Blunt, has a warm rapport with a certain Herr Bosendorfer, a bearded trick-cyclist and close personal friend of Van der Pump. His new passion, shared by the Widow, is for what he calls 'ze divine Mozart', who, it transpires, was resident in an adjacent watering hole where he worked for many years as a bandleader before coming to a sticky end from over-indulgence. When the Boss and I checked in at the beginning of the week, we therefore found that we were booked on a season ticket for the next three nights to listen to the Maestro's oeuvre at what was described as 'nearby Salzburg'.

On with the bib and tucker, crammed into the back of Herr Hanfstaengel's obsolete hearse, Bosendorfer reeking of Old Swiss Rocky Mountain Shag and bubbling through his meerschaum in a most disgusting manner and off down the hairpin descent. Three hours later, green at the gills, we are deposited by the smirking little bugger at the wheel outside the Festspielhaus to be greeted with a barrage of Kraut flashbulbs and the oleaginous Master of Ceremonies one Hubert von Caravan, soon slobbering over Margaret's paw and babbling away about the honour she has bestowed on their 'leedel Fest'.

Hanfstaengel, I realised, had every reason to grin as he was going to spend the evening with his companions in the Golden Horn, beyond whose welcoming doors I could see a number of obese burghers in leather shorts all getting stuck into the flaming brandy and stone jugs of Heineken. Von Caravan caught me gazing wistfully in this direction, slapped me powerfully on the back with a sadistic leer and said 'Come on, Herr Thatcher, only five hours to go to the first interval.'

The pong of aftershave and fancy French scent almost swamped that of Bosendorfer's pipe. No air conditioning and too dark in the box even to read the newspaper. There was a bit of the usual scraping and sawing from the M.U. down below decks, then absolute silence. Von Caravan, it emerged, is a very bumptious bugger and had trodden on the toes of the local Scargill, prompting a down tools on the orchestra floor. The curtain finally went up at about nine o'clock, by which time my throat was like the Sahara and I was in no mood to appreciate why the Count had dressed up as a woman and jumped out of the window into the arms of the gardener, also for some reason dressed as a woman and singing in a high soprano voice. I may have got this slightly wrong, because shortly afterwards I drifted off into a profound sleep and dreamed that you and I and Maurice were playing golf on an ocean liner with Edmundo Ros conducting a choir of trained seals in the saloon.

Bosendorfer, to whom I confided this experience in the

interval, said the sea always betokened sexual frustration and the symbolism of the golf clubs should be pretty obvious, even to me. Dirty Bugger. During the second half and on subsequent evenings I succeeded in hammering myself into insensibility with miniature stickies smuggled in at a price by Hanfstaengel. I find that if I wear a very stiff shirt it stops me from keeling over.

Back at the Schloss we discovered that the Widow G's initial enquiries about spiritualism were no mere ploy to put us off. On the first non-musical evening, hoping for an early night, I was slinking away from the table only to be beckoned back. Menials having cleared away the biscuit crumbs and bubbles of mineral water, a stout, swarthy woman with a bristling moustache called Frau Balogh who had kept pretty quiet during dinner closed her eyes and asked us all to place our hands palms down on the table, our little fingers touching. She then enquired in a foghorn voice whether anybody was there. There was silence for a time. Then the old bird began making burbling noises and asked if one of us had a friend called Stebbings. Quite frankly, Bill, I never thought there was anything in this sort of caper and you could have knocked me down with a bargepole. Before I could own up, Reggie's voice came through clear as a bell, sounding as though he'd had a few, and describing his life 'over there'. 'We're all very, very, very happy', he said with a bit of a German accent. 'Jolly decent crowd in the Club House and I'm now living with a nice Red Indian woman. Give my best to Maurice and the Major and let me know when you're coming so I can bag you a place at the bar. It doesn't sound very jolly where you are.' Luckily the old boy signed off at this point or it might have got rather embarrassing. The next caller was Mozart, speaking with an even thicker German accent, thanking us for motoring all that way, and did anyone have a bit of manuscript paper as he had a new waltz he wanted to dictate. The old bird then burst into song, but it sounded to me very like the Blue Danube.

Talking of people going into a trance, I saw in the Airmail Edition of the *Daily Telegraph* (25 Swiss Francs) that poor old Hopalong has taken to nodding off during his brief spells on duty and that Nancy now has to be on hand to answer his questions for him. But he's clearly not like that all the time and I thought his plan for bombing Russia was very sound and proves that at that moment at least he was absolutely on the ball. I wonder if the Boss will soldier on into her dotage. I shall certainly be elsewhere by then, whooping it up with Stebbings and Co. in some far-off pavilion, so she'll have to rely on the Boy Gummer to blow into her ear trumpet.

Must toddle down to the Edelweiss Tea Rooms to 'catch the post' (code for a bottle and a half of the gentian-flavoured firewater at Herr Davis's Pull-Up for Goatherds).

Yours till the shadows fall,

DENIS

10 Downing Street
Whitehall

21 September 1984

Dear Bill,

Hope you got my p.c. frae Bonnie Deeside. An unusually dreary episode this year, even by the standards of Castle O'Doom. The D of E had invited some miserable little Japanese Johnny called Prince Fujiama in the hopes of winning the hissing Nip round to support his Ban the Whale Campaign. Quite frankly I'm beginning to think our Greek friend, though a doughty sniffer of the cork and teller of ribald yarns over the stickies and cigars, is just a gnat's out of touch with the modern world, and I speak as one against whom the same accusation has from time to time been brought by certain pushier members of the Club.

Margaret, who now seems to have the Queen very well trained, had led the ladies off to watch a re-run of The Two Ronnies in the Highland Lounge, leaving me, the Nip and His Grace to toy with the tiny thistle-shaped sticky-thimbles. 'One thing I wanted to ask you, Thatcher,' said the D of E, 'what's this thing called Income Tax? You don't have it down your way, do you, Hiro?' The Japanese bird, somewhat the worse for wear after a couple of hours with the Queen Mum, picked a piece of shot out of his oversize dentures, inclined his head and said 'Ah So' a couple of times in the way that they do, leaving it to me to enlighten old Rip Van Battenberg on how us working class folk had to hand over every brass farthing we earn to Lawson and Co. to give away to layabouts, drones, scrimshankers and striking miners. I may say it crossed my mind to add that a hefty slice of the hard-earned caboodle was siphoned off to keep His Nibs and numerous family in the style to which they had become accustomed, but discretion intervened. I discover since I got back that the economics lesson I had unfolded was regurgitated word for word for word by HRH in that magazine they give away free on aeroplanes.

Strictly entre nous I think poor old MacGregor's finally blown a gasket. You probably saw the photograph of him running round with a plastic bag over his head pretending to be a chicken. Friends said afterwards he was in fact about to be sick at the

238

thought of another confrontation with King A. the Kremlin's friend, which is very understandable, but anyway the talking shop appears pro tem to have been closed down once again. M. is pretty pleased at the way things are going. I think she has always had this vision of a forty-eight round contest to the death in the square ring and at the end of it the once-proud King Arthur, battered and bleeding, being led in chains from the arena with his gumshield knocked down his throat. The wets, including Dead Eye Whitelaw who always whimper at the sight of blood, have been pleading for the referee to go in and stop the fight. However Mr Munster (Tebbit N.) is urging her to go on till the final bell, by which time they hope there won't be any pits left to close down and everything will be hunkydory.

Poor old Fatty Prior, the while, has wisely taken his copper handshake and buggered off to the boardroom, for which I cannot say I blame him. He is to be replaced by the stuck-up ex-FO greaser Hurd, who has about as much chance of bringing peace to the war-torn province as Danny la Rue, and will be hindered in his endeavours by Muttonchops Boyson, who between ourselves has been hitting the optics pretty heavily of late. The other new recruit to the Cabinet is a friend of Maurice Picarda's called Young who used to be in property and has spent the last few years shimmering about Finchley making a bob or two out of various big deals. His task is to foster the illusion that Margaret is worried sick about unemployment and has numerous schemes up her sleeve to create jobs and scupper the opposition's little tricks on that front.

Must go now. That little runt Gordon Reece has blown in to put us through our paces for the Conference. The Boss, as I understand it, is to appear in battleship grey with steel handbag and accessories to suggest a resolute Autumn Mood, with myself in beige to strike a note of mellow optimism. We get the words later. If I can lay down smoke and beetle over to Pyecombe we might manage a few rounds and I can assure you that Deadeye will not be asked this year. God knows what he might do with a niblick after lunch.

T.T.F.N.

Yours aye,

DENIS

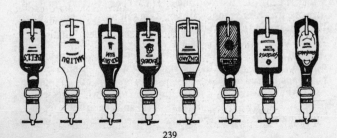

5 October 1984

Dear Bill,

The more I think about it, the more I regret my weakness in not insisting on Archie Wellbeloved being given the Canterbury job. Admittedly, as I may have said before, the poor old sod had one foot in the grave (as opposed to the present score of two), and his sermons had become pretty weird to put it mildly, but no power on earth would have persuaded him to allow a rabid revolutionary like Bishop Jenkins to occupy any senior position in the firm. Runcie in my opinion is a walking disaster, utterly spineless, in very much the same mould as the padre we had at Aldershot who tried to have the Clap Parade held behind closed doors on compassionate grounds.

As you may recall the Boss had to carpet the silly bugger after his boshed Thanksgiving Service for the Falklands which he turned into some kind of pacifist rally. Unrepentant, the daft old sod appoints this dreadful god-botherer to Durham, despite the fact that Comrade J. has made it clear he thinks the whole bang shoot is a lot of rubbish. I myself as you know am not a deeply religious person, though I've always believed in turning up for church parade, but I must confess when the bolt of lightning struck the Minster the morning after he'd been wheeled in, it did give one pause for thought. Bishop Trotkins however failed to get the message and the first thing he did on climbing into the pulpit was to trumpet away at the top of his voice to the effect that MacGregor was past it and should be shipped back pdq to the US of A. All of which may be perfectly sound over the stickies and cigars and indeed coincides with my own opinion, but it is not the sort of thing a senior sky-pilot is employed to say when dressed up in his full rig with the cameras turning and the grubby reptiles squatting under the pulpit, pencils poised, waiting to seize on anything remotely controversial.

As you can imagine, the Boss blew her top in no uncertain manner. She may not be a very religious person either but she is firmly convinced, quite rightly, that the Almighty is one of us, and that Old Nick lines up with Arthur Scargill and his Moscow minions. I made the mistake of toddling in with the clubs just after she'd seen Trotkins' outburst on the news and got it full in the neck.

Wasn't there a King in the history books who was always getting stick from some rabble-rousing saint or other and in the end dropped a hint to a couple of his heavies that he wouldn't be all that depressed if the aforementioned Red Cleric was rubbed out? On this occasion it turned out that I myself came within a whisker of having to get in the motor, drive up the M1 and pump lead into the troublesome bish. Eventually, however, wiser counsels prevailed and M. snatched up the blower to give an earful to Runcie. Pretty good stuff, entre nous, and I had refilled my glass no less than four times before she replaced the receiver. The gist of it was that if it hadn't been for her he would still be ladling out the swill on the pig-farm down in St Albans, an object of ridicule and contempt. As it was he was now an international star, allowed to dress up in silly frocks for the delight of millions of viewers all over the world. Point Two, MacGregor was her oldest and closest friend, very prone to depression and already under considerable strain, and remarks of the kind made by Runcie's Red appointee could very well cause him intense personal distress.

Cantuar I don't think managed to get a word in though I could hear him bleating faintly at the other end whenever Margaret paused for breath. Anyway, upshot was that he was to bike a letter round to old Mr McGoo personally apologising, and then get on to Trotkins and boot his spine through the top of his mitre. M. then telephoned Sir D. English, smarmy little creep, and told him to clear the front page of the *Daily Mail* for the shock exclusive that Runcie was on his knees praying for forgiveness.

The moment he spies the paper the next morning, of course, Runcie being Runcie and having no sense of dignity, goes on the wireless and says he hasn't apologised at all, Jenkins a damn good bloke, quite right to sound off, a shepherd responsible for giving voice on behalf of his sheep, which only drove the Boss into further paroxysms.

My plans for Brighton are as follows: Check in Hotel Metropole Tuesday a.m. Photo-call to establish presence. Mid-morning unexpected Telemessage arrives announcing Emergency Board Meeting Picwarmth Ltd. Arrive Pyecombe 12.15 view copious snorts with yourself, Maurice and the Major. Hideyhole chez Maurice's aunt Freda, Pyecombe 312, ask for 'Mr Simpson'.

Yrs unquenchably,

DENIS

19 October 1984

Dear Bill,

Very decent of you to ring following the Brighton bomb blast. Your concern much appreciated. I'm afraid I can tell you very little about the 'incident' itself as I had retired to bed following a pretty heavy fringe meeting of the Conservative Friends of Grape and Grain (F.O.G.G.), at which I had done perhaps a little too much research into the second category. Hardly had my head touched the pillow than I was plunged into a dreamless state of oblivion, from which I was only woken by the Night Porter telling me that the Grand had collapsed during the night, and would I make my way quietly down the fire escape.

The Boss, needless to say, took the whole thing very much in her stride, rather like that Campbell woman who was catapulted out of Bluebird at a hundred and fifty m.p.h. After a few comforting words to the Boys in Blue, she resumed the preparation of her speech to Conference. I myself tottered down to the TV lounge, where a jolly Red Cross lady was ladling out medicinal snorts to those suffering from shock.

Oddly enough the whole thing seemed to have rather an encouraging effect on the general morale, until then the moaning minnies having had the best of the argument. Bloody Runcie started it all. The sheep-featured primate himself claimed that it was all fixed by the press, he had no idea the Conference was coming up etc. etc., but there he was across half a page of *The Times* on the opening day, just like Parkinson the year before, bleating away about the unacceptable face of the Boss and the need for everyone to come together in a spirit of woolly benevolence. Usual *Guardian* rubbish, time for Scargill and McGoo to kiss and make up etc.

The effect of this was to put new spine into the wets who all promptly came popping out of the woodwork berating the Proprietor for her lack of compassion. I don't usually have much time for Mr Munster but I thought he was very sound, particularly on TV, in putting Runcie in his place. In case you missed it, the point he made was that the chap in the Bible who lent a helping hand to the poor old Samaritan or whoever it was who got mugged, wouldn't have been able to get him into intensive care at a local hotel had it not been for the fact that he was a businessman of enterprise and initiative with a pretty healthy credit balance at the NatWest of the day. A very good point, I thought, that Runcie might well put in his pipe and ponder before he next sounds off.

Just before the bomb put an end to the bickering, Walker threw his toupee into the ring with a few scarcely veiled cracks at M., egged on no doubt by the usual seedy gang of Yesterday's Men, e.g. Cemetery Face Gilmour, gloomy little Pym and poor old Sailor Ted. However all these things were forgotten in the Warrior Queen Reborn scenario: show must go on, men of violence whether in the bogs or down the mines to be resisted to the last breath, law and order to be upheld, Old Bill given pat on back, but delegates never to forget that M. deeply concerned about the plight of the unemployed etc. far more so than any woolly-haired cleric or whingeing wet like Walker. All of which may or may not be true, though in my experience compassion has never come all that high on the Boss's list of Top Ten Virtues. As for Lawson, if you ask me he is about as compassionate as a traffic warden with a hangover.

We've had the odd chuckle watching poor old Hopalong getting the bird for his TV debate with Mondale. My own view is that he was perfectly all right so long as he had his prompter screen with all his words written out in capital letters and the sincere bits underlined, but that it was tantamount to insanity to let him go on without his apparatus. At Burmah he'd have got his golden handshake years ago. Why they can't introduce compulsory retirement for politicos the same as anyone else I cannot understand. You've only got to look at Hailsham gazing round and trying to remember where he is to realise the folly of letting these old boys hang on. I saw some wag suggesting that Hopalong should submit to a senility test which consisted of starting at a hundred and counting backwards in sevens. Some of us tried it in the bar the other night and only Prothero got down past eighty before he had a brainstorm and frothed at the mouth. Which only goes to show.

Are you coming to Maurice's birthday party at the Bay Tree?

Yours in one piece,

DENIS

16 November 1984

Dear Bill,

Glad to see you for our regular binge after the Cenotaph. I finally found out who the crumpled little bugger with the fifth wreath was, the one we all had such a good chuckle over. Apparently they decided to put Owen's nose out of joint after he'd insisted so much about being allowed in on the act by getting hold of some undertaker bird from Ulster to represent the Orange Extremists. As you could see, security was pretty tight. The Queen Mother was frisked on the way in and even I had to produce means of identification which made me very cross I don't mind telling you.

It's rather amazing, isn't it, about old Hoppo staying in the saddle for another four years? Our American cousins really are a very rum crew. The poor old boy is plainly gaga, a fact which emerged on the one occasion he was allowed out without his prompter. But it's all fixed by a bunch of Hollywood smart-arses with big cigars, and whenever anyone asks a difficult question they let off a lot of balloons and hundreds of chorus girls come in twirling drumsticks, everyone sings 'God bless America' and they all burst into tears.

A far cry I may say from the malodorous Orient whither I was propelled on the sad demise of Mother Gandhi. I never had much time for the old trout myself, but she went down very well with M. and also, for that matter, with H.M. and as you may remember even starred in the Sandringham Christmas Spectacular last year, which I thought was an error of taste. One could see that despite differences of caste, creed and colour, both the ladies' hearts went out to her for taking a firm line on everything – castrating any males caught wandering about the streets looking randy, clapping her opponents in jail at the drop of a turban – all ideas, I may say, that the Boss has been secretly toying with for some time. Given the excitable nature of her subjects, I agreed with the Major that she had been rather asking for it when she blew up Johnny Sikh's Holy of Holies, as those of us who have been out East could have told her. But with a woman like that there's no point in arguing the toss.

Having had my backside punctured like a colander by the medico at London Airport against swamp fever, beri beri etc., I was in no mood to appreciate the obsequies, especially as I had to share a mini-van in the cavalcade with Steel, Owen and little Kinnock, all of whom had been tucking into the Duty Free and were sweating pretty heavily in their outfits from Tropiccadilly Off-the-peg Department. I said to Kinnock, who very generously offered me a swig of his Warrington Vodka, what a good thing it was we didn't do things over here the way they do them over there. Imagine the Boss, which heaven forfend, being set fire to on the Albert Embankment, and then distributed in brass bowls by Red Star throughout the length and breadth of the Kingdom.

Kinnock made the good point too, I thought, that it was a bit ripe the way young Reggie Gandhi stepped into his mother's shoes without so much as a by your leave, and how would I feel if the Boy Mark automatically took up the reins of office in similar circumstances? After this and a few more libations from the domestic vodka I began to take quite a shine to brother Neil and to think that on several other points he was reasonably sound. He told me, entre nous, that he regards Friend Scargill as a prize twat and would be more than ready to crack his skull open with a walking stick should the opportunity present itself. Obviously he's not allowed to say that in public, otherwise he might get the walking stick treatment himself from the hooligan pickets.

Re your enquiry about whether you should buy into British Telecom. Lawson's so snooty he won't even give me the time of day, but Maurice P. says they're going to be a goldmine so I should draw your own conclusions.

May Shiva's many arms fill your pockets with good things.

DENIS

10 Downing Street
Whitehall

30 November 1984

Dear Bill,
I don't know whether you ever have the wireless on in the bath? If so you may have heard the very entertaining cabaret last week when the Smellysocks ran amuck at Halitosis Hall, shouted down poor little Fowler, called him an animal, tried to pull his trousers down and stamped on his sandwiches. Heffer, the ring leader, even breathed on his spectacles, so I was told.

The whole thing was got up by Scargill's paid agents in the House, who claimed that M. was ruthlessly robbing the piggy banks of widows and orphans in the Yorkshire Wastes in order to induce their menfolk to join the trickle back to work. I may say if it had been left to me every damn penny would have been docked. Why we should pay out all our directors' salaries and other dividends so that the miners can go on lobbing petrol bombs at the Boys in Blue quite passes my understanding. Margaret agrees, entre nous, but couldn't get it past the Saatchis.

Despite this setback they seem to think it'll be all over by

Christmas, and the only real talking point is what to do with the defeated King Arthur. Should he be led in chains through Threadneedle Street or will there be a lot of pie in the sky from the Wets about no one being the winner, now is the time to kiss and make up etc? My own solution, which the Proprietor seems ready to rubber-stamp when the time comes, is for

Scargill to be doped, crated up and dispatched on a one-way ticket to Moscow via Aeroflot. Act Two: A full-scale Thanksgiving in St Paul's to be conducted by the snaggle-toothed Archbishop and his Bench of Trots, at gunpoint if necessary.

Since I saw you last at the R.A.C. – and thank you for a slap-up blow-out with all the trimmings (I assume you can swing it on expenses – next one on me) we have been entertaining Fitzgerald the Dublin Teasock, a tall gangling bean very much out of his depth, but like most of his race no mean sniffer of the cork. Despite the rigorous security (every field and hedgerow within miles of Chequers bristling with Panzer Divisions) and the For Your Eyes Only timetable, all the reptiles were on parade at the gates, including those who had just returned from interviewing the World's Most Wanted Woman in her attractive terraced house in Dunleary, who in fact was obviously somebody quite different.

Fitzgerald plainly had no idea what was coming to him. He turned up with a file of suggestions about the way ahead which it took three men to carry and which the Boss proceeded to tear up one by one in front of the television cameras, while that oily little Hurd sniggered obsequiously at her side. You could see from FitzG's eyes that this made him very upset as they'd spent months working on them and after it was over I felt obliged to lay an arm round the poor old boozer and lead him away to the smoking room where we killed off a brace of Jamieson's King Size.

He's actually very sound on most topics, agreed with me that Hurd was a four-letter fellow of the first water and seemed reassured by my own view that we should hand back the whole bang shoot to the natives a.s.a.p. As he pointed out while demonstrating a very amusing penny-throwing game they play over there, the only result of M. getting on her high horse was that his lot would get the heave-ho and she would find herself having to do business with that little shyster Haughey and serve her bloody well right. I think it might have been at the back of his mind that I would share this thought with Margaret in the privacy of the boudoir, but that only goes to show he doesn't know much about how to deal with the Boss.

The only thing that's really got up the old girl's nose of recent days was old Walrusfeatures Macmillan coming back from the grave and attempting with shaking hand to plunge the dagger

 between her shoulder blades. According to a friend of the Major's who runs a lupin farm near Birch Grove, what brought the old bugger out of the woodwork was Emmanuel Shinwell slipping in to do his soft-shoe number in the Other Place at the age of a hundred. Bovvermac was determined to show that even if he was a mere stripling of ninety he could knock spots off Manny any time and, unlike his competitor, still put the boot in. Picture the scene. Massed ranks of ermined geriatrics weeping quietly into their pocket handkerchiefs. A lot of guff about the old days, First World War, camaraderie of the trenches, and what it all boiled down to was that Margaret was a heartless little woman who was leading us all up the garden path. Fortunately they were all blubbing so much they didn't understand what he was talking about, but the Boss got the message and quickly crossed his name off the Christmas Card List.

Talking of Christmas Cards, did you see Margaret's favourite poem she quoted in *Women's Realm*? You might like to know that it came off a card she got last year from Maurice's Antique Hypermarket lady:

> When skies above are dark and grey
>> And troubles get you down
> A smile will chase your cares away
>> And soon replace your frown.

Try saying it when you've had a few. I find it jolly moving.
Yours in tears,

DENIS

10 Downing Street
Whitehall

14 December 1984

Dear Bill,

I was sorry to hear that Maurice came a cropper over the Telecom issue and had his application sent back. But I do wish he would refrain from ringing me up on these occasions in such a highly emotional condition, especially as he knows full well that relations between Number Ten and Number Eleven, at least between the menfolk, are decidedly frosty. Even so, with the Yuletide nearly on us, I did poke my nose around the door in a charitable manner and ask what was up. Old friend, good war record, scraped together his savings to have a flutter, usher in the new age of shareholder democracy, only to receive bum's rush. Lawson, who obviously thought it was me and not my friend at all, turned up his enormous hooter in the usual snooty fashion and said that thousands of other entries had been disqualified on technical points to do with the application form. 'And if you will insist on doing your paper work after lunch, Denis' – this with a great smirk and his waistcoat going up and down as he chuckled – 'you have no one to blame but yourself.'

As you may have seen, the Mad Monk is under sedation after being duffed over by Margaret's Bovver Boot Boys. It's often baffled me why the crinkly-haired old loon soldiers on, especially when every time he sticks his head out of the door he gets pelted with a couple of dozen standard, medium or large. However there has always been a strange rapport between him and my better half, going back to the time when she entered the ring against Sailor Ted with the Monk in her corner flapping the wet towel. His latest wheeze for once seemed reasonably sound. You know my view about students: layabouts, troublemakers, unwashed fornicators and dope-fiends living it up at my expense and yours in agreeable listed buildings. Why not, the Monk reasoned in a rare moment of lucidity, make the parents of these long-haired slugs cough up a goodly whack towards their breakages, magistrates' fines etc?

Shrill squeals might have been expected at this from the Moscow-funded Smellysocks, but no one had anticipated any trouble from our own side. What they don't realise of course is that with a swing like they had last time, the place has filled up with some of the most grisly detritus of common little yoiks ever seen on the Tory back benches, all of them keen to cash in on anything that's going, all wanting their spotty offspring turned into gentlemen scientists and upwardly mobile computer programmers. Not surprisingly, the prospect of having to put their

248

hands in their own pockets to this end soon had them up on their hind legs, baying for the blood of the Monk.

I don't know which was worse for the poor old boy, being debagged by the yoiks or getting the laser beam treatment from Queen Boadicea in one of her chillier moods. I met him in the corridor coming out of the study, fumbling with a big bottle of green pills and muttering to himself about making a terrible mistake and having to atone for it. He clearly had no idea who I was. It crossed my mind to propose a stiffener but remembering what happened to Maurice when he washed his Uppers down with a tumblerful of neat Pernod I let him pass. All to no avail as he proceeded to slosh the contents of the pill-bottle back with a large G and T and stumbled out through the front door, where needless to say a quorum of egg-chuckers was waiting for a spot of target practice.

Christmas comes on apace. I did ask little Brittan off the record if he could get the boy Mark's re-entry permit chewed up in the computer, but I fear we may have to grin and bear it.

Stay low (some chance!),

DENIS

10 Downing Street
Whitehall

28 December 1984

Dear Bill,
I'm sorry you couldn't join Maurice, myself and his Antique Lady when they came up for their last-minute Christmas Shopping spree. Probably just as well under the circs. The idea was to R.V. at the R.A.C. mid-morning and then sally forth to Regent Street to find a few stocking-fillers for the nearest and dearest, take in a light lunch at Selfridges, load up a taxi with our purchases and then back to Number Ten for fortified tea before popping the happy couple on the Flying Wino back to Dover Priory.

Alas, events fell out otherwise. Our first mistake in my view was to accept a seasonal snort in the Ladies Annexe from that awful buffoon Frank Longford, who has taken to coming into the Club to use the swimming pool. Maurice's Antique Lady took a tremendous shine to Old Baldy, sat on his lap and told him he was a bit of all right. Maurice naturally got very shirty about this and asked Longford to step outside. I said why didn't we all step outside and get on with the shopping but then suddenly they became very friendly and decided on one for the road, followed by a splash in the pool to cool off. By the time they got back to the Bar they seemed to have lost Longford but claimed their teeth were chattering and ordered trebles. Next thing I remember the Club Secretary was having a word in my ear to say that there had been complaints from Members about our lady guest standing on the table in the library to sing carols. By this time the restaurant was closed, the usual mob in the bar were in jocular mood, and the prospect of getting our heads down in the scrum at Lillywhites began to seem less and less attractive. Maurice became very matey with a pretty shifty looking old cove under the impression that they'd been in the R.A.S.C. together, his lady disappeared to powder her nose and that was the last we saw of her. I myself struck lucky, as I thought at the time, in that I ran into a bloke who'd just taken delivery of a consignment of cut-price hampers from Fortnum's: no questions asked, cash in hand, drop them off by plain van later that night. As I recall I handed over a monkey in readies, only to discover next morning that the damn fool had tried to deliver at Number Eleven and got a flea in his ear from Mother Lawson. Like Maurice's lady he has not been seen since.

As you may gather from the foregoing mousey adventures the cat has been away, whistle-stopping round the globe a la Superwoman, girdling the planet in a matter of moments. I couldn't see the point of it quite frankly, as she could have easily signed away Hong Kong to Mr Dung by Telex and bending Hopalong's ear might have been done a great deal more effectively over the blower, deaf though he be. Shouting would have been considerably simpler than all that air-travel. Originally it was ordained that I too was to tag along. However you may have seen that we played host to Mr Gorblimov and his very presentable Missus. (Don't ask me why. Six months ago it was a non-speaks situation with the Bear, source of all evil in the universe etc., suddenly it's all hunky-dory, lunch out at some derelict pile beyond Wimbledon, Howe slobbering over the snow-covered boots of Yesterday's Enemy as if he was a human being.) Anyway, when I was introduced I naturally asked the interpreter why Comrade G. was wasting his time with our lot, when his friend Arthur Scargill was no doubt keeping a fish and chip lunch hot for him on the picket lines and expecting his usual cheque from Moscow Narodny Bank. I could see the interpreter blanch a bit at this, and Margaret immediately jumped in to divert the conversation onto heavy engineering. Later I was told brusquely by an aide that my presence would not after all be required on the jaunt to Honkers. I did my best to look upset.

Before leaving, the Boss went on the TV to blast the Wets, doing her Mrs Scrooge act and saying that in future there would be no more free handouts to school-leavers, no going back, blood, sweat, toil, tears and champagne corks cracking in the boardroom. But if you ask me the yoiks on the back benches have tasted blood. No sooner was her back turned than Jenkin was being debagged to universal cheering.

You are very wise to spend Christmas in Lanzarote, even if, as you say, you don't intend to put a foot outside the door. Remember me as you knock back the Pina Coladas, enduring the pains of Purgatory in the bosom of the family round the tree at Chequers. We are once again threatened wih the Howes on Boxing Day. And Mr Munster is coming to stay for an open-ended convalescence. I suppose that's something to look forward to.

Yours while life lingers,

DENIS

CHATEAU
ST. DENIS

1985
BOTTLED

10 Downing Street
Whitehall

8 February 1985

Dear Bill,

I am amazed by what you tell me about the Major putting it round the Club that the lapse in our correspondence was due to my having been 'dispatched to dry out at Broadlands'. The fact is that following this Ponting business, the Boss has instituted a major security blackout, with the result that even my private correspondence has been gone through by two buggers in trench coats who have obviously fed my last two screeds into the shredder. Not that there was anything remotely sensitive in them, other than a few offensive remarks about Lawson. Talking of whom, I couldn't resist rubbing his nose in it a bit when the solids hit the airconditioning last week over the OPEC circus. Fatty had been trotting round saying the pound would find its own level, everything tickety-boo, never fear, Skipper Nigel at the helm etc, when Wham, slap into the iceberg, lifeboat stations and arse-end out of the water. I was fortunate enough to collide with him as he sidled into Number Ten for Correction with Madame T. and made some jocular reference to his navigational skills. 'What of your famous Tax Cuts the noo?' At this he purpled up no end, stuck his nose in the air, made an odd snorting noise, and ponced off to take his medicine.

If truth be told, 14% is pretty good news to those of us who've got a bit under the bed for a rainy day, but I obviously couldn't tell him that.

You would have thought, at this stage, with our lot hacking about in the rough, that little Kinnock would have seized his chance to sink a putt or twain. Not a bit of it. Smellysocks put down some frightful-sounding censure motion, all channels of communication booked for a full-scale coverage, but as usual little Ginger Pillock having danced into the ring and sparred about for a few seconds was stopped in his tracks by the Grantham Gouger and left looking like a piece of knotted string. As I said to Maurice in the House of Lords Snug afterwards, they should all take a leaf out of old Snaggleteeth Stockton's book. He may be a hundred and six, but he certainly knows how to put the boot in. I don't know whether you saw his performance on Geriatrics' Half Hour. Personally I thought it was a lot of piss and wind, but he had Boris sobbing into his vodka like a child.

You ask if the Boss was miffed when the Oxford egg-heads black-balled her from their Funny Hats and Gowns Club. I happen to know that when the idea was first mooted by some young brown-tonguer from the dreaming spires, she became quite misty-eyed; in fact I distinctly remember the scene at the breakfast table when she dropped the EPNS with a clatter in mid-egg. 'I little thought, Denis, as I biked out to the Labs all those years ago as plain Margaret Roberts that I should one day return to Oxford to receive the highest honour that our greatest university can bestow. An Honorary Degree in the Sheldonian Theatre.' At the time I refrained from pointing out that these old codgers distribute honours of this nature with a packet of cornflakes to every tin-pot coon and mafioso who takes the trouble to check in at the Randolph. Even I myself, if you remember, had to go and dress up in some damnfool dressing-gown and cowpat hat at Peebles when I was on the board at Burmah to be made an honorary Doctor of Applied Lubricants. However the Boss had obviously set her heart on the Oxford Accolade and had even got the little woman round the corner to run up a frock to go with the outfit. If you ask me she also had half an eye on the prospect of getting her own back on old Stockton who in his role as Chancellor would have had to parade through the streets at her side trying to look as though he was enjoying it. Instead of which some band of barmy Lefties and long-haired Trots got up a protest motion at the last minute and scuppered it.

I was all for pulling the rug from under those fat cats with their sherry parties and eight-course dinners pretty sharpish and letting the Monk loose to make a few judicious cuts. I ventured to suggest as much to the Boss but she claimed to have forgotten all about it and said that Oxford had always been a hotbed of Communism even in her day; it was of no concern whatever to her, these tinsel honours were meaningless, she was too busy running the country etc. All very well, but if you ask me it was not a coincidence when that same evening the wild-eyed Rasputin de nos jours was summoned round to discuss annual MOTs for all university lecturers, with special reference to those working in large car-manufacturing towns within a sixty mile radius of London.

Are your Americans still coming over on Thursdays to do their marketing? If so I could warn Lillywhites to lay in some of their electric buggies with the cocktail cabinet attachment. If they felt like taking half a dozen we might even get a commission on it.

Yours in the spirit of enterprise,

DENIS

10 Downing Street
Whitehall

8 March 1985

Dear Bill,

I'm sorry to hear that Daphne wasn't amused by my prezzo from the US of A. I wasn't suggesting for a moment that either of you had AIDS, but these do-it-yourself detector kits are selling like hot cakes in the Big Apple, and I thought you'd be amused by the little rubber gloves. Why don't you forward it anonymously to that curate you were telling me about who made a pass at Maurice in the Long Room?

I'm afraid the Special Relationship beano was a bit of a dead duck. The old girl was absolutely over the moon, bless her heart, when they invited her to be the first British P.M. since Winston to talk in their equivalent of Halitosis Hall. (I can never remember which is the Senate and which is the Congress, I don't suppose it matters very much.) Anyway, the Corsican Brothers laid on a team of copy-writers including Sir Custardface, armed with the Reader's Digest Golden Treasurehouse of Wit and Wisdom, little Gordon Grease was choppered in to add herbs and spices to the brew, I was driven round to Harley Street for a tough talking to from Bosendorfer's friend Dr Gropius about loss of self-esteem and mixing with social inferiors and handed a milk-bottle full of the Antibooze pills Maurice used to take, which I of course flushed down the loo the moment I got back to H.Q.

I had hoped the flight to Washington would include a Western with suitable Ambassador Class refreshments, but the Captain told me the Boss had ordered all the seats and the bar unit to be taken out so that she could rehearse her speech without the distraction of revelling winos from the Cabinet Office.

Hopalong was waiting on the tarmac with the red carpet and the customary damnfool drum majorettes prancing up and down: the anorexic spouse was clutching his paw as usual, and dropped a curtsey to the Boss obviously thinking she was someone else. The old boy himself seemed to have had another couple of tucks taken out of his face since we last met, and his hair is now ox-blood. The next day we all filed in to the Washington H.H., and I must say the Boss got a very nice round of applause from the white-haired cowpunchers and Colonel Sanders lookalikes there assembled. She then stepped onto the rostrum and gave them forty minutes' worth of what they fancied, references to Sir Winston, Dark Days of the War, Yellow Peril, Red Menace, Hands across the Sea, bung everything into space including the kitchen sink, U.S. know-how an inspiration to the entire world etc.

I could see some of the old grandpappies sobbing into their

bandanas, and everything seemed to be entirely tickety-boo. The whole point of all this, as you will have realised, was to butter up Hopalong to such an extent that she could them twist his arm on letting some steam out of the dollar, at present putting the kibosh on all Mr Nicely Nicely Lawson's Springtime Tax Cuts. At a suitable moment therefore as she was receiving congratulations in her dressing room afterwards, M. took him aside and explained her dilemma, how the high price of the dollar was threatening her stability and could lead to a Communist Government in Britain, headed by Kinnock. The old ham seemed to be drinking it all in, his face registering grandfatherly concern, compassionate twitch of an eyebrow, arm round the shoulders and so on. However, no sooner were our backs turned than he went on Coast to Coast television to say they hadn't seen nothing yet, the dollar was going to ride even higher and those who were squealing had nobody but themselves to blame. As you can imagine, the Boss, who had been expecting a rapturous welcome home from her historic mission with the dollar obediently tumbling on arrival, was pretty sore at having browned her tongue in vain. The Smellysocks were quick to rub her face in it, and the old girl took it all very badly, saying she had been cruelly let down and that it was distressing to find one's hero not only had feet of clay but also played a pretty dirty game of poker. Personally I put it down to general deterioration of the grey cells. The old boy I'm sure had meant to do his bit, but he clearly can't retain anything for more than a few moments, and as their conversation wasn't in the minutes it probably went clean out of his mind on the way to the TV studio. We had the same trouble with that Chairman at Burmah who used to blow bubbles at Board Meetings and always had odd socks on.

The Boss's revenge is to be taken on the Barnsley Lenin, King Arthur. For the first time in years the tramp of hob-nailed boots was heard in the hall, and the new leader of the horny-handed sons of toil Mr Willis and his cohorts came round for the old traditional beer and smoked salmon sandwiches. The Boss was surprisingly polite, and told them that she greatly valued their views on any topic. Willis and his chums were obviously a bit bewildered by this, having expected the usual fire-breathing dragon act and a lecture about the need for hard work. While they were still groggy from the shock Walker produced a form of words to settle the strike and said he was grateful to them for having drawn it up and that he was sure he himself could agree to a good deal of it. Still stunned they were then shunted out the front door and exposed to the reptiles for a group photo. This in turn made Arthur livid at being left out, and he retreated to his bunker. However finally on Sunday even he had to admit defeat and come out with the white flag flying. The Boss decreed that there was to be no talk of any victory but since then the champagne corks have been popping non-stop.

Yours sub rosa,
DENIS

10 Downing Street
Whitehall

22 March 1985

Dear Bill,
You enquire why no national junketings following Comrade
Scargill's fifty-nil defeat at the hands of my good lady the
Grantham Mauler. That was precisely my reaction. You'd think
that after a year spending millions on well and truly humiliating
the wretched little Bolshie, the least they could do would be to
blow a couple of thou on a really good celebration, be it in the
form of a whole holiday for schools, a Thanksgiving Service at St
Paul's with Runcie under lock and key, or possibly a firework
display with Arthur burned in effigy.

To be fair to the Boss, she agreed with me that such a scenario
was in order. Enter then however the Corsican Twins, Alberto y
Luigi, flourishing the results of their overnight market research,
which purported to show that the Boss's shelf-life would be
drastically reduced were she to indulge in any such exercise.
Selected housewives had been asked for their opinion, and they
all plumped for a kiss and make-up reconciliation between the
warring factions, and a low-key business-as-usual pay-off. In
view of the shrivelling pound and Kinnock's ten-point lead in the
polls this eventually won approval.

It didn't stop me, I may say, from funding my own private
beano down at the Club, where a lot of the boys got pretty tight
and set fire to some of the soft furnishings.

I imagine poor old Hopalong must be rather feeling the
draught now that Chernenko has turned his toes up. The one
thing that kept him going all these years was the thought that
however senile he may be, his opposite number at the Kremlin
has always hitherto been allotted the bed nearest the door. Now
the Russkies, pretty sozzled and never very quick off the mark,
have finally hauled in the fact that things proceed rather more
smoothly if the Chairman of the Board can at least find his way to
the Gents without assistance. The upshot is that instead of another
incontinent OAP they have handed the baton to a younger
bugger, one Comrade Gorblimoff, who you remember toddling
over here recently to see the sights, bringing with him a very nifty
little wife and making a great impression on the Boss, who can
spot a fellow bone-crusher miles off.

Naturally she leapt at the idea of climbing once again into her
Moscow Funeral Outfit, which is beginning to look a bit shiny at
the elbows, to be there as Most Favoured Foreign Dignitary
while they were wheeling the stiff round Red Square to the
strains of solemn music. A further inducement for M. to shine as

258

the funeral baked meats were being snapped up in the Hall of Mirrors was that poor old Hoppo failed to show, the official word being unavoidable business engagements – the truth, if you ask me, was that the medicos rightly advised that three hours standing to attention in minus thirty degrees while they rolled past every available jalopyful of rockets in their arsenal could well sound the old fellow's death knell.

Frankly, after the fiasco of Mother Gandhi's send-off I didn't fancy sharing a mini-bus with Kinnock and Steel, so I usefully filled in the time by tooling down to the Major's Bring and Buy in aid of Police Horse Trainers, and got in a few rounds at Rye with Archie Wellbeloved's brother, the one who was drummed out of that Prep School at Broadstairs for allegedly jumping too low in the leapfrog. Don't say I'm not a tolerant man – though personally I never believed the story and have always found him a very sociable bloke when it comes to knocking back the doubles until four-thirty a.m. in the Residents' Lounge.

As you probably saw, Sailor Ted has been let out of his basket again, making his customary snide observations, this time on the TV. If you ask me, our chubby friend was extremely miffed about the Boss's victory over the Miners, particularly in view of the fact that that was where he came unstuck himself. I suppose the thought has also crossed his mind that he's not getting any younger and that he'd better put his best foot forward, ideally up the arse of the leadership, if any hope of a comeback is to be entertained before the Chernenko phase sets in. I know what he feels like.

Hope you managed to get the consignment below decks before Mr Nicely Nicely slapped his new price labels on.

Yours to the bitter end,

DENIS

10 Downing Street
Whitehall

5 April 1985

Dear Bill,

A propos the Budget, I am as delighted as you are to see the smile wiped off the face of our fat friend from Number 11. A year ago, you may recall, the sun shone from out of his fundament, causing Margaret to don her dark glasses whenever he held forth and mark him down as a dangerous rival on a par with Tarzan and Mr Munster for the take-over stakes. Now, at a stroke, as our seafaring friend E. Heath used to say, the Golden Boy has become the dunce in the corner, and Ladbroke's won't give you much more than 100 to 1 on his finishing in the first four.

I couldn't resist rubbing his nose in it a bit when I espied him over the garden wall taking one of his sprogs to task for insubordination. 'Sorry about your getting boxed in,' I called, 'no doubt we shall have to wait till next year for the tax cuts you were telling us about.' This provoked one of his predictable jibes about me having to go and drown my sorrows at the R.A.C., but I thought it was Advantage D.T., especially as his sprog kicked him in the shin just as I toddled off to follow his advice.

Talking of Mr Munster, word round the Power House is that the wretched little creeping Jesus of the Lower Fourth, Gummer, is about to get the boot with ten minutes' notice to clear his desk. I never liked him since he handed me a tract at Blackpool with a disgusting caricature of a decrepit wino staggering down the Primrose Path and a spruce teetotaller in a bowler hat and pin-stripe smugly ascending the Hill Difficult to the Heavenly City. Sod him. His place is to be taken by Mr Munster, who is trying to mellow from punk bother boy into kindly avuncular patriarch, cracking jokes and handing out fivers to the children of party workers. Not a role, I may say, that comes naturally to our Norman, but he toddled in for a screw-driver or twain the other night when Margaret was slumming it out in the sticks and told me, when Boris went out of the room for a moment, that he was very much impressed by my own personal image and asked whether I had any tips on how to win a reputation for bonhomie. I said the secret, like the Genie, was to be found in the bottle.

You'll be pleased to hear, a propos Margaret's intended reshuffle, that she has finally seen the light about her dancing partner from the Bromley Charm School, friend Cecil, who will not after all be asked back on the bus, where he once gave her the benefit of his aftershave and obsequious smiles. The powers that be have decided that despite his gifts as a TV salesperson, he is a bit too rich for the pudding. No great loss in my view, but the Boss shed a few quiet tears into her hankie after she crossed his

name off the list, and said it was a tragic case of a man brought down by a fatal weakness – glancing sternly at myself as she spoke.

As you can see from the foregoing, some of our chaps here have got the wind up, following Mr Nicely's lamentable performance with the battered leather case. Kinnock's personal rating has leaped ahead, which says something for the state we're in. The Corsican Brothers, having completely buggered up the Victory Celebrations after the Miners' Strike by advocating a low-key softly-softly scenario, proceeded to recommend to Margaret that she should demonstrate her great concern for the plight of the unwaged by entertaining a charabanc full of pimply Scouse layabouts to tea and cucumber sandwiches at Downing Street. I myself was told to be on hand to provide light relief and keep an eye on the silver. At the outset, all seemed pretty much under control. The yobbos filed in, rubber-necking round at the fixtures and fittings, and were ushered upstairs to the drawing room, where Boris was standing by the tea-urn, assisted by a couple of old bags from Charlie Forte's outfit, who ladled out a plateful of fancies and they all went off, sat on the edge of their chairs and munched away. The Boss then blew it. Never keen on anyone getting something for nothing, she delivered a stern lecture on the need for them all to get off their fat arses and start window-cleaning or set up multi-million pound computer businesses. Whereupon they all fell out of the front door snarling and growling, much to the delight of the reptiles who were waiting with microphones at the ready to record their thoughts.

Did the Major or Maurice get on to you about our proposed weekend of thwacking the pill in Rye? I'm told the Mermaid is full of Americans, but there's a very jolly little woman called Polly Carter-Ruck who does B&B at Appledore. Own front door key, no questions asked. Does this appeal?

DENIS

10 Downing Street
Whitehall

19 April 1985

Dear Bill,
Wasn't there some story or other about a chap in the olden days who went whizzing round the world in a balloon for a bet and was so dazed when he got back that he didn't realise what day it was, let alone that the Club Bar was still open? I can't remember how it turned out, but I can quite understand how the poor old cove felt.

I woke up at three o'clock this morning, got dressed and bowled down to the R.A.C. for lunch. I thought first of all it was a rather murky sort of day, not many people about, but when I got there the Night Porter very decently took me into his box and administered a tranquillising draught of Jap whisky from the jerry-can under his chair. It was then I realised that my bodyclock, as the medics call it, had gone on the blink.

Not that one can blame it in the circs. You ask what was achieved apart from knocking a good five years off one's natural span? The answer, as far as I'm concerned, is sweet F.A., or sweet F.O. might be nearer the mark. As you know, these trips are all hatched over the duty-free vodka by the reds and weirdos at the Foreign Office on a Saturday morning when they haven't got much to do. No earthly purpose is served, but the Boss can't resist a chance to rip off her tweeds and twinset, revealing the Wonderwoman leotard and cloak, and circle the globe in a shower of sparks.

As you can well imagine, I did my best to be excused the exercise, pleading an important business lunch at the Savoy with Maurice P. and his boy Kevin who is setting up some kind of dental equipment emporium in the Mile End Road. However the powers that be dictated otherwise, and in the end I think this was probably a good thing. It's usually me who doesn't know which day of the week it is, but on this occasion the old girl dropped a trail of clangers rather in the style of old Prosser-Cluff in his butter-flicking period. At one point when she began to hail the achievements of the brave Indonesian people while addressing the Singapore Businesswomen's Anti-Communist League, or it may have been the other way round, I felt obliged to lean forward and put her right on her geography. Not that I got a word of thanks, and indeed took a full dose of gamma rays while the oriental ladies tittered nervously into their hankies.

Talking of Prosser-Cluff, I mentioned his name to Mr Lee, the very sensible little man who runs Singapore, knowing that he shared with P-C a liking for a round of golf and a toughish line with the Unions. Lee's face immediately lit up and he paid a glowing tribute to the man who had brought the workers to heel by setting fire to their living quarters, and repeated what I had heard before, i.e. that they all adored him for it. It was at this stage, I think, that the Boss got rather carried away and made a fiery speech extolling Mr Lee as the hammer of the Trots, venturing to boast of her own achievements in settling the hash of Friend Scargill. Naturally the reptiles picked it up, and the Smellysocks, desperate for anything to throw into the stew, immediately made the most of it. (On that topic, I'd like to see Brother Kaufmann attempt the Nineteen Cities of the Orient in Four Days Dash. One blast of hot air off the tarmac and Baldie would melt into his terylene tropical suiting.) Not but what the travelling media circus, ever on the look-out for a bone to chew, immediately started bombarding the Boss with namby-pamby comments from him and the other whining pinkos at home, accusing her of selling the British worker down the river and crying stinking fish in someone else's back yard. Margaret's answer, which these morons didn't seem to grasp, was that your wily oriental businessman has been under the impression for years that this country is inhabited by a rabble of work-shy Trots living off the state, with barely sufficient energy to heave back the blanket and toddle down to the corner to pick up the dole. You and I know that nothing has changed, but the Boss is trying to push the line that the old firm is now under New Management, and Scargill's bleeding head is held up as an example of what happens to those who don't like it. A point well worth making, in my view, considering the hopeless balls-up that the Corsican Twins made of our Victory in the Pits.

This unseemly controversy apart, I came back with my respect for the good old D of E very much enhanced. Having watched twenty-six displays of Native Dancing, shaken hands with four hundred and fifty-three diplomats and their wives and even been obliged to feed a suitably engraved coconut to the sacred elephants, I now realise there is more to being a Royal than meets the inexperienced eye. By the way, did you see that barmy Scotsman in the *Sunday Express* suggested I should be given a peerage for my pains? I was rather touched by that, quite frankly. But if you'd spent any time in the Bar at the House of Lords, you'd share my reluctance to don the ermine. You may think the R.A.C. has some pretty hard cases, but that gaggle of geriatric winos at half-past ten in the morning trying to pick up their tonic bottles make you, me and Maurice look like outpatients.

I brought you back one or two exotic curiosities which came by Diplomatic Bag. I don't want Daphne to see them particularly, so I'll wait until our lunch at the Praying Dog in Tonbridge on the 20th.

Yours garlanded with flowers,

DENIS

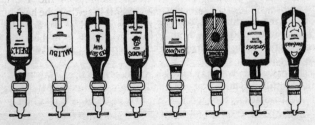

10 Downing Street
Whitehall

3 May 1985

Dear Bill,

I'm glad we see eye to eye about the Princess Michael business. As you rightly surmised, it was all got up by a grubby little nest of Trots round at the *Daily Mirror*. And I also happen to know that Robert Maxwell is very thick with the Kremlin and has already signed up Gorblimov to write his memoirs. So it doesn't require much second sight to see what's going on, i.e. the discrediting of the Royal Family as a last desperate bid, after the failure of Scargill, to bring about violent revolution.

I felt I had to write to poor old Reibnitz's girl, spelling it out for her, because sometimes these people are a bit out of touch with the political realities and take it personally. As it happens I had a bit of an 'in' with the distaff side of the Kent set-up, having bumped into the Baron a couple of times on business in South Africa. He always seemed to me to be a perfectly decent old cove, very sound on the Red Menace, labour relations, the welfare state, etc. He was very pally with old Mrs Keffirbesher Senior, as he was with many of the good ladies on the Joburg circuit, where he was known as the Baron von Randypants. Of course the word was that he'd been mixed up with the Ribbentrop lot, but as I understand it his main interest was bagging the local wild life, plus any Russky trouble-makers who happened to cross his sights, and what better recommendation could one have than that? I remember one particular evening at Mrs K's under the stars when the Baron had had a few and got rather weepy about the old days, saying that if only Winnie and Adolf hadn't been so touchy we could all have joined forces in '45 and flattened the Reds once and for all.

Of course no one's seriously suggesting that the Palace didn't know about this all along. For a start most of the D of E's relatives were on the other side, mixing cocktails for the German High Command. No reason at all therefore for them to blackball Prince Michael for going through with it. Even so I didn't think he made a frightfully good showing on this occasion. After all, if in a purely hypothetical case, the Boss were to be ostracised as the daughter of a raving Grantham Mosleyite, I think the least I could have done would be to toddle along to TV-AM and sit beside her on the sofa, nodding supportively while she made her tearful appeal to the nation for sympathy.

Hopalong, as you may have observed, is no longer Flavour of the Month. No doubt moved by the plight of Princess Michael, the old movie star took it into his head to celebrate VE Day being filmed laying a wreath on the Tomb of the Unknown SS Man during his forthcoming trip to Krautland. Needless to say this went down like a lead balloon with the New York fraternity, and the Boss, who in view of her setbacks was feeling like putting the high heel in somewhere along the line decided that Hoppo had had it coming to him for a long time, and blasted his so-called reconciliation bid from the Front Bench at Question Time.

Talking of that sort of thing, we were hoping to have a reunion of the Veterans' Lodge at the Savoy on VE Day itself. The plan was to get Bomber Harris to say grace, but now he's turned his toes up we're a bit stuck. Whiffy Heatherington suggested Runcie, but I trod on that p.d.q. despite the fact that Rev. Snaggleteeth in his day was no mean slayer of the Boche. What about that old Chindit you ran into in Folkestone who had spent time inside for pyromania? I'm sure if we had a word with Wontner and told the waiters to keep him out of reach of the matches he'd do the job as well as anybody.

Give us a bell to let me know your thinking on this.

Sieg Heil from all of us here in the Bunker,

DENIS

10 Downing Street
Whitehall

17 May 1985

Dear Bill,
What a wonderful celebration of my 70th! I may say that when I received Maurice's invitation to address the East Sussex Small Businessmen's Association on 'Some Experiences on and off the Rugby Football Field', I never twigged for an instant what lay behind it. Right up to the moment when I took my place on the platform next to the Padre and the curtains were drawn aside to raucous cheering from the DT Fan Club and the Bells' Yew Green Footwarmers struck up 'Where Shall We Be A Hundred Years From Now?' I seriously believed a bona fide evening of decorous boredom lay ahead with little more in prospect than half a bottle of Cyprus Sherry.

Of course you were perfectly right in thinking that I'd never have been let off the leash, had the Boss herself known the true nature of the beano. I fear that even so she may suspect something from the bits missing off the Roller and the fact that I strolled into breakfast next morning, so I'm told, still in my bib and tucker. Did the Fire-Brigade get to the Almshouses in time? I knew it was a mistake to ask Maurice's Chindit.

Nonetheless our little booze-up made me feel that there was

after all something to be said for notching up the Three Score Years and Ten from which no traveller returns. The only other advantage I can think of is that it gives one a chance to cock a snook at the Gummers of this world who maintain that a hundred a day plus the firewater is certain death before thirty. Of course there are unlucky ones – Prosser-Cluff's brother springs to mind, not to mention P-C himself – whose system produces some

chemical reaction with unpredictable results but as I said to the Boss on Sunday when she started waving her arms about in an exaggerated way to disperse the smoke between courses, 'Look at Winston. He was your hero. All this VE Day guff and so forth. If it hadn't been for the brandy bottle and fifty Corona Coronas a day we'd never have won the war. And he kept going till he was over ninety.' I could see a cloud pass over Margaret's brow as she envisaged the possibility of having me toddling about putting the foot in it for another twenty years. But she seemed to accept the logic of my argument.

I should say that this little contretemps sprang up during the official 70th Birthday luncheon at Chequers, graced by the presence of the boy Mark, plus yet another floozie, Howes, Mr Munster and the Corsican Twins. A far cry indeed from the good-natured bonhomie of the Frog and Loincloth. From the Boss's point of view, the highlight was the delivery of a wire from Hoppo congratulating 'The Duke of Thatcher' on being eighty.

Talking of which, the wrinkled cowboy seems to have got the bird on his Grand Absolutely Final Appearance Tour of Europe. His progress through the continental capitals reminded me very much of the Monk on his peregrinations, with the egg-stalls doing a roaring trade and in one case, as he was about to address some bunch of big-noise wops, a pigeon being released, presumably well dosed with laxative – a prank which reminded me very strongly of the time Reggie Stebbings employed the same device to clear a shareholders' meeting about to discuss the Chairman's expenses.

Needless to say I was far from being the main topic of conversation at my own seventieth birthday lunch. Almost as soon as Lady Howe had made her usual damnfool remarks about the charm of the floral arrangements, up spoke the Corsican Twins, embarking on an in-depth analysis of our failure at the polls in the Local Council Elections and the inroads made by the smarmy Doctor and his plonk-swilling Pinkos. To my astonishment, either Alberto or Luigi, I can never tell the difference, actually had the effrontery to lay the blame on the shoulders of the Boss. (I could only assume that Boris had laced his pre-lunch tomato juice with something a little more substantial.) At any rate his tongue was loosened and out he came with it: how her style was engendering consumer resistance and her packaging would have to be re-thought at a creative level. Not surprisingly our Italian friend got it clean between the eyes. How dare he say such a thing after they'd vetoed her Victory Parade at the end of the Miners' Strike, a mistake that had kept her awake night after night? If anyone was to blame for the polling figures it was Walker, a power-crazed financier manque who had waited till she was fighting for British jobs abroad before launching a cowardly attack on her. And now little Pym was organising his Private Army of wets. I had already heard this several times before, so I switched off, my thoughts reverting to the F & L, and the wonderful moment when Maurice did his gorilla on the overhead light and went through the stained glass window.

However, believe it or not, I tuned into the old girl doing her animal training act at Halitosis Hall a couple of mornings later, and it seemed our spaghetti-stained adviser's words had not fallen on entirely deaf ears. There was definitely a new note of pained condescension in her voice as she dismembered the wretched Welshman. But I am happy to say it didn't last long and when some yobbo caught her on the raw, the whip once more began to crack and he was soon up on his perch again licking his paws with his fellow chimps.

See you on VJ Night. God knows what they'll dredge out of the archives for that. I hope not the photograph of us and Prosser-Cluff in the fountains at Trafalgar Square kissing those Russian Lady Soldiers.

Onward into the Vale of Tears,

DENIS

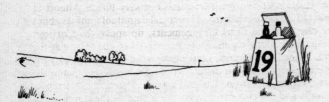

10 Downing Street
Whitehall

1 June 1985

Dear Bill,

I don't know if you've heard the joke Maurice picked up at the Club which is going the rounds about me? Question: 'What were Denis Thatcher's last words?' Answer: 'He didn't have any; his wife was with him to the end.' Quite amusing, I suppose, if you've had a few, which I had when I heard it from Maurice's lips, but looking at it written down it strikes me as being rather silly. Maurice says he sent it into Peterborough of the *Daily Telegraph* so you may have to read it again.

Entre nous, a certain amount of whistling in the dark has been going on here during the last week or so. Little Furniss who I had a snifter with in his office at the NatWest really put the wind up me by saying that the big boys in the City are only waiting for the moment to what he calls 'go liquid'. I said I'd done that a long while ago, but he didn't seem to get the point. I don't think matters have been helped in the Square Mile by this Lloyds business. You probably heard about poor Ferdy Trapnell-Braine's missus, who had been drawing a very nice little couple of thou over the last few years, and suddenly got the buff envelope at the breakfast table saying she owed some Libyan Oiltanker man half a million quid. Ferdy says they'll have to sell their place in Majorca for a start, and he was even talking about making do with just one Roller instead of the three. Now they've brought in Lord Goodman to try and bale them out, though a more unsuitable person to drop into an over-crowded lifeboat it seems hard to imagine.

According to Furniss, the City Mob have finally come to the conclusion that Margaret is all gong and no dinner, largely because of the inflation rate taking an upturn. I haven't really dared tell M. this, but she has no one to blame but herself, allowing her fat friend at Number 11 to jack up the price of everything in sight. What do they expect? Up till then, of course, beating inflation was the only feather in her cap, and now that's gone she's looking a bit thin on top. The hoi polloi seem to have reached the same conclusion at the same moment, and Moron, or whatever they're called who do the opinion polls, came out with a real shocker, showing Kinnock and Steel neck and neck well out in front, with the Boss trailing along behind only a whisker ahead of Screaming Lord Sutch.

The only shot left in the Corsican Brothers' locker is to press full steam ahead with plans to put Halitosis Hall on TV every evening, the idea being that the punters will be impressed by the Grantham Gouger nightly throttling the wretched Ginger Nuts and tossing little Steel out of the ring like a piece of thistle-down, while the winos behind her bay and brawl. In my own view this scheme is doomed to failure, and may well be the end of democracy as we know it. As soon as Joe Public is allowed to lift up that particular rock and glimpse the slimy and disgusting creatures that infest the Palace of Westminster I would have thought it was only a matter of time before the Army had to be called in.

The only other scenario on the drawing board, an absolute non-starter, is the promised reshuffle in the Cabinet. However, despite heavy hints Hailsham is refusing to allow them to wheel him away, so force may have to be used to make him see reason. These geriatrics can be very obstinate, as you remember from all the trouble we had getting the Major's father to take down the barricades when he locked himself in the drinks cupboard at the Old Contemptibles. The Monk has also been letting it be known that a period of absolute rest in the House of Lords might be finally called for. But if you ask me any chances will be merely cosmetic, as the admen have it, and there isn't a hope in hell of shifting either little fuzzy-bonce Brittan or Matey Next Door.

The only laugh we've had has been Pym's little rebellion. A perfectly decent fellow, no doubt, but hardly the man to sound the trumpet call and bring Margaret's walls tumbling down. At the first feeble blast from his party squeaker all his followers were taken short and vanished over the horizon.

I got a belated birthday card from Rudolf Hess, extending his sympathy. Did I detect the Major's handwriting?

Yours for Life,

DENIS

FICTION

THE PRINCESS OF POOR STREET	Emma Blair	£2.99 ☐
WANDERLUST	Danielle Steel	£3.50 ☐
LADY OF HAY	Barbara Erskine	£3.95 ☐
BIRTHRIGHT	Joseph Amiel	£3.50 ☐
THE SECRETS OF HARRY BRIGHT	Joseph Wambaugh	£2.95 ☐

FILM AND TV TIE-IN

BLACK FOREST CLINIC	Peter Heim	£2.99 ☐
INTIMATE CONTACT	Jacqueline Osborne	£2.50 ☐
BEST OF BRITISH	Maurice Sellar	£8.95 ☐
SEX WITH PAULA YATES	Paula Yates	£2.95 ☐
RAW DEAL	Walter Wager	£2.50 ☐

NON-FICTION

NEXT TO A LETTER FROM HOME: THE GLENN MILLER STORY	Geoffrey Butcher	£4.99 ☐
AS TIME GOES BY: THE LIFE OF INGRID BERGMAN	Laurence Leamer	£3.95 ☐
BOTHAM	Don Mosey	£3.50 ☐
SOLDIERS	John Keegan & Richard Holmes	£5.95 ☐
URI GELLER'S FORTUNE SECRETS	Uri Geller	£2.50 ☐

All Sphere books are available at your local bookshop or newsagent, or can be ordered direct from the publisher. Just tick the titles you want and fill in the form below.

Name_____

Address_____

_____

Write to Sphere Books, Cash Sales Department, P.O. Box 11, Falmouth, Cornwall TR10 9EN

Please enclose a cheque or postal order to the value of the cover price plus:

UK: 60p for the first book, 25p for the second book and 15p for each additional book ordered to a maximum charge of £1.90.

OVERSEAS & EIRE: £1.25 for the first book, 75p for the second book and 28p for each subsequent title ordered.

BFPO: 60p for the first book, 25p for the second book plus 15p per copy for the next 7 books, thereafter 9p per book.

Sphere Books reserve the right to show new retail prices on covers which may differ from those previously advertised in the text elsewhere, and to increase postal rates in accordance with the P.O.

HENRY ROOT'S

A-Z of Women

'The Definitive Guide'

*I know what you're thinking.
You're thinking: Women, eh? What's there
to say about women? The bedroom and the
kitchen. The duvet and the blender. The corset
and the rubber glove. That covers it,
you're thinking. But Root on women,
that's different...that's very
different indeed.*

*So to balance the current spate
of books by women on men, the
incomparable Henry Root
has gone out in the field
and up at the sharp end –
and has come back with
the ultimate guide to
women today.*

0 7221 3067 8   Humour   £2.50